"It is rare these days to find an unequivocal non-dual communication. Attempting to describe that which is beyond understanding, process, or path is hardly ever embarked upon. However, Richard undertakes this task in his own inimitable style. He also includes relevant stories and perceptions about the human condition gleaned from a rich and varied experience."

—**Tony Parsons**, author of *The Open Secret*

"The reader is guided on an exceptional journey into the unknowable by an expert in psychology and spiritual traditions who awakened from the dream of separation."

—**Christian Salvesen**, MA, author of *Advaita*

"Richard Sylvester fields a spectrum of questions that covers personal journeys and non-duality culture. He barely breathes on questions and…they disappear. To try to say what remains would invite more questions, yet it is present on every page."

—**Jerry Katz**, editor of *One*

Non-Duality Questions, Non-Duality Answers

Exploring Spirituality & Existence in the Modern World

RICHARD SYLVESTER

NON-DUALITY PRESS
An Imprint of New Harbinger Publications

Publisher's Note

This publication is designed to provide accurate and authoritative information in regard to the subject matter covered. It is sold with the understanding that the publisher is not engaged in rendering psychological, financial, legal, or other professional services. If expert assistance or counseling is needed, the services of a competent professional should be sought.

Distributed in Canada by Raincoast Books

Copyright © 2016 by Richard Sylvester
          Non-Duality Press
          An Imprint of New Harbinger Publications, Inc.
          5674 Shattuck Avenue
          Oakland, CA 94609
          www.newharbinger.com

Cover design by Amy Shoup

Library of Congress Cataloging-in-Publication Data on file

18   17   16

10 9 8 7 6 5 4 3 2 1   First Printing

With deep appreciation to Tony Parsons for communicating
non-duality so clearly and with such love and humour

Also by Richard Sylvester

I Hope You Die Soon

The Book of No One

Drink Tea, Eat Cake

Too many people have contributed to the writing of this book to list them all here. However, particular thanks are due to Tony and Claire Parsons and to the following: Allan Bloxham, Brett, Cha, Dawn, Jason Lee, Jay Mistry, Jeremy Robinson, Jonny Roth, Karin, Michael Dobias, Rosemary Cochran, Rupert Peene, Seamus Gilroy, Terry Murphy and Thorsten.

"I have no use for traditions or traditional knowledge. If you do the slightest research on tradition you will see that it is all a concept."

Nisargadatta Maharaj

"A day will dawn when you will laugh at all your past efforts."

Ramana Maharshi

"There is no rider on the horse."

Sam Harris

THE TOPICS IN THIS BOOK INCLUDE NON-DUALITY AND...

a course in miracles angels anger anxiety astrology attachments awakening bliss buddhism celibacy channelling children choice and choicelessness christianity conflict between teachers of advaita conflict with family and friends consciousness contraction and localisation death de-personalisation depression despair detachment drugs electronic voice phenomena emptiness evolution evolutionary enlightenment fear god gratitude gurus john rowan karma liberation madness maslow meditation mindfulness mystical experiences mystics negative habits negative thoughts neuroscience neurosis nisargadatta maharaj non-action non-duality trolls out-of-the-body experiences paranormal phenomena past-life regression paths and practices positive thinking post-modernism pre-destination projections psychosis psychotherapy quantum physics ramana maharshi ramesh balsekar ramtha rebirth and reincarnation relationship difficulties religion sacred cows sadhana seeking self-enquiry separation spiritual fascism spiritual paths spiritual people suffering superstition teachers of awakening the cosmic ordering service the golden rule the laws of attraction the mind the secret the shadow the tiger's mouth the witness thinking time transcendence unconditional love wei wu wei zen

For about ten years people sent me questions on non-duality by e-mail and usually I answered them. I am no longer able to do this, so I have put some of these questions and answers into this book. If you have a question, I hope you will be able to find the answer here. Alternatively, you could come to a meeting and ask it and you will get a cup of tea and a biscuit as well.

Most of the questions have been edited to maintain anonymity. Where names have been given, this is always with permission.

❋

IS AWAKENING A CHANCE EVENT?

Question: *You say that there is no separate person and therefore no free will. So is it simply a matter of chance whether the sense of self drops away?*

Richard: Answers to questions such as this one will always be frustrating for the mind. Liberation, or the seeing that there is no separation, is either seen or it is not seen. That is all that can be said.

As soon as we suggest that it is a matter of chance, or of fate, or it is willed by God, or it is earned by spiritual striving or purification, or it is the result of karma or grace, we are entering into another story.

Of all the stories that there are about this, I quite like the one that says that it is grace. But that is also a story.

❋

AWAKENING AND PRACTICES

The same experience that you and Tony Parsons describe is very familiar to me from several years ago. At the time I felt very joyful. In fact I laughed out loud. I felt a tremendous sense of peace, freedom and relief. This state lasted for about two years, during which life was simply living itself and there was no searching for anything else.

But then somehow I found myself searching again. I started reading about non-duality, going to meetings, talking to all sorts of people about this. I've become terribly frustrated with trying to understand this and very confused by what different people say about it. Some teachers tell me that I should develop awareness, others that I must become totally present in the here and now. Could you comment?

What you describe is quite common. There can be an unequivocal seeing of This, Oneness, Presence. Then after a while the mind can come back with all its theorising and with its suggestions that maybe, just maybe, there really is something more than This. That is how the mind tries to clamber back onto its throne, or into its Managing Director's chair.

So heigh ho, we are back on the hamster wheel and searching again, with all the terrible frustration that this can entail. Many people who write and talk about non-duality encourage this, wittingly or unwittingly. They may suggest that the seeing of Oneness can be used instrumentally in a variety of ways, for example to improve our life and our relationships. Often they teach that we can approach closer to Oneness by increasing our Awareness or by practising being Present.

And then off we go on another merry-go-round of inadequacy and searching.

If I gave advice, I'd say "Forget all that and relax."

"Becoming totally present in the here and now" is a phrase which is time-bound and space-bound. It has nothing to do with the seeing of non-duality. It encourages people to think that they can be more present by making an effort. Indeed, some people can, but it usually doesn't last more than a few minutes.

Seeing Oneness has nothing to do with making an effort or being totally present or anything else that a person can do. No amount of effort will reveal presence. There is only This, only presence, which is either seen or not seen.

❊

HOW SHOULD WE LIVE?

Does it matter how the apparent person lives their life? Does it matter if I simply eat, drink and be merry? How free am I?

It is not a question of how free or not you are. Ultimately it may be seen that there is no you, so you can neither be free nor bound.

In the meantime, life will be lived as it is lived. I am not sure whether your question is about morality, but if it is, the golden rule covers a lot of eventualities. It says simply "Don't do to others what you wouldn't want them to do to you." It can be written on a postcard and it is simple enough for a child of five to understand.

❊

LIBERATION EVENTS

The event that you describe as liberation happened at a definite time and place. Have you come across other individuals for whom similar events have happened? And if you have, is this becoming more common?

Tony Parsons describes an event. He was walking through a park, then there was just walking through a park but nobody walking. Nathan Gill describes an event. He was riding a bicycle down a lane, then there was just riding a bicycle down a lane but nobody bicycling. I describe an event. I was walking through a country town, then there was just walking through a country town but nobody walking.

Others also report events like these. The realisation of liberation may come with such an event, or afterwards, or not at all. Or the realisation of liberation may come without any event. There are no rules in this, because liberation is all-embracing and therefore excludes no possibilities.

The trouble with hearing these stories about 'liberation events' can be that they set up an expectation that something has to occur. This can lead to yet more searching. However, if searching for an event happens, then it happens. I know this is a tautology, but it expresses nicely the hopelessness of our case. If that hopelessness is realised, then there might at least be some relaxation.

It is becoming more common for people to report these events. It cannot be known whether that is because the events themselves are becoming more common or because more people are communicating about them. For other people there is no event, just a gentle gliding into the realisation that liberation is already the case.

❋

EVOLUTIONARY PATHS

I live in Tehran. Today I came across you by chance on the internet. I appreciate the beautiful sharing that you're engaged in. I have a question for you.

I know someone who claims that liberation can be achieved only by following a guru tradition, involving many spiritual techniques that will purify the emotional, mental and body systems of all their accumulated toxins from the past. I've met a guru from such a tradition. He says that those who claim self-realisation without following any method have done many techniques in their past lives and this is why they have now reached liberation. I don't have any way of judging whether they are right or whether this is just another story. I have used spiritual techniques, but I find it hard to persevere with them. They seem to provide temporary relief, but then my suffering returns. And while I'm doing them, I seem to lose contact with the moment.

The seeing of liberation is not something that the person can achieve by following an evolutionary path because the seeing of liberation is impersonal. In other words it has nothing to do with the person. I also agree with you that, while we are doing a 'future-orientated' technique, we may be missing this moment. However, some of these techniques can be helpful psychologically and emotionally. I meditated and engaged with different forms of therapy for about thirty years and I do not regret this.

Of course, as you indicate, there is always a story that can justify to an individual whatever they wish to believe. So if someone believes in rebirth, they can explain 'sudden' liberation as the result of good karma accumulated in past lives. But how would they—or you—ever know whether this was true? It may seem like a reasonable hypothesis, but it is not even testable. So it can never be more than an opinion. Some people would call it a superstition. A superstition is an improbable belief, held without sufficient evidence—often in fact with no evidence at all. Another phrase for this is 'baseless supposition'.

If someone is drawn to doing 'evolutionary techniques', then that is probably what will happen. If not, not. Meanwhile, all there is is This, and in this the seeing of liberation may arise.

❋

PRE-DESTINATION

Is the life of a person already written in advance?

No, the life of a person is not written in advance, because there is no person who has a life.

As soon as we start speculating that our lives may be written in advance, we engage with a story which takes us away from presence, from the miracle that is This. We might also notice that the idea that our life is written in advance is only one of many different possible stories. Why should we choose that story rather than any of the others?

When it is seen that there is no person who has a life, our fascination with stories about the future or the past tends to drop away. Then what is left is this ever-changing play of consciousness.

But I think that what we have to experience from birth to death is already written when we are born.

That is a story which appeals to many people. There are other appealing stories, such as that we can create the reality that we desire through understanding and practising 'the laws of attraction' or that we should accumulate good karma and avoid accumulating bad karma.

But what I am pointing to is that there is no person who has a life, or who creates their own reality, or who accumulates or avoids karma. And that there is no birth or death or time. All there is is This, whatever is apparently manifesting in Oneness, this present outpouring of unconditional love.

Then why are there people? Surely it's because Oneness wants to have the experience of being a person.

The mind lives in a world of time and of cause and effect, so it cannot help asking "Why?" It is its inescapable fate. The mind loves to entertain itself with questions about meaning and purpose and it creates answers of ever greater complexity so that it can silence its own doubts. Its answers may be religious or spiritual or existential. They are immensely varied, colourful and entertaining. And they often contradict one another.

If one of these answers appeals to you, then have it. But meanwhile the joy of presence is likely to be missed and this moment becomes a shadow, drained of energy and glimpsed only through a veil of speculation about meaning and the future.

You can have stories about meaning and purpose and endeavour or you can have presence, the simplicity of the leaves rustling in the breeze. You cannot have both.

❀

PRACTICES

I feel that I can still do something to help myself see through my illusory self. It's not that I'm trying to achieve anything. It's rather that I'm trying to let go of whatever it is that keeps me in a state of separation.

Does it not make sense for us to practise letting go, through Zen for example? Can we not learn through daily practice how our mind keeps our illusion of separateness intact?

I am going to try to undercut your question by pointing out that everything simply unfolds of its own accord. If there is an interest in following Zen, then following Zen will probably happen. If there is no interest in following Zen, then following Zen will probably not happen. Neither of these possibilities has anything to do with you, nor any relevance to liberation.

Zen may be followed and liberation may or may not arise. Zen may not be followed and liberation may or may not arise.

If you are drawn to Zen, it probably makes sense to practise it. If you are not drawn to Zen it probably makes sense to avoid it. In either case, I wish you well.

❋

DEATH

What is the difference between liberation and death? If these two events are equivalent, what is the point of even talking to anyone about their realisation? I know there is no point to liberation, but if this body-mind is extinguished at death, why work to see what will happen at that instant?

The difference between liberation and death is that in the first case the dream story continues, but now it is seen to be a dream story. In death the dream story ceases.

There is no point in talking to anyone about their realisation and it is not theirs. There is no point in working to see what will happen at death, but if that happens, then it happens. In other words, everything is exactly as it is and it cannot be any different.

❋

TRANSPERSONAL LOVE AND PRACTICE

I really enjoyed the conscious.tv panel discussion. I noticed a differ-ence in the answers the three of you gave to some of the questions. There seemed to be an especially clear difference in the answers about whether anything can be done to 'get closer' to Oneness, with one of the three of you claiming to run workshops in which people had this experience. Could you comment on this?

The differences about whether anything can be done arose because we were talking about different things. One of the panellists was describing workshops in which the participants are encouraged to experience emotions which are less egoically based than those we normally experience in 'everyday life'. Sometimes these emo-tional experiences are referred to as 'transpersonal', because they take us beyond our usual personal boundaries. However, they are still experiences, albeit experiences of a refined kind.

This part of the discussion reminded me of my training many years ago in the transpersonal psychology and human potential movements. From my experiences at that time I know that it is quite easy to take a group of people who are willing, and invoke in most of them an experience of these less egoic emotions.

This can have benefits on a personal level, for example feelings of increased well-being and of kindness towards others. Usually these don't last very long. These practices also often create dif-ficulties on a personal and relational level. I have witnessed this many times. Sometimes this leads to spectacular break-downs of existing relationships and the forming of often very short-lived new relationships amongst workshop participants who have shared a very intense experience. In the heightened atmosphere of the group, it is very easy to 'fall in love' in what seems like a very pure way. But as soon as daily reality hits, there can be a sudden coming down to earth. Mariana Kaplan wrote "You can't stay in God's world for very long. There are no restaurants or toilets there." We could add "And there are no mortgage payments, colour schemes or electricity bills to squabble over either." Ram Dass also describes very well the difficulty of coming down from the spiritual mountain and trying to live daily life from that heightened state.

An Australian acquaintance of mine summed all this up very succinctly. She said "We go on these workshops. We feel wonderful. We're in love with everyone. And then our lives fall apart!"

Nevertheless, doing intensive group work of some kind can be a very effective way of dealing with personal issues.

The seeing of non-duality has nothing to do with transpersonal experiences. Liberation is a paradigm shift which does not relate to any experience we have ever had, whether it be transpersonal or not. It is the seeing that, although experiences of many kinds arise, there is no experiencer.

❀

ASTROLOGY

On the one hand astrology seems to fit with the idea of non-doership, because it suggests that everything that happens is 'written in the stars' and can be found in our horoscope. On the other hand I have the feeling that astrology is just another story. But if it is just a story, why do our horoscopes so often match our experiences of life?

The variety of phenomena that occur in this waking dream are so varied and numerous that if you wish to you can find evidence to support any story. If you wish to believe in astrology, you'll focus on the evidence where it seems to have got things right. If you wish to discount astrology, you'll focus on the evidence where it seems to have got things wrong. The same will be the case for dream interpretation, psychic readings, shamanic prophecies, hand analysis, numerology and many other systems such as the Myers Briggs Type Indicator and Jung's theory of psychological types. These systems go in and out of fashion. Few people try to determine the future through the augury of birds' intestines anymore, luckily for the birds. But many people still have their astrological charts plotted.

We all suffer from a cognitive bias known as the Forer Effect and this contributes to the continuing popularity of these systems. The Forer Effect describes our propensity to rate as highly accurate generalised descriptions of personality when we believe that they have been individually tailored for us. Many psychological experiments have been done which have proved beyond doubt the power of the Forer Effect. For example, in one experiment subjects were invited to supply the date, time and place of their birth and apply for a free individual astrological reading. Most subjects rated their reading as highly accurate. They did not know of course that the same generalised reading had been provided to all of them. Psychics and others adept at the art of cold reading also know—or intuit—the usefulness of the Forer Effect in pursuing their chosen trade.

Meanwhile there is only This, presence, in which any kind of story about life and its meaning may arise. All these stories are essentially meaningless, an entertainment with which we structure time and try to inure ourselves against the pain of separation.

❋

BEING IN A DESERT

I have experienced a spontaneous shift in perception, and it is clear now that I'm not this body-mind organism, but awareness itself which witnesses everything. This has brought a great sense of freedom. It is clear that there is only 'now', and that the past and the future are just present thoughts. It is also clear that everything is simply happening, so there has been a dramatic reduction in the sense of responsibility and guilt.

Nevertheless there is still a sense of separation. I relate to what you write about a period of being in a desert, without hope, help or meaning. I see that nothing can be done to bring about the end of searching, but I am still waiting for it to happen, and this is sometimes very painful.

I would be really grateful if you could comment on my hopeless situation.

In awakening it is clearly seen that there is no doer, there is only the unfolding of whatever is apparently happening, and you give a very clear description of this. But awakening is only seeing the emptiness from which everything arises. The fullness, the loving unconditionality of Being, is not seen in awakening. This leaves a sense that there is still something to be realised, yet it is also known that there is nothing that we can do to realise it. Hence the sense you have of being in a desert, without help or hope, still waiting for liberation.

I don't give advice, but if I did it would be to relax and take enjoyment in some simple everyday thing that you like doing. It could be a walk in the park, a cup of coffee, a trip to the cinema, a drive in the car—whatever it might be for you. You'll recognise, I think, the paradox in my writing this, because of course there is no one who can choose to do any of this. But if it should happen for us, then we are really blessed.

❋

DISAGREEMENTS ABOUT NON-DUALITY

I've just been reading a book by Nisargadatta and I'm very confused. On the one hand he states quite clearly that there is nobody and that all there is is This. Several other books on Advaita say the same. But then he says that there is something prior to consciousness. Another contemporary writer on Advaita tells me that there is the 'I', the 'I am' and the 'I am Sarah'. He also says "It never ends" and "Next time you may be born as a worm." This seems very different to what you say.

I find the messages given about this very confusing. They are like the contradictions found in religions. Are these all just concepts? After many years of searching, I feel that I know nothing more than when I started. But paradoxically, I cannot give up the search.

The mind will spin endless stories about Advaita and make them ever more complicated. These stories are indeed like religions and some of them actually become religions. As long as the mind takes an interest in these stories, there will be confusion.

However, when the sense of being a person collapses, or is seen through, or evaporates, then it is seen that there is just This and the stories that the mind tells become irrelevant. Then statements like "You may be born as a worm next time" or "There is something prior to consciousness" or "There is the I, the I am, and the I am Sarah" will probably lose their fascination.

If I could recommend anything I would say forget about all these stories and take a walk in your local park. But of course there is no one who can choose to forget about these stories. They will be there till they are not and then they will be gone.

❋

CHANNELLING

In a recent talk you briefly mentioned angel channelling. I suppose that the existence of angels is a story of the mind, so I am wondering where the channelled words come from.

For some time I seemed to be channelling messages. These were full of advice about what people should and should not do. Now I feel that there is no need for such advice.

Where does channelling come from? Does it come from the mind? My channelling sounded different to my usual speaking style and I've noticed the same with others.

Yes, angels are a story of the mind and channelling comes from the mind. This is the same as saying that it comes out of Oneness like all other thoughts. Psychologically, channelling comes from a somewhat deeper level of the mind than everyday conscious thoughts do, but not from a deeply unconscious level which the everyday mind cannot access so easily.

What channelling requires is that we simply open ourselves up to this slightly deeper level of the mind. Almost everyone can do this quite easily if they simply relax and allow the thoughts to begin to flow. Of course most channelled messages are obvious and banal. "Be nice to one another." "Be kind to one another." "Try not to destroy the planet." "Deal with your fear if you are able to." "Try not to kill one another." These are not revelations of deep spiritual wisdom that require the intervention of angels, archangels or cosmic beings from beyond the dog star Sirius.

As to the different style of these communications, this is very common. For example, many people channel in archaic English, which they might hope will make them sound much wiser than they really are. J. Z. Knight's channelling Ramtha is particularly amusing in this way. Get her (or him) up on youtube, sit back and enjoy a good laugh.

By the way, I understand that the latest fashion is to channel unicorns. But I may have got this wrong.

❋

REALITY, APPEARANCE AND ILLUSION

I have heard you say that this is an appearance and it is very convincing. Could you explain in more detail how it is that we think that this is real but it is not?

Sometimes I suddenly have the realisation that of course there is nothing, that this is simply obvious. These moments make my 'reality' wobble.

And what do you mean by "There is no mind"? Some people describe the mind as an energy field surrounding the body. But if there is no mind, then what are thoughts? Are they simply brain activity?

I do not say that we think that this is real but it is not. The closest I can get to explaining this is to say "It is both real and unreal", rather as quantum physics suggests. A metaphor that I like to use is the quite traditional one of comparing this to a night-time dream. While we are having a night-time dream, it is utterly real. Or we could say that its appearance seems utterly real. To the one who is having the dream, it makes no difference whether it is real or whether it only seems real. However, as soon as we wake up we can see that actually nothing happened.

Some people call this waking reality 'the waking dream' and some call it 'an appearance'. I like both those expressions. Others call it 'an illusion'. I don't like that expression, because, as most people understand the word 'illusion', it is misleading. If the word 'reality' has any meaning, which it clearly does, then this is the only reality there is. By 'this' I mean whatever is happening in presence, right here, right now. Of course whatever happens can only happen in presence in any case. There is no other time and no other place for it to happen in.

Most of us think we have a mind because thoughts come so thick and fast and they have so much energy that they create the impression that there is an entity, the mind, thinking them. But actually thoughts arise out of nothing, or No Thing. We could say that there is a brain which transforms the pure energy of Being into thoughts, and then we imagine that there is a personal mind thinking these thoughts. As a metaphor we could say that the pure undifferentiated white light of Being enters a prism (the brain) and emerges as the differentiated colours of the rainbow (thoughts and other perceptions).

You ask what thoughts are. Thoughts are Oneness thinking. Feelings are Oneness feeling. You are Oneness 'Mary-ing' and I am Oneness 'Richard-ing'.

14

Thank you for your reply. It seems as if the thoughts which arise out of Oneness are based on the past experiences of the body-mind, as if our conditioning causes our thinking to be a certain way. Is this true?

Yes, within duality there certainly seems to be cause and effect, and past experiences apparently condition present thoughts and feelings. When Oneness is seen, it is quite likely that this conditioning will be seen as less important or not important at all.

❋

LSD AND OTHER PSYCHO-ACTIVE DRUGS

I have some friends who take LSD for spiritual reasons, although I've never tried it myself. Do you think psycho-active drugs can help people destroy their concepts about being a person?

I last took psycho-active drugs over three decades ago, so I'm not very up-to-date. Their effects are very individual, but for myself, I would say that taking LSD revealed that our normal experience of reality is provisional. In other words it is just one possible version of reality. So how reality is experienced can depend greatly on our individual circumstances. If you meddle with the brain even slightly, an entirely alternate reality may appear.

Later on I took Thai magic mushrooms, and I described that experience at the time rather pompously as "Knowing God and understanding the nature of the Universe". Of course, by the next morning I had no idea what this meant.

Taking psycho-active drugs can profoundly alter our concepts of who we are as a person. But this has nothing to do with the seeing of non-duality. Drug-induced experiences are still experiences—that is, they still happen to a person. The seeing of non-duality is not an experience, because it doesn't happen to a person. And our concepts about ourselves and about non-duality have nothing to do with the seeing of non-duality.

I was recently invited to take part in an ayahuasca ceremony but I turned the invitation down. I am no longer interested in taking psycho-active drugs. The experiences they offer are another ride in the fun-fair of life. Sometimes they are an exciting ride like the ferris wheel, sometimes they are a frightening ride like the ghost train. But once Oneness has been seen, the ordinariness of life tends to be seen as so extraordinary that an interest in fair-ground rides usually dies away.

❋

SUFFERING AND FEELING REAL

Can the person return and go back to their previous ways after awakening, and lose all the transparency? Although this has not just been concepts for me, I've become very involved in the story again. It seems to me that suffering is especially good at making the person feel real once more.

Anything is possible. Especially after awakening, the person can come back and become completely immersed in the story again. Suffering can have a particular hold on us and make the person feel extremely solid.

Sometimes, even when liberation has been seen and there is nothing left to be realised, there can be 'neurotic mechanisms' which still have their own momentum and which can still be running. It can simply take time for these remaining neurotic energies to run down or dissipate. Remember in any case that being asleep and being awake are the same. Life goes on as before, it is simply seen that it is not going on for anyone.

❋

PSYCHOTHERAPY, DETACHMENT AND PRACTICES

I've heard you say that some spiritual practices are very good for people but others are damaging. You've specifically mentioned, as bad, practices that encourage people to distance themselves from their experience through detachment. Could you tell me a bit more about why you regard those practices as damaging and also which practices that includes? Do they for example include mindfulness?

I am interested in this because I teach meditation to people as a way of coping with stress and I would not want to cause them any harm. In my psychotherapy training we are also taught to use the Observing Self as a tool with clients.

There is evidence that mindfulness practices can be helpful in dealing with suffering, whether they are taught in a spiritual context such as Buddhism, or in a secular context as they are within the National Health Service. Observing thoughts and feelings, especially feelings, can also be therapeutically beneficial. I have myself taught Focusing to people as a way of doing this. Meditation can also be extremely helpful in reducing stress and in other ways.

Techniques that seek to develop detachment, which is the opposite of the connectivity of mindfulness, can be quite unhelpful or even damaging to an individual. Although they can create a bulwark against suffering, this is often at the cost of our aliveness. It is healthier to connect with our suffering in an open way and see where that takes us. Techniques that encourage us to try to control our thoughts can also be counter-productive and create more stress for us. This is partly because of what psychologists call 'the rebound effect', whereby the more effort we put into excluding unwanted thoughts, the more intrusive they become.

As an experiment in this, for the next thirty seconds try not to think of rabbits.

It is healthier simply to pay attention to our thoughts and notice what happens.

I wish you well, both with your teaching of meditation practice and with your psychotherapy training.

Thanks very much for your reply. I'm really pleased to hear that you feel mindfulness is safe and useful.

Could you explain more about the unhelpful practices that encourage detachment? What might a teacher of such techniques say to a student? For example, are you talking about Advaita teachers who encourage students to try to discover their true nature as some kind of pure awareness?

No, I'm not talking about the techniques recommended by some Advaita teachers, generally known as self-enquiry. I'm talking about certain techniques, often yogic ones, which encourage detachment, often through many hours of meditation practice a day.

Unless an individual has made an informed decision to live the life of a recluse, such techniques are not suitable for them. In other words they do not suit the majority of us who are living as 'householders'. They can provide a certain level of protection against the pain of everyday suffering, but only at the cost of being cut off from life. If you have the sort of rare personality that craves reclusiveness, you will probably already know this.

Similarly, techniques which encourage an individual to control or avoid their thoughts or emotions, rather than pay attention to them, can be very damaging to our aliveness and spontaneity. I hope this helps to clarify what I have said.

Thank you very much for taking the time to reply to me. I had never thought about it in that way and so it's been very helpful. I can see now that even meditation has its shadow side.

❉

SENSE OF SELF, CHOICE AND CONTROL

You say that things just happen and there is no authority on any level. However, in my daily life I feel that there is a 'me' inside my body. This body doesn't do everything I would like it to do, but nevertheless I seem to have some control over things. For example, I can decide whether to continue typing this or not.

Are you saying that this sense of control, admittedly a limited one, is an illusion? If so, could you explain how this can be? As long as the sense of self exists, it seems undeniable, at least to me, that there really is some kind of control. As an example of this, I could have decided not to write this message.

Firstly I would not call "this sense of control" an illusion, but rather an appearance which is absolutely convincing until it is seen through. As you say, "as long as the sense of self exists, it seems undeniable". However, when the sense of separation comes to an end and the self is seen through, it is equally undeniable that the self has always been an appearance within a dream. Then life goes on as before, but it is seen that there is no one living it.

When the sense of separation drops away, the absence of a central self is seen directly. However, many neuroscientists, psychologists and philosophers would also deny the existence of a separate self from the evidence that is being gathered from research into the brain and into perception. If you are interested in reading about this, you might enjoy David Eagleman's 'Incognito', Sam Harris's 'Free Will' or Julian Baggini's 'The Ego Trick'.

❋

CONFLICT WITH FAMILY AND FRIENDS

The more I find myself drawn into non-duality, the worse my relation-ship with family and friends gets. Whenever I see my parents I find myself behaving like a teenager again. This causes both them and me considerable hurt. I'm also finding it more difficult to get on with my friends as we seem to have less and less in common.

I know this is all a story, but it's a story I don't like!

I doubt whether you'll give me any advice but I've still felt like writing this to you.

It is quite common for individuals to go through a radical re-alignment of their relationships when non-duality bites. Sometimes this can happen catastrophically, sometimes not.

As far as your relationships are concerned, especially with your parents, all I would suggest is "Follow your heart". I'm in favour of a stress free and relaxed life and that's difficult to have when we're feeling incomplete with significant figures in our story. Our sense of incompleteness binds us as well as them. So if you want to be able to wish your parents well, I hope you're able to find a way to do that.

Of course none of this is advice.

❁

DE-PERSONALISATION AND AWAKENING

Could it be that awakening is simply depersonalisation disorder?

And what is meant by "This is all there is"? I can't see you right now, so who is reading this message? Is there any 'out there'? If there is no 'out there', does the reply just come out of nothingness?

When an attempt is made to describe awakening, that description can be confused by some people with depersonalisation. However, when an individual has experienced depersonalisation, and at another time awakening has occurred, there will probably be no possibility of confusing the two.

As to your question about "This is all there is", I can only answer it by referring to the metaphor that this is like a night-time dream, in which many things are happening and yet in the morning when we wake up it is realised that nothing actually happened. This makes no difference to the dream as it is experienced. We could say that you and I are both dream characters who can only have experiences within the dream. The dream unfolds, and yet it is also seen that This is all there is. There is no possibility of the mind understanding this. It is either seen or it is not seen, and it doesn't matter which.

Yes, the reply comes out of nothingness, just as everything else does. That includes you, me, puppy dogs, the smell of coffee and rain on an autumn afternoon.

AWAKENING AND RELATIONSHIP DIFFICULTIES

After an awakening event this year, experience has taught me not to say anything about it to my family and friends. But because I don't have anyone else to talk to about this, I'm beginning to feel hopeless.

I am feeling very frustrated after this event. During it, there was only pure being and 'my story' disappeared in a gentle way. I didn't even really realise that anything had happened until a few days later. The person who had been looking for Paradise wasn't there anymore and suddenly instead there Paradise was, beyond any experience of time and space.

But now the seeking energy has started again even more power-fully than before and I feel I'm back in the 'story'. At the same time I now know that seeking is hopeless. My friends and family are finding it very difficult to cope with the changes that have come over me and cannot understand why I no longer share the interests we had. This is even threatening my marriage. Can you suggest anything?

This is quite a common problem after an awakening event. I don't usually give advice, but you could simply be as patient with and kind to your partner, family and friends as you're able to be. It can be a great challenge for them to be confronted with the changes that may suddenly come about when someone they know well undergoes an awakening event.

❋

POLITICS AND A GREAT UNKNOWING

You may find this a weird message. I've been reading about internet surveillance, the infringement of civil liberties, and the Orwellian State. I used to be shocked by stuff like this. In a way I still am. But somewhere deep inside me I know that I just don't care anymore. There's no one here who can care anymore.

Whether you find this weird or not, my friends certainly are having a problem with it! I don't want to save the world anymore, but they still do. In fact, these days I just feel quite ignorant about everything. How do you feel now?

Thank you for your 'weird' message. The personality is still the personality, so an individual who has seen through separation may or may not still be engaged in social and political matters. There are no rules and in any case it doesn't matter. However, if their engagement had been neurotic, it's likely, though not certain, that it will lessen when Oneness is seen.

Awakening tends to burst the stories of meaning that we used to believe in. Liberation tends to bring them completely to an end. 'Ignorant' is a good word to describe where this leaves us, although I prefer 'not knowing', as this seems a little kinder to myself and others. What we are talking about here is undoubtedly a plunge into A Great Unknowing.

❄

NEITHER A BLESSING NOR A CURSE

Dear Richard, Nothing has changed except that life no longer seems to be happening for anyone. Every thought gives way to This. Stories peter out and I have no influence over them.

Nevertheless my feelings have grown stronger. I am affected very deeply by the suffering of others. But all of this passes quite quickly. I relate to your mantra of "Hopeless, helpless, meaningless".

There is almost no desire to visit the past or the future and my memory gets worse and worse. But life still seems to happen quite effectively.

So it seems that seeing Oneness doesn't necessarily make life easier and it is neither a blessing nor a curse. It is just what it is. Best wishes, Jonny

Dear Jonny, I love your descriptions. And what you describe is so commonly experienced when Oneness is seen. Feelings tend to become stronger but don't stick around for long. Memory gets worse. The past and future are no longer visited so much. Nothing about this necessarily make life easier.

Best of all is your "It is neither a blessing nor a curse". As a Zen monk said to a seeker, "Why do you want liberation? How do you know you'd like it?"

Best wishes, Richard

❀

SEARCHING AND DEPRESSION OR DESPAIR

I am in my sixties, and for many years I was searching, sometimes through politics, sometimes through psychotherapy and sometimes through spirituality. Then one day I came across Tony Parsons' 'The Open Secret' and I knew that my searching had ended.

But I am still a person and in my case a person who often feels despair. In the past I could always do something which felt worthwhile to try to fix myself, but now I feel that nothing helps. Books, psychotherapy, spiritual techniques and even my friends can't help. Worst of all, my friends can't even understand what's going on for me. They try to be helpful by for example suggesting psychological exercises that in fact I did years ago, but I can't do these again because I don't believe in them any more. I wonder if I'm becoming depressed. All I want to do is play games on my computer and read books. Do you have any suggestions for me?

Thank for sharing your story with me. Like you, I spent many years involved both with psychotherapies and with spiritual paths. Like you, when I came across Tony Parsons and non-duality I couldn't engage with any of that any more and it all fell away, leaving a certain amount of despair. From the people who write to me, I would say that this is quite a common experience.

When in the past I was in despair, I used to talk to Tony and he would suggest that I find something simple that I enjoyed doing, such as walking round the park. Now, although I do not give advice, I find that this is what I suggest to others. It may not sound deep, but it has the virtue of being simple.

❋

PROOF OF LIBERATION

How do you deal with the environment? And did you ever look for proof that liberation had happened?

Here everything seems transparent. Sometimes there seems to be more 'me', sometimes less, but there is always a constant. Sleeping and being awake are known to be the same.

Doesn't a decreased interest in the story make it difficult for the character to function and be involved?

I don't deal with the environment. Life goes on, stuff happens, and in separation we think we're doing it. When separation ends, it's seen that everything is unfolding of its own accord.

No, I never looked for proof of this. When Oneness is seen, it is simply seen. What happens after that can take many forms, none of them important.

'Transparent' is a word which I think many would relate to. And yes, the ultimate seeing is that in any case, being asleep and being awake are the same. It's just that while we're asleep, that can't be known.

A decreased interest in the story might make the character less involved. In some circumstances that might actually make action more effective. And it's possible that the character might still take a lively interest in aspects of the story depending on their nature.

❋

EXPECTATIONS

Awakening is not what I was expecting. I'm less neurotic now but I still worry about whether I turned the gas off on the stove. I don't really behave any differently but there is no person behind my behaviour any more. Really anything can happen.

Isn't there something profoundly relaxing about resting in the realisation that everything, all states and ways of being, can simply be allowed to be? No special experience is required or necessary. It's okay to be whatever the character is. It's okay still to be somewhat neurotic. We can finally let go of all our stories and projections and expectations about enlightened states of being with a mighty exhalation of relief. That can be a blessing, although it's not what anybody is expecting.

❊

PSYCHOTHERAPY

I believe you've been involved professionally with psychotherapy. I've been in psychotherapy for many years, having had a traumatic childhood. My feeling is that it works for the person, especially where there's a 'resonance' with the therapist. Do you agree with this?

For the apparent person, living in apparent separation, there are many ways of making life more comfortable. Where neurosis and childhood trauma are concerned, engaging with psychotherapy for a while is one of the most intelligent things a person can do. If there is a resonance with the therapist, the therapy will probably be more effective. However, it would be a mistake to assume that the process of psychotherapy has anything to do with the seeing of liberation.

Even after liberation, there is still an individual who will probably prefer to be comfortable. So psychotherapy may still be engaged in, although that is less likely. Other ways of keeping the body-mind healthy, such as yoga or tai chi, may also be followed.

Remember that liberation has no necessary implications. Life just goes on, only now it is seen that nobody lives it.

❊

FRIENDS

I have a close friend who thinks that we are on a path and need to reach a spiritual goal. Sometimes I want to talk to him about non-duality but I don't want to start sounding like a guru, even though I know that seeing liberation has absolutely nothing to do with me.

When you first started giving talks about non-duality, did you feel schizophrenic? What do your family and friends think of this?

By and large I tend to avoid talking about non-duality except to people who are really interested. But I'm noticing that more and more people seem to have a feeling for this. For example today I was talking to a friend who, after following Buddhism in a small way for a long time, simply came to the conclusion that "This is it". As she said "There is no point in searching for anything else so I might as well get on with enjoying it."

No, I didn't feel schizophrenic when I started giving talks about this. It's usually a delight to be able to talk about this to people who are interested in it. In fact it's a privilege. As to my family and friends, some of them are interested in this and some are not. It doesn't matter.

❋

UNEXPECTED JOY

Does liberation always follow awakening? I feel like I have been in the desert for a long time, although unexpectedly joy arises at the oddest moments, like yesterday when I was doing the washing up.

There are no rules. Liberation can happen soon after awakening, or at the same time, or after a long time, or not until physical death. Sometimes I talk to individuals who are still waiting for something else to happen, yet my feeling is that they have already seen everything that there is to be seen. They simply have an idea persisting that there must still be something more to find.

Taking joy in doing the washing up sounds good to me.

❀

WATCHING A PLAY

I feel increasingly lately as if I am watching a play. My thoughts simply appear and then dissolve again. It feels like everything is being done without 'me' doing anything. I cannot take the sense that I am a person seriously anymore.

What you describe is often experienced in awakening, particularly the feeling that everything is being done without a person doing anything. "Actions there are, but no doer thereof." You were never doing anything. It just seemed as if you were.

❀

AWAKENING OR CLARITY AND ASTROLOGY

Recently I've had the feeling that things are just happening, that events are simply unfolding. I used to be very interested in philosophy, but now I'm becoming very bored with philosophical discussions about life and how to live it. I'm also becoming bored with people telling me about what is happening in their lives, although this used to fascinate me.
   Is this awakening or is it just clarity?

What you describe is often experienced by individuals as they become drawn to non-duality and they open to awakening and liberation. There can be a lessening of interest in the stories of people's lives and in philosophical speculation and an increased connection with the simplicity of whatever is arising in presence.
   I tend not to use the word 'clarity' in my description of awakening as it can imply mental understanding which has nothing to do with the seeing of Oneness. It sounds as if what is happening for you is a more fundamental shift than a change in ideas.

Thank you for your reply. It leaves me, delightfully, with nothing. However, I have one more question. A few years ago, an astrologer gave me a very accurate description of my character and also predicted that I would go through a difficult period at a specific age. Although I don't believe in astrology, everything happened as he said it would.

If there is no time, how is it possible to 'see into the future' in this way?

In liberation it is seen that there is only This and there is no space and time. However, until there is physical death, this 'waking dream', to use a common metaphor, continues apparently to unfold in space and time.

In this dream, time, space, people and events all apparently continue to happen. Your astrologer reading your character and predicting your future is part of that dream which is arising without any meaning or purpose. That is its beauty and magnificence—that it needs no meaning or purpose, but simply is what it is.

✺

HOW IS LIBERATION KNOWN?

If liberation is seen, how does the person know that it has been seen?

There are no rules about liberation, but sometimes there is a sudden 'event' in which liberation is seen. In this event, the sense of contracted separation that belongs to the person dissolves and it is seen that there is no one, there is no central identity or self. Words really break down at this point and perhaps the best we can do is to say that Oneness sees itself, or if you prefer, Oneness recognises itself. There is a knowing that all is empty, but also full, and that the nature of that fullness is love.

Whatever is happening right now is also Oneness experiencing itself. But included in that there might be the sensation that this is not the case, that there is a separate person who is doing the experiencing.

There is a kind of hopeless delight in your answers. They refresh me and plunge me into despair at the same time.

✻

A FORMULA FOR LIBERATION?

I used to assume that if awakening or liberation happened, there would be constant joy. But now I can see that you were right in your description. It is simply the seeing that there is no one here and that everything is just happening. Apart from that everything remains the same.

If there were a formula to express this it might be GJ + GD − TP = N + IM

(Great Joy + Great Despair − The Person = Neutrality + Intense Moments)

I like your formula, but it often settles down into a bit better than neutral. Often there may be quiet joy.

✻

NO GROUND TO HIT

I've just heard that you won't be coming to Munich this Spring. That's a pity because I wanted to buy you a beer.

I'm not sure what's happened here. Perhaps I would describe it as a shift in energy. Everything that was happening before is still arising including ambitions and neuroses, but somehow they're not taken seriously anymore.

It's not a state of bliss and it's clear that there's nothing to be gained from this. It's as if this was always known although it wasn't seen.

I read somewhere "The bad news is that you're in free fall and there's nothing to hold on to. The good news is that there's no ground to hit." I like that.

I'm sorry to miss the beer. Maybe another time.

Yes, seeing This is not especially about bliss, although of course bliss may sometimes arise. Your description is very good. There's an energy shift and then life goes on.

I like the quote very much.

✸

TRAUMA AND THERAPY

At the moment I find myself feeling quite desperate. This seems to be because of a particular trauma that I experienced. I see a therapist and a lot of powerful emotions come up with him, but there still seems to be a deep unease underneath my feelings.

Do you think that trauma can be alleviated? Or do you think it is just a story? Do you have any suggestions as to what I might do? I've glimpsed liberation and I think this makes it difficult for me to really engage fully with therapy. My glimpse seems mainly to have left me with despair.

I'm sorry to hear that you're having such a hard time.

It is quite common for people who have been through an awakening to go through a difficult period afterwards. Your description of deep unease and despair is very similar to how some other people describe that period. Indeed I relate to your description myself when I remember how the time after awakening felt for me.

Beyond that, it is difficult for me to make suggestions. For myself at that time, I valued certain therapeutic activities, particularly ones such as Focusing, which helped to direct me to the feelings involved rather than to the story in my head about them. I also found certain transpersonal techniques of some help, as well as doing simple everyday things that I could take some enjoyment in. But of course we're all different and we each have to find whatever's most helpful in getting through this period for ourselves. I send you my best wishes.

✸

THERE IS ONLY LOVE

Liberation to me is indescribable, but the words "There is only love" come closer to touching it than any other. For me there was a profound and dramatic unfolding and then the drama of life simply went on as if nothing had happened. What was seen was completely impersonal. It was seen that there can be no mistakes and life flows as it has to. The individual who is left cannot really know what happened because it has nothing to do with them. That sense continues now in spite of doubts sometimes coming in.

One other thing. Can you cast any light on why it is that, after total expansion, a sense of localisation returns?

You describe this very well. As you say, there is a sense that life just happens and that there can be no mistakes. Strangely enough, the neurotic mind can still come in at times and doubt this, because anything is possible in liberation. Yet somehow that doubt is seen to be just a thought and it is known that this is simply life flowing "as it has to". However, we need to be careful with that phrase, as it is very easy for the mind to start weaving more stories around it. Perhaps it's better just to say that "Life happens."

I can't throw any more light on localisation returning. From what you write, you have sensed that yourself, and it is a common experience. First there is no sense of localisation or separation, then localisation returns but separation has ended. As far as I know, localisation always returns eventually. Perhaps it's necessary to protect the body-mind organism.

✸

JUST THIS

When you say there is just This, do you mean that literally? Do you mean there is only whatever is happening right now?

Yes, when I say there is just This I mean it literally, just as you describe. It really is that simple. But the sense of there being a separated person with a past and a future and all their other concerns gets in the way of seeing this.

❋

RECOGNISING OR NOT RECOGNISING LIBERATION

I've never really felt that the stuff that's happening in life was important in the way that everyone else seems to experience it. I've never felt like rejecting it and it's always somehow felt like a dream.

I have had two liberation experiences exactly as you describe them. Consciousness suddenly and unexpectedly expanded and was seen to have nothing to do with 'me'. It was seen that everything is literally appearing out of the void or abyss moment by apparent moment, just as you describe. This everything includes me, thoughts, experiences, feelings, other people, all natural phenomena and all objects. From clouds to cars to trees, it's all nothing being something.

I have listened to a lot of so-called non-dual speakers suggesting that if we do some process or other we will become liberated. I know that all of that is ridiculous. I liked your 'Buddha at The Gas Pump' interview and thought it was very funny, but not as confrontational as Rick Archer's note about it suggested. I found it funny listening to someone determinedly wanting to know how the character could become liberated. The character cannot bear to hear that it has no more persistence than a cup of coffee. It arises, seems to exist in time and space and then disappears.

I feel I have always understood non-duality and yet there is still a sense of self. The character is still somehow regarded as real. Therefore 'I' still experience the pain of separation, even though I know it is only an idea. And I know that everything is as it 'should' be. I don't really understand why, even though I have had this understanding of non-duality, there is still something here trying to escape from a sense of separation. But in spite of this, there are many times when the self fades away and at those times there's no confusion about this at all. Then even the simplest things in life are seen as amazing.

I seem to exist in and out of two worlds, sometimes an 'I' and sometimes nothing. It's as if Consciousness is flickering back and forth. At one moment I'm a 'me' and then it is seen with total clarity that the 'me' seems to pop into existence but isn't real. There is everything and nothing at the same time and they are both somehow the void.

In spite of what I have written, I lead a very ordinary life which I enjoy a lot. I want to thank you for communicating about this so clearly.

I very much enjoyed reading your description. You write with great clarity about this.

Sometimes when I talk to someone about this, I get the impression that everything there is to be seen in liberation has been seen. Nevertheless there may still be a remaining thought or an idea that there is something still missing. Maybe they feel that the experience of life after liberation (excuse the time-bound language) should be different and better in some way. But everything is simply what it is. It will probably tend to go on as before, except now it is seen that it isn't going on for anyone. From your description, it sounds like you may have always recognised this in some way, so the shift probably won't seem very dramatic for you—not as dramatic as for someone who had previously had a more solid sense of separation. I don't know if that's what's happening in your case but it might be worth thinking about.

Thanks for your reply, Richard. I neither reject the world nor experience it as entirely real. And I've always experienced the dramas that people enact as a kind of play "signifying nothing".

I listen to you and Tony and it seems like a great joke that the 'me' is still waiting for liberation to take place. It really is a great joke.

I like it that in your communication about this there is nothing for sale. And when someone says "So what you're saying is there's nothing I can do? I should just stop trying?" I almost laugh out loud. The 'me' just can't hear this.

✲

TOOTHACHE

I felt a resonance on reading your books, but I have two questions. Firstly, you seem to be saying that there is no cause and effect. So if you have a toothache, do you go to a dentist? And if so, isn't this a contradiction?

Secondly, when you say that there is nothing happening, do you mean that events take place but without any purpose?

In liberation, this is seen to be a waking dream and then everything goes on as before. So if a dream character has a dream toothache, the sensible thing to do is to go to a dream dentist. You see, liberation makes no difference to this.

Seen from the perspective of liberation, there is nothing happening because there is no time. Past and future exist only as thoughts arising in this. However, you are also right to say that events are (apparently) taking place but without a purpose. Life does not need a purpose. Life is its own justification. A flower does not need a purpose for being here and neither do you. The flower and you are already Oneness manifesting as a flower and as an individual.

May I ask you two more questions? Some time ago I was sitting in my room and just for a moment there was no more seeking. There was just looking around, hearing the sound of a car, feeling the summer breeze on my face. There was no need for thoughts about any phenomena. Everything was perfect. Everything was still. Everything was simple. Everything was connected to everything else. Is liberation really that simple? You say that there is just This. Do you mean that literally? Is there simply a room, a character, sensations, and nothing else, nothing happening, no cause and effect?

And what about suffering? This seems to be such a problem. Does suffering really have no meaning?

In liberation it is seen that there is emptiness, and out of emptiness this waking dream that we call life arises. Just as in a night-time dream, there is apparent cause and effect, and just as with a night-time dream, this cause and effect can be seen through. It is seen through in liberation. But when liberation is seen, the waking dream goes on until there is physical death, so as I said before, if there is a tooth-ache, it is sensible to go to a dentist.

As to suffering, if you want to reduce your own suffering there are lots of things you can do. Similarly, if you would like to reduce other people's suffering, there are also clearly many things you can do. And if you want to perceive a meaning in suffering, then you can buy into any one of the many religious or spiritual or psychological stories. And in the meantime, there is still only This, in which stories about suffering and many other things arise.

"Nothing is happening" is meant literally. There is nothing happening and yet this dream of time and space arises. The mind can never make sense of this, yet in liberation it is clearly seen.

✸

SPIRITUAL FRIENDS

I notice that your German publisher says that one of your books will "give life meaning and value". I think that's very funny, because you are obviously saying that there is no meaning.

Recently I asked you what someone could do when all meaning and purpose had been seen through and all previously-held concepts and theories had fallen away, but the person was still there. You described it as being like a desert and that is my experience of it.

Because I have changed so much, my friends and family are very confused about what may have happened to me. We used to share a common belief in the importance of following a spiritual path, but now I've lost all interest in this. The people I hang out with most are very concerned about this and hoping that I can be persuaded back into spirituality. But now that all just seems like a game to me—a game that the ego plays. Even though I'm uncomfortable with what's happening now, I know I can't go back to the old spiritual ways.

Whenever something negative happens to me, like I have an illness, my partner feels that I must find the deep reason why this has happened so that I can learn from it. She means well, but I can't take these beliefs seriously now.

I resonate with what you say, especially about the time spent in the desert, and about the impossibility of believing any longer in stories which seek to give an explanation for everything from the 'spiritual' level. All such stories come under the heading of 'baseless supposition' or 'superstition'.

I hope you come out of the desert soon.

✿

MIND, SELF AND EGO

Is the mind the same thing as the ego? Are these just synonyms describing the same thing? And what is self-realisation?

The mind is simply the process of thinking. In other words there is no mind, there is a thought and then another thought and then another. These thoughts arise from nothing and fall back into nothing, but the sense that they arise from a mind creates the impression that we live in separation.

The word 'ego' is used in different ways, which makes it very confusing. Sometimes it is used to mean the sense of 'I', or in other words the sense of 'self'. But often it is used to mean our sense of self-importance, as in "He has a very big ego". And sometimes it is used in the Freudian sense, to mean the 'Reality Principle', or the part of ourself which mediates between the moralistic demands of the super-ego and the pleasure-seeking demands of the id. In this third sense, the ego is like the Managing Director of our life, which sits behind a large desk believing that it controls things.

But in whatever way we use the word 'ego', when separation is seen through these are all seen to be meaningless phenomena, like waves crashing on a shore.

Ironically, self-realisation is the realisation that there is no self.

❀

PRACTICES

Sometimes I still find myself doing spiritual practices, as if I am doing them automatically. Then I may not do them for a while. At the moment I feel that practices are futile, but I know that it's at least possible for them to start again. I feel that self-enquiry is particularly futile and yet I know that even that could re-assert itself.

Sometimes I walk round the park with my dog. Sometimes I watch television. Sometimes I phone Tony Parsons. I know there's still a sense of separation here, but I suppose I could lose it at any time, regardless of what I am doing. Do you have any comments?

Walking round the park with your dog sounds good to me, whether you lose your sense of separation or not.

What you describe is often experienced by others as well. Sometimes there's practice, sometimes there isn't. Sometimes there's the belief that practice is useful, sometimes there isn't. And sometimes there's the knowing that nobody is doing any of that. Everything simply arises of its own accord.

'You' can't do anything, which is why I sometimes suggest to people that they find something simple that they enjoy and go out and do it. I hope that doesn't sound too paradoxical—that's just the nature of language. I know that Tony sometimes suggests the same.

❀

REPORTING ON THE NON-DUAL STATE

I loved your book but I have a question. How can anyone report back from a non-dual state if non-dual awareness is not even aware of itself?

I'm glad you enjoyed my book. I don't recognise the description "non-dual awareness is not even aware of itself". I don't know who it's from, but it's not from me. My description would be that non-duality is either seen or it isn't. If it is seen, it is seen impersonally. In other words its seeing has nothing to do with the character of the individual who is reporting back on it. That's why liberation cannot be induced by an individual working on their emotional, psychological or spiritual state.

Of course, although there's always only Being, if there is no individual around to report on it, there will be no description, either accurate or misleading.

The description was from a book by John Wheeler. It made me wonder what the point of being in a non-dual state was if there was no one to recognise that this is the case. The individual would still be as ignorant of liberation as they were before. Perhaps I'm still hoping for a liberation experience but I can't understand how there can be an experience without an experiencer.

The seeing of liberation is an energy shift, not simply a change in cognition. When non-separation is seen, it is incontrovertible. This seeing tends to have a transformative effect on the character of the individual who remains, unless of course it coincides with physical death, in which case there is no more individual and no more character.

There is no one who is either ignorant or not ignorant. Being asleep and being awake are the same thing, except that in being awake it is known that they are the same thing, whereas in being asleep it is believed that they are different. This knowing also tends to transform the individual, because all the stories of meaning and searching that ran their life tend to drop away.

Thank you for your reply. I once had a drug-induced energy shift that I described to Tony Parsons. My 'sense of self' included everything— the fields, the trees, the river, the sky. Everything felt like it was me. I described it as like walking through myself. Tony said that was because 'I' wasn't there.

Yes, I agree with Tony about that. But the trouble with drug-induced 'energy shifts' is that they often do not have the transformative effect that tends to happen when the sense of self collapses of itself, without any help from pharmaceuticals, opiates or hallucinogens.

✳

CONFLICT BETWEEN TEACHERS

Dear Richard, I've been watching the discussions on conscious. tv between yourself and two other non-duality teachers. I found it interesting and informative, but I noticed that there seemed to be differences in opinion between you. So it seems that even Advaita speakers fall into the trap of disputation.

I have also noticed that various books on non-duality seem to dis-agree with each other, and some speakers declare that other speakers are misleading.

So is Advaita descending into the same mess that has happened to the major world religions? Are divisions, dogmas and conflicting teachings appearing?

I'm sorry if I sound like one of the Advaita Police, but I'm inter-ested in your view on this. Best wishes, Jason

Dear Jason, The terms 'Advaita' and 'non-duality' are umbrella terms that do cover quite a lot of ground. So yes, you will find different points of view expressed, and it is probably inevitable that sometimes one speaker will comment adversely on another's point of view. As you point out, we can compare this to the schisms in religion which inevitably arise from our somewhat combative psychology. I like to mis-quote the New Testament on this: "Where two or three are gathered together in my name, there will be discord, disharmony and a punch-up."

The antidote to all this, I suggest, is to remember that no point of view really matters. If you find yourself taking it too seriously, have a cup of tea and a walk round the park, or whatever else you enjoy doing. All the versions of Advaita are stories. None of them can really encapsulate the reality of liberation. Other than that, I would simply steer clear of anyone who has an agenda about non-duality, that is, anyone who seems to think it is important that you buy their version.

The conscious.tv discussions were great fun to do, but you are right, there were definitely differences in what we were saying. One speaker, for example, was talking about leading groups through transpersonal experiences. It is not difficult to evoke transpersonal experiences in a group of people as long as they are willing to be taken there. I have done it myself many times as a transpersonal trainer and I have experienced it many times as a participant in workshops.

Transpersonal experiences are lovely, although their intensity can wreak havoc in your personal life afterwards. However, they have nothing more or less to do with liberation than any other experience. Liberation is not transpersonal, it is impersonal, and it cannot be reliably evoked during a weekend workshop, not by me, not by anybody. It has no reference to any experience, whether transpersonal or not. It has nothing to do with me, and if it is seen where you are sitting, it has nothing to do with you.

I like the idea of you acting as the Advaita Police. It's a tough job, but somebody's got to do it. Best wishes, Richard

❀

SELF AND NO SELF

Non-dual speakers say that the personal self has no existence, but I suspect that they are not talking from a wide enough perspective.

For example, I have a strong feeling that I am responsible for my actions. I can even carry out simple experiments to demonstrate that I have free will. For example, I can choose to raise my arm or not, choose to make myself a cup of tea or not and many other actions.

Perhaps the self really exists in some form prior to awakening, and dies during liberation. If there is really no self at all, why does our everyday experience feel so much as if there is a self?

The only perspective that anything worth saying about non-duality can come from is the perspective of direct seeing. As no other perspective can have any bearing here, it doesn't matter whether this perspective is too narrow or wide enough. There simply isn't any other valid perspective to draw on.

Life as you describe yourself experiencing it is simply what it is like to feel that we are separate. When that sense of separation ends, it is over. What is experienced after that may not change very much, but it is seen then that there is no one doing any of it.

You suggest that the self may exist prior to awakening and die during liberation, rather than there being no self at all. But ultimately what difference does that make? These are just alternative ways of trying to describe that which cannot be described. However, if you think that the self might exist in some form prior to awakening, it might be interesting for you to speculate about what that form might be.

You comment that you can carry out simple experiments to demonstrate that you have free will. Neuroscientists can carry out sophisticated experiments that demonstrate that your sense of free will is illusory.

❋

WHO OR WHAT IS AWARE?

If there is nobody, who is aware of that?

Rather than ask "Who is aware of that?" it might make more sense to ask "What is aware of that?"

No one is aware of that, it is simply seen. Or we could say that Being, or Oneness, is aware of that. Being is aware of itself. But this is a little misleading because now it sounds as if we are personalising Being. Unfortunately that is just the way language works.

We could equally say Nothing or No Thing is aware of itself.

The thought "There is nobody" apparently arises for a person in a mind. But the direct seeing that there is nobody occurs when neither the person nor the mind are there. The thought "There is nobody" has no value but the direct seeing that there is nobody may transform everything.

My mind seems to come up with more and more questions and wants to become doubt-free. I think this is because the reality of Seeing seems so far off that it's a relief to get some concepts clear. The trap for me of course is that as soon as my mind gets an answer to one question, another question immediately appears.

Yes, that is the nature of the mind. The point I made about language is simply that there are many different ways to answer these questions, and the apparent differences, paradoxes or even contradictions, don't really matter.

The reality of Seeing can seem so far away, but actually it is closer than we are to ourself. But it can't be seen as long as we are there, blocking out the view.

❃

IS THIS JUST ANOTHER RELIGION?

I'm troubled by the thought that non-duality might be just another religion, like Buddhism, Christianity or Judaism.

What makes this communication different to a religion is that there is no agenda attached to it. With religions, and even with spiritual paths, it is usually felt that it's important that others should get the message, and that people should do what the teachers, priests, rabbis, swamis or gurus tell them to do.

However, with this communication there is no suggestion that it matters whether it is understood or not, and certainly no suggestion that anyone should do anything in particular about it. It is simply a sharing among people who feel drawn to share in this way.

Of course non-duality can be turned into another religion. I'd be very wary of anyone who tries to do that. A big clue is if they suggest that this could be useful in any way. I recently participated in a conference on non-duality where one of the speakers wanted everyone there "to help move non-duality into the mainstream" so that it could "help people with their suffering." It is in this way that 'Non-Duality' as yet another religion is born.

What I love about this communication is that it's so refreshing after all the religious stories I heard as a child with their instructions to do what the priests told us to do.

Nevertheless I am feeling a lot of fear which seems based on those childhood stories. In recent years I've been following spiritual teachers rather than priests, and now, instead of fearing hell if I don't do what the priests say, I fear bad karma in my next life if I don't do what the spiritual teachers say. How crazy is that! Yet I don't seem to be able to free myself from these stories about death.

You are experiencing something very common. Many people feel that their life is ruled by fear. Much of that fear may be focused on death, especially if they've been brought up with the cruel threats of an unkind religion.

Dealing with fear takes us into the therapeutic area. I don't venture into that area much anymore, but I will simply share with you what I feel after many years involved with therapy.

One of the simplest and most effective ways of dealing with fear, or indeed any uncomfortable feeling, is to spend a certain amount of time each day tuning in to the bodily sensation of the feeling. You could keep your attention on it without trying to change it in any way, but if it changes of its own accord, just allow your attention to follow whatever change takes place. This has a completely different effect to paying attention to the story about fear in your head. Gradually the feeling may release and transform. If you want to know more about this process, you could look up Focusing or some similar technique on the internet.

Certain transpersonal techniques, such as meditation or Symbol Therapy, might also be helpful. You can also find out more about these on the internet.

As you can see, this communication comes more from 'The Therapist' than from 'The Non-Duality Communicator', because that's what feels more appropriate at the moment.

❋

FEAR AND DEPRESSION

I frequently wake up with a feeling of overwhelming fear. Although this is terrifying, I also find it interesting. Do you have any suggestions as to what I can do? Should I just let go?

I also feel depressed and anxious. This seems to have started when my relationship broke down a year ago. Can depression precede awakening?

Nothing in this reply should be construed as advice. Nevertheless, you ask "Should I just let go?" Many people would suggest that this is probably the best thing to do in the circumstances that you describe, that if possible you don't resist this kind of experience but allow it to unfold. In psychotherapeutic circles this is some-times known as 'experiential non-avoidance'.

As to your question about depression, yes, it is possible that a period of depression can precede awakening. But it's also likely that your depression is associated with the end of your relationship. Of course it might be unrelated to either of these. I believe that Eckhart Tolle wrote about his severe depression, and Suzanne Segal wrote about her profound anxiety. You might like to look at some of their writings.

When I was still searching and in despair, I used to ring up Tony Parsons. Fundamentally, what he said to me came down to "Find some small simple thing that you enjoy doing, and do it." I would say the same myself now, although I recognise that this is not easy when we are feeling depressed and anxious.

Thank you very much for your reply! I understand that it's not possible for you to give me advice. In fact as soon as I had written to you I realised that my questions can't be answered by anyone. Nevertheless, the answers you gave are what I wanted to hear.

I have read Eckhart Tolle and Suzanne Segal and I thought they were both very interesting.

❈

DEATH

Does awareness persist after physical death? If so, how can it do so when there are no sensory organs?

It is natural for the mind to speculate about death and to create endless stories about it. But it is also, in a profound and rather obvious way, a waste of time. All I can say is don't worry, it will be okay. When Oneness is seen, it is seen that death is not a problem. This is partly because it is known then that what you really are was never born and so can never die, and partly because the mind grows bored with baseless speculation. Of course, all speculation about "after physical death" is baseless.

However, in separation, we will do with these statements whatever we will. We will embrace them or reject them and it doesn't matter which.

MORE DISAGREEMENTS ABOUT NON-DUALITY

I would like to know what you think about the different views on non-duality that are being expressed at the moment. I feel that what you and Tony Parsons say has little to do with what most non-dual teachers are talking about.

They say things like "You are already present awareness, but to discover this you must investigate the belief in 'me'." One teacher says that you must have the courage to live as awareness. Another one says that you must stop believing in the concept of 'me'. I've been given lots of advice, most of which seems to be designed to put me firmly in my place.

But you, Tony and a few others say that seeing Oneness is a kind of energetic shift and that it has nothing to do with how much we self-enquire or how much we understand about non-duality.

So there seems to be a lot of confusion around the subject. This can be very puzzling for the seeker. But waiting for an energetic shift to occur can also create a lot of expectations. Can you throw some light on any of this?

The clue is in the word 'teacher'. Speakers who say that they are teaching non-duality are usually prescribing a path of becoming, some version of the story that separation can be seen through by some kind of effort. It can't be. Whether separation drops away has nothing to do with the one who feels themself to be separate. However, paths and practices can have psychological and emotional effects, and these can be pleasant or unpleasant and make life less difficult or more difficult.

Understanding concepts about non-duality, or believing or not believing in the concept of 'me', are irrelevant, because they are things that a person can do and the person can never see non-duality. As for having "the courage to live as awareness", I have no idea what this means, nor how you would go about doing it. But it sounds painful and therefore appealing to those of us who are masochists. It would also enable us to beat ourself up every time we 'failed' or become pompous every time we 'succeeded'.

I would be very suspicious of any teacher who tells you that you must or should do anything. Many psychotherapists have a good understanding of the negative effects of 'musts', 'shoulds' and 'oughts'. They warn against the perils of 'hardening of the oughteries' and 'musturbation'.

You are right that waiting for a shift can also create a lot of expectations. These will neither delay nor hasten the seeing of Oneness. If advice were possible, which it isn't, I would suggest that rather than waiting for a shift, you find some simple thing you enjoy doing and do it, perhaps taking a walk in the park, or drinking a cup of coffee in a café, or whatever seems pleasurable to you.

I find that doing something simple may be sufficient for five minutes, but then I start thinking "OK, what's next?"
If it's so simple, how come we keep missing it?

You are right. For the person who lives in separation, doing something simple is not sufficient, or not sufficient for long. That is why there is no point in giving advice about this.

The reason we miss it in spite of its simplicity is that there seems to be a person there looking for it in some other imaginary place and in some other imaginary time. When the sense of the person collapses, it becomes obvious that "This is it" and there is no need to look for it anymore.

✳

AWAKENING CRISIS, FEAR, ZEN

From my own experiences, I recognise a lot of what you say in 'I Hope You Die Soon'.

I practised Zen and some years ago there was the experience that I wasn't there anymore. This lasted for a while but then my sense of self returned.

Recently the self has disappeared again. My sense of time has changed a great deal and my relationships with people do not feel important any more. It's as if the physical world isn't quite real now. But very strong feelings can come up, sometimes of intense peace and sometimes of intense fear, although it doesn't feel as if I 'own' them. Sometimes this is wonderful, but sometimes I feel that I could be going mad.

I have no one I can talk to directly about this, so I'd really appreciate it if you could comment.

The experiences that you describe are quite common in awakening. They are not experiences necessarily to be overly concerned about, even if some of them are sometimes disturbing. Awakening is often a shock and in both awakening and liberation all kinds of feelings can still arise. These can include fear, anger and sadness among others. From the point of view of managing them, probably the best thing to do is simply to pay attention to them as they arise in the body and let them, as it were, unwind.

Of course anyone who is concerned about their experiences might find it helpful to seek out a therapist if they feel drawn in that direction. Unfortunately not many therapists are familiar with awakening. However for those who feel very disturbed by awakening, there is an organisation called The Spiritual Crisis Network which might be worth looking into. (www.spiritual crisisnetwork.org.uk)

Thank you for your answer. I'm feeling less fearful and more peaceful now.

I've read that, like me, you are a psychotherapist. Since the realisation that neither I nor other people are 'real', practising as a psychotherapist feels quite difficult for me. Nevertheless, I'm still practising and observing what happens in the sessions.

In a way it seems quite ridiculous for 'no one' to work with 'no one' to try to help the person become healthier, especially as I see now that there's really no such thing as a relationship. But although my mind thinks that this is a problem, inside me there's a knowing that it couldn't be any other way.

Can you comment? Do you think there's something wrong with me? Do you still work as a psychotherapist?

I trained in therapy, counselling and humanistic psychology but then worked as a lecturer and trainer rather than as a practitioner. I have recently retired from lecturing and training work.

The concerns you express are quite common among psychotherapists when non-duality is seen. It doesn't sound to me as if there is anything wrong with you. My own view is that a psychotherapist who is not there (I hope you know what I mean by this) is preferable to a psychotherapist who is there. The psychotherapist who is still there as a person will probably have some agendas, which may get in the way of them being present for the client. When the psychotherapist is absent, there can be more presence. In that presence, the client may flourish.

Although it is seen that there is no such thing as a fixed relationship, an entity, a noun, relating continues as a fluid and ever-changing process, a verb.

When you say that your mind thinks this is a problem, but inside you there is a knowing that it couldn't be any other way, you sum up very clearly the experience of many individuals where Oneness is recognised. Even when there is an undeniable knowing, the mind may fight against so many of the implications of this knowing. But that 'mind energy' will probably diminish over time.

In your reply to me you wrote "relating continues as a fluid and ever-changing process, a verb." I cannot understand this because that would imply the existence of time, but there is no time.

Before awakening, a relationship seemed like a movie to me, but now it seems like a series of separate photographs with no process linking one to another. Yesterday I saw my closest friend. Today she is not here and there is no experience of having this friend. This frightens me, because all my roles have disappeared. I am no longer a friend, a sister, a colleague or a daughter. I am nothing. My mind rebels against this.

Last year I heard Tony Parsons say "There is no London. There is only This." Inside I feel that he is right, but my mind says "No, he is so obviously wrong!". I am sitting here writing to you. But is there really a man called Richard who I'm writing to? Inside I feel that there is no one to write to, but my mind still thinks there's a reason for writing.

Can you cast any light on my confusion?

In this waking dream, which continues when liberation is seen unless there is physical death, an apparent process of relating, of thinking, of feeling, of perceiving, even of writing to apparent other people, continues. This process can only unfold in time. If we want to be more scrupulous with language, we could say "This process can only unfold in the appearance of time." The appearance of time unfolds in consciousness. There is nowhere else for it to unfold.

That is why you are apparently able to write to me in one place and time and I am apparently able to read your words in another place and time. Perhaps you could see yourself as writing to yourself in order to ask yourself to clarify some confusion for yourself.

In awakening it is seen that This is all there is and there is no friend, no sister, no colleague, no daughter, no relationships of any kind. This is certainly sometimes experienced as frightening. You describe all this very well. But to the mind, this can make no sense, because the mind lives in time and in a world of cause and effect and continuity, so of course to the mind all these relationships exist and continue. However, after awakening, even for the mind these continuing relationships will probably be somewhat transformed.

What is seen in awakening is not seen by the mind and cannot be understood by the mind. If we want to have an argument between the mind and Oneness about the nature of reality, the mind will always win. But this makes no difference to the seeing of Oneness.

If you want to harmonise what is seen in Oneness and what the mind thinks it knows, you are on a road to nowhere. You will always fail. And yet Oneness is still seen, no matter how much the mind may revolt against it.

I have lost all reference points for my physical existence. All sense of a physical body has gone, even though there are thoughts and feelings in the 'space' which the body used to occupy. Awareness is just everywhere with no location at all in space. Sometimes this feels beautiful, but sometimes it's frightening because everything that happens seems to be happening within 'me'. I seem to have no physical boundary at all, so when I am with a client, for example, she and I seem to be part of the same 'everything'.

I feel conflicted about this. I love it and I don't want it to end, but it's frightening so I do want it to end.

The experiences you are having are not unusual. The disappearance of the person often provokes both joy and fear. I don't give advice, but if I did I would say just allow the fear to be and stay with it while it is there.

Very few people actually die of fear, you know.

When the fear isn't there, simply enjoy the disappearance. And don't be disappointed when the intensity of this event comes to an end, as it inevitably will. It might feel then as if you have lost something but you won't have, except of course for yourself.

❊

CONTRADICTIONS IN NON-DUALITY

I understand you as having written that there is nothing beyond what is happening here in my room, and that there is nothing beyond what is happening there in your room. There must be a contradiction here as both cannot be correct.

This is the construction that the mind puts on the words that it hears. Remember that words can in any case never describe Oneness.

The mind may hear these words as contradictory. That's okay. But I would say instead that these and many other words about non-duality are paradoxical.

The mind absolutely cannot understand non-duality. There is a complete disjunct between how the mind perceives reality and what is seen in awakening or liberation. Then it is seen that there is neither a person nor a mind and that This is all there is. This is why seeing non-duality can be such a shock.

The mind may try to work out this puzzle, but that has no importance. Working it out, if that were possible, would not bring liberation any closer. Not working it out will not keep liberation at bay.

Perhaps you could view this metaphorically as like a zen koan, which defies logic and goes beyond the mind.

As you have mentioned koans, from the point of view of non-duality, how would you reply to koans like "What is the sound of one hand clapping?"

Although I mentioned koans, they tend to make my head hurt so I don't pay them much attention. I'd rather take a walk round the lake in the park and have a cup of coffee in the café there.

However, I recently saw someone respond to "What is the sound of one hand clapping?" by simply striking the table they were sitting at with one hand. I thought that was very clever. However, I don't think cleverness is really the point where koans are concerned.

Here for you to puzzle over is my own non-duality koan: "How do you get out of a prison that you are not in?"

✻

SEEKING BEFORE AND AFTER LIBERATION.
DO THINGS REALLY CHANGE?

Why are you not still seeking? If life continues after liberation unchanged, surely the body-mind will still be seeking, just as it was before liberation?

You and Tony Parsons both say that nothing changes after liberation but then you say that seeking is over. But this is not what you would have said prior to liberation. So apparently liberation does have an effect on the dis-identified body-mind after all.

The most important word in your what you write is 'apparently'. What I say about liberation is that nothing is changed, yet everything is transformed. Everything goes on just as before, but now it is seen that it is going on for no one.

Once it has been seen that This is all there is, that there is only Oneness, that there is unconditional love, that there is no need for meaning, how could there be any need for searching? What could there be to search for?

Communication about non-duality is bound to be paradoxical. To anyone who objects to this, all I can do is apologise on behalf of Oneness and remind them that they are doing it themselves. Before we go off chasing after any more hares, let me say that this last phrase is only a metaphor.

Thank you for that reply. I think I understand this much better now.

But it's time for my next question. Can I trust that events will proceed normally once liberation happens? Or is this really a non-question? Would there even be an 'I' to be concerned if events did not proceed normally?

I have a fear about the possibility of losing the ability to function normally on an everyday basis in liberation. This might really be a fear about something as basic as survival.

I wonder what 'events not proceeding normally' could possibly mean.

Whether you trust or don't trust makes no difference. This is still all there is, Nothing appearing as everything, the One appearing as the many.

Perhaps you have a fear that 'you' could somehow get in the way. But the very sense of 'you' is false and so it cannot interfere with anything.

Fear around this is a common experience. It's probably best just to pay it some attention as it arises in the body and then afterwards do some simple thing that you enjoy. Of course some people, if fear becomes very intense, like to deal with it with a therapist. In this case, a therapist who understands something about non-duality might be a good choice.

I do not understand how there can be no 'I'. After all, I have conversations. Do the words simply arise of their own accord?

What would have happened in history if everyone had been liberated, including great thinkers like Darwin, Marx and Freud? Would they still have thought of their theories?

I think that really I'm feeling the need for reassurance that the realities of life if I am liberated will be okay.

You ask "Do the words simply arise of their own accord?" Yes, that is exactly what happens. Everything is proceeding quite satisfactorily without there being any need for an 'I'. Oneness is writing these words and Oneness is reading them.

Pretending for a moment that there is such a thing as time in which history can unfold, Darwin was Oneness Darwin-ing, Marx was Oneness Marx-ing—you get my drift. And all our memories, thoughts, ideas and speculations about your question can only arise in This. Why is that? Because This is all there is.

No one is liberated. No one has ever been liberated. No one will ever be liberated. There is only liberation, in which the existence of people who believe they are not liberated arises.

❄

TRYING TO KNOW WHO YOU REALLY ARE

Many teachers emphasise that we need to discover who we really are. You and Tony talk about who we are not, but you don't say much about who we are. Could you comment?

I wouldn't worry about discovering who you really are unless you are interested in exploring yourself through psychotherapy, self-development or other means. Knowing who you really are will not help the seeing of non-duality. What (not 'who') you really are is Oneness, Being itself. As a person living in separation we are unable to see this, but when the person drops away, it is seen in non-separation.

❋

CAUGHT BETWEEN AWAKENING AND LIBERATION

I may be one of those unfortunate beings who is stuck between awakening and liberation.

From a young age I was searching for enlightenment and some years ago I went through powerful kundalini experiences. I don't think they actually had anything to do with enlightenment but they were certainly disturbing and painful.

Then I began to realise more and more that everyday life is a dream. This seems so obvious to me that sometimes I find myself laughing out loud at the joke of it.

My reading about this has produced some clarity but some of the authors, such Nisargadatta and Balsekar, have also really pissed me off. I do get that there is no one who owns their actions and there is no point asking "Why?", but your 'The Book Of No One' really shook me to my foundations. It's very hard for someone like me to lose all sense of meaning and hope but still be 'trapped' as a person.

I'm progressively losing my sense of a future or a past. I can't project myself imaginatively into the future anymore or even plan quite simple things. And it no longer seems to me that I have an actual past that I lived through. I have a strong sense that our whole life only consists of the present moment. 'I' seem to be gradually disappearing.

Of course the autobiographical material stays intact. I know where I live and, if pushed to it, I can even find where I parked my car. But there's nothing 'inside' that feels as if it is essentially 'me'. Nevertheless, there's still a painful sense of separation and a longing to be free.

You write about the despair that can be felt when meaning has been seen through but the sense of separation is still there. That's what it feels like for me. It's really terrible to realise that I don't want anything out of life anymore.

Reading your book has sometimes produced a real sensation of shock in which my mind simply shudders to a halt. I really want to lose 'me'. Is there anything you can say that may bring about 'my end'?

I relate to a lot of what you say, especially the pain that can be experienced between awakening and liberation. Even when this is seen through in liberation, suffering can still arise, sometimes even more strongly than before. This is because the filters of separation have come off. However, in liberation it is common for suffering to become more visceral, to be sensed directly in the body rather than indirectly as a story in the head. I think it was Koho Zenji who said "No one knows sorrow like a Zen master." However, if suffering does arise, it is likely that it will be moved through more easily. It might be more intense but it will probably be less long-lasting.

I wish very much there was something I could say "to bring about your end", but you probably already know that there isn't.

❊

SUFFERING AND PSYCHOTHERAPY

I've heard you say that even in liberation, suffering (including depression) can arise.

But who is it who suffers, if the person has been seen through? Some people seem to live very relaxed lives, but I find myself suffering a lot. I'm thinking of having some psychotherapy. Do you still think that psychotherapy has some value?

Anything that happens before liberation is seen can happen after it is seen. However, depression and boredom are much less likely to arise.

Who is it who suffers? No one suffers. Thoughts, feelings, physical sensations and perceptions, whether of suffering or of pleasure or of anything else, all arise out of Oneness and fall away again. In separation, it appears to be "my suffering", or "my perceptions" or "my feelings". But in liberation it is seen that this never was the case.

You mention psychotherapy. In dealing with suffering, it may be a very good idea to have some psychotherapy. Psychotherapy belongs to the drama of the waking dream. Non-duality sees through the drama of the waking dream. But the drama still goes on, just as the waves still go on even though it may be known that they are the same as the ocean. If the boat is leaking, it might be a good idea to plug the leak. If life involves a lot of suffering, it might be a good idea to see a psychotherapist.

❋

IS THIS REALLY ALL THERE IS?

It disturbs me when I read statements like "This is all there is", "What's happening is all there is" or "When you are inside a lift, that's all there is". These are sweeping statements about the nature of reality, but I cannot see any proof of their accuracy. You might say that nothing exists 'behind me'. Nevertheless, when I turn around, I always see something. You could say that there is nothing outside my closed front door, but when I open it, behold! It's my front garden!

The fact that something is not being observed at the moment does not guarantee that it does not exist, although I grant you that it does not guarantee that it exists either.

So how can you be so confident of what you write?

The points you raise make perfect sense to the mind. But a statement such as "This is all there is" is not a concept which I would want to argue for or against with the mind. Instead, it is simply an attempt to describe what is impersonally seen when the sense of separation drops away.

If you find these statements disturbing, it's probably best just to leave them alone and forget about them. They have no importance and after all what difference do they make? Whatever concepts the mind may hold about them, if you open your front door and look out you will probably, as you say, behold your front garden. And when the lift reaches the ground floor and the doors open, my bet is that the lobby will appear.

There is a well-known Zen saying that after liberation "Mountains are no longer mountains". The shock of seeing through everyday reality can be extremely profound and sometimes there is a desire to try to put into words a description of what is seen. "This is all there is" is a part of that description. But the Zen saying continues "Then mountains are simply mountains again". In other words, this new way of seeing eventually becomes the normal way of seeing. After that there might be less excitement about trying to communicate about it.

❀

LANGUAGE—'CONSCIOUSNESS' AND 'AWARENESS'

Some people who communicate about non-duality avoid the words 'consciousness' and 'awareness' believing them to be misleading. They prefer the word 'being' because it is more neutral and has no specific qualities. But I have heard you talk about both 'awareness' and 'consciousness'. And sometimes I think that words have to create confusion and arguing about them is just a mind-fuck. Could you comment?

I'll comment on the point you raise, although these things often simply come down to how different people use specific words differently. On that level arguing about them can indeed, as you suggest, be a mind-fuck.

As language never really gets close to describing Oneness, descriptions that may sound different are sometimes actually not. I understand the reluctance of some people to use the words 'consciousness' and 'awareness' and their preference for 'being'.

The trouble with using 'consciousness' and 'awareness' is that many people immediately personalise these terms and think of them as 'my consciousness' or 'my awareness'. Then they may go racing off down the path of trying to 'develop' their awareness or consciousness as a way of finding non-duality. There are many teachers who will encourage them in this futile endeavour.

This is less likely to happen with the word 'being'. It is more difficult with 'being' to interpret it as an internal quality which needs to be developed.

Nevertheless, there are circumstances where the words 'consciousness' or 'awareness' may throw some light on what we are trying to describe, as long as we resist the temptation to personalise them. For example, it is self-evident that there is 'being'. Without 'being' there would be no appearance. But we might also suggest that it is self-evident that there is 'consciousness' or 'awareness', because without 'consciousness' or 'awareness', the appearance would not be known to exist.

The problem is that this description immediately sounds dualistic, as we now appear to have at least two things, 'being' and 'consciousness'. If we add that there is also 'unconditional love', we are in an even worse pickle. But this is just the inevitable effect of using language.

We could try saying that there is only Oneness and that it has three characteristics. There is a well-known precedent for this, which is described in the traditional *satchitananda*. The three characteristics could be named as 'being', 'consciousness' and 'love'. But this too can sound hopelessly dualistic.

At this point I can only apologise on behalf of Oneness because we have reached the limits of language. Language is always determinedly dualistic, dividing Oneness into this and that and the other. We have also reached the limits of the mind.

Of course none of this has any significance at all. If Oneness is seen, it is seen regardless of what language we use to describe it. If Oneness is not seen, it does not matter what language we use to describe it, we will not get any closer to seeing that there is nothing to seek.

✳

DOES IT MATTER WHAT WE DO?

I'm reading your book 'I Hope You Die Soon' and I want to thank you for this gift. I can see that the body-mind arises within presence, as do all phenomena including thoughts, emotions and all other perceptions. I can see that I am not living life but that life is living me and all other people, but we make the mistake of thinking that it is we who are living life.

But I don't agree with you that it doesn't matter what we do. When I notice suffering, I am moved to help however I can, and especially by helping people to see that it's all a story. So is it not the case that Oneness acts through us, in order to express unconditional love?

You say that nothing brings about awakening, but surely Oneness is calling out to us. Surely Oneness wants us to realise Oneness. Meditation may not bring about awakening, but doesn't it help to create the right circumstances for awakening to occur and encourage us to let go of 'me'?

Thank you for your kind words about my book.

I have never said that it doesn't matter what we do. I have said that there is no one who does anything. That is quite different.

When you (Oneness) see suffering, you (Oneness) may be moved to help. Oneness may also be moved to get drunk or to cheer at a football match or to shop for a new hat.

Oneness doesn't act through us, because there is no 'us'. This is the revelation that is seen when the separate self collapses; that there is no need of 'us' to help, to drink, to cheer or to shop for a new hat. All of that is going on quite satisfactorily without any need for 'us' at all. As for unconditional love, whatever is apparently happening, unconditional love is the case.

Everything is calling out to us constantly to notice Oneness. That is the nature of this waking dream. But to say that Oneness wants us to realise Oneness is to personify it misleadingly and to add yet another story to the simplicity of This.

I have found meditation to be wonderful, but there are no right or wrong circumstances which will create or hinder the seeing of Oneness. That is simply another story. If a person is letting go of 'me', they are still a person, and if there is no person there, then there is no need to let go of 'me'.

❦

DEATH AND REINCARNATION

I have a concern about death. I am wondering whether death might turn out to be temporary, the end only of this particular incarnation.

When 'I' die, another 'me' might arise out of the void. This would be a new embodiment, arising as the old one did. Then 'I' might have to go through the whole bloody process again, or it might be even worse!

Ramesh Balsekar was once asked this question but his answer wasn't satisfactory. Maybe he didn't understand the question or maybe he couldn't answer it. I am not asking it frivolously. I would really like to have a satisfactory answer.

There will always be stories, either to torture ourselves with or to inspire us. Any speculation about death is just that, a story. We may also notice how contradictory many of these stories about death are.

When liberation is seen, it is realised that there is no separated self. Then concerns and questions about death have a tendency to drop away. This is partly because it is seen that what you really are was never born and so can never die. It is also recognised that the question that you ask belongs to the unknowable and, once this has really been recognised, the mind tends to become bored and lose interest. I would also add about death "Don't worry, it will be okay."

It is also possible, although not guaranteed, that when the self is seen through and This is seen for the miracle that it actually is, life will no longer seem like a bloody process but might be enjoyed with gratitude.

I hope you didn't find my previous question daft. Ramesh Balsekar talked about 'The Pool of Consciousness' in which the impressions of a past body-mind are 'recycled' into a new body-mind.

This is really about God observing itself, isn't it?

There really is no such thing as a daft question. I have read some of Ramesh's theories on death, including the theory you refer to. I thought he was very confused and confusing. I was tempted to throw the book across the room, but as I was in Watkins Bookshop at the time this seemed ill-mannered.

Yes, this is about God observing itself. God is typing these answers and God is reading them. Or if you prefer a different kind of language as I do, Oneness is asking questions and Oneness is answering them.

❋

CONSCIOUSNESS, AWARENESS AND DEEP SLEEP

Consciousness has the apparent aspects of awareness and the content of awareness, and these cannot be separated. They are one. But content and awareness are not there in dreamless sleep. So how can Consciousness remain in deep sleep?

To me it sounds confusing to say that awareness is something that Consciousness has. I use the words 'Consciousness', 'Awareness', 'Oneness', Non-duality and 'Being' synonymously. My description is that there is only Consciousness (or Awareness, Oneness, Non-duality or Being) in which content apparently arises as all phenomena.

Deep sleep is not simply an absence or a gap. As we have to use words, misleading though they are, we may as well say that there is consciousness in deep sleep, but this is not, of course, consciousness as experienced by an individual.

As there are no phenomena in deep sleep, there is nothing more that can be said about it. It's quite a boring topic really.

❋

AWAKENING AND DESPAIR

I found your book very helpful in understanding what has happened for me. There has been an awakening here. It happened with the force of an explosion. It was very frightening to see that free will and life purpose do not exist and that there is nothing 'sacred' about 'enlightenment', it is just very ordinary.

Although my everyday personality took over after this 'event', I live with the knowledge that there is no free will and nothing to regret or hope for.

I do not have anyone I can talk to about this. Sometimes I feel despair and hopelessness, so when I read that you also felt these, it was comforting. I get the impression that many people are awakening but without feeling despair or isolation.

I know you can't give me any advice but I'd appreciate your comment.

I hear from many people who experience something similar to what you have experienced and find themselves sometimes feeling despair and hopelessness as you do. So in a way it is a shared experience. But many people also find that it is impossible to share about this with others that they know, especially with friends and family.

As you say, there is no advice that I can give you. However, if it is possible for you to do some small simple things that bring you some pleasure, that is as good a way to pass the (non-existent) time as any other. When I was in despair I used to talk to Tony Parsons about this, and in his own way this is also what he said to me.

❊

NOSTALGIA AND DEPRESSION

I've always felt burdened by a strong feeling of nostalgia. I've also always yearned for a deep connection with others. But somehow my relationships with others never fully satisfy me and leave me feeling depressed and lonely. I find this paralysing. Have you any advice that might help me?

There are a variety of things that an individual can do to make the prison of being a person more bearable. But I don't give advice because different approaches suit different people. Some find therapy helpful, some a practice such as mindfulness. Some find reading useful. If you are drawn to reading, 'The Happiness Trap' by Russ Harris might address your situation. Ultimately, finding some simple thing that we enjoy doing may be as helpful as anything—a walk round the park, a cup of coffee—whatever it may be for you.

❊

BEING IN A LIFT—IS THIS REALLY ALL THERE IS?

You say that all there is is This, but do you mean that literally? If that's the case, what happens to you when I get into a lift? If you are sitting in your room when I get into a lift, do you and your room disappear? If so, that would seem to put me in a rather privileged position.

Does the world literally disappear when we close our eyes?

The mind can never understand this although it is natural for it to try. So all questions of this philosophical nature are futile. When I say "This is all there is" I am not making a philosophical statement. I am describing what is seen when the person falls away. Then it is known that This is all there is and nevertheless the dream of 'you' being in a lift and 'I' being in a room goes on.

In much the same way, you might have had a dream last night in which you were in a lift and I was in a room. But now you can see that none of that was real.

❊

DEATH AND USELESSNESS

Can you write something to me about death and impermanence? It all seems so useless.

When it's seen that there is no person who can die, death becomes irrelevant, a non-issue.

There is only This, whatever is manifesting right now. When This is seen for what it is without the person filtering it, then it is enough, it is all that is needed. Then questions about its usefulness or uselessness fade away.

❊

WHAT HAPPENS AFTER DEATH?

I read in your book that after death there is enlightenment. But how can this possibly be known? After all, as Hamlet pointed out, no one has ever come back from death to talk to us about it. Even though I know that on one level this question is just the mind up to its monkey tricks, on another level it really bothers me.

It's important to notice that the words I quoted, which are from Max Furlaud, are *"At* death there is only liberation" not *"After* death there is only liberation". Death is the end of the dream of time, so there is no *after* death. But don't expect the mind to be able to understand this, because the mind always wants a story and stories can only unfold in time.

Wondering what happens after death makes no more sense than wondering what happened in your dream last night after you woke up.

The answer to your question, which will not satisfy the mind, is that you can never know this. The person, having a mind, always looks for stories about what will happen next … and after that?… and after that?… and finally after death? But when the person drops away and it is seen that in actuality there never was a mind, all the stories collapse. Then it is seen that there is only liberation and that there is no one who could die because there is no one who was ever born.

❄

WEI WU WEI, IRRITATION AND MEANINGLESSNESS

I find my struggle with non-duality and with life, and the sense of helplessness that it invokes, quite unbearable sometimes. Someone suggested I look for inspiration in the writings of Wei Wu Wei. But I find his books deeply irritating because I have very little idea what they are getting at. I start wondering whether I'm not intelligent enough to understand them.

I am becoming quite angry with my whole involvement with non-duality as my search becomes more and more desperate. But everyday life seems meaningless in comparison. Can you comment?

I tried a few pages of Wei Wu Wei (Terence Gray) myself some years ago but I couldn't get anywhere with him, so I have some empathy with your irritation.

Mental engagement with non-duality can be very irritating for some people, partly because of the paradoxes involved and partly because the mind can never actually get it. This can generate a lot of frustration. I used to feel angry at meetings about non-duality, but nevertheless something kept calling me back to them.

If it's possible to relax the mental effort that you are engaging in and enjoy some simple pleasures, that might be good. The mental effort won't get you anywhere, after all. But of course relaxation and enjoyment will either happen or they won't. That's frustrating, I know.

Thank you for your reply. For reasons I can't explain, I feel somewhat relieved by it. I do know that liberation will either happen or not and that is the crux of the matter.

I'd like to ask you another question. Can non-duality explain what consciousness is?

No, non-duality cannot explain what consciousness is. On the one hand consciousness is self-evident, but on the other hand there is almost nothing that we can say about it that makes any sense. Many psychologists and philosophers acknowledge this. The problem of consciousness is not amenable to a scientific explanation because science deals with the material and objective, but consciousness is non-material and subjective. In writing that I am not introducing any superstitious woo-woo about some mysterious non-physical effluvia, I have simply reached the limits of language.

Nevertheless, we could say that consciousness is embedded in the very nature of existence. The ancient yogic way of characterising the Absolute, which is of course in reality indescribable, is *satchitananda*. One element of this portmanteau word can be translated as 'consciousness'. It is not quite correct to say either that the Absolute is conscious, or that it is consciousness, or that consciousness is a characteristic of the Absolute, but nevertheless that is about as close as we can get to a description in words.

You say that consciousness is non-material. Many physicists say that consciousness is simply a product of brain function, in other words entirely material. However, some physicists say that ultimately even matter is non-material. So who is right?

The current standard scientific paradigm, which is sometimes known as 'material realism' or 'scientific realism', holds that consciousness is an accidental by-product of the increasing complexity of matter as it evolves in brains. Many scientists also believe that consciousness has some Darwinian survival function, but acknowledge that they do not yet know what this is. Philosophers of consciousness posit the (at least theoretical) possibility of 'zombies', beings who behave identically to us but who have no interior awareness. They ask why it is that we are not zombies in this way.

We could express the scientific paradigm in this way: "The material creates consciousness. Consciousness is an epiphenomenon of matter."

But if the scientists had asked a mystic, he or she would have told them that a more accurate description would be to put it the other way round and say "Consciousness creates the material." Even more accurately, we could say that just as the Absolute and the relative are one, so consciousness and the material are one. Matter is consciousness, consciousness is matter, there is only Oneness and now it's time for a cup of tea in the park café.

By the way, saying that "consciousness creates the material" has nothing to do with the comforting but facile beliefs expressed in books like 'The Secret' or 'The Cosmic Ordering Service'.

❈

TRANSCENDENCE

Does transcendence exist? Is it the same as seeing non-duality?

Yes, transcendence exists. It is experienced by many individuals when for a variety of reasons, or sometimes spontaneously, they go beyond their egoic self.

However, this has nothing necessarily to do with the seeing of non-duality. Transcendence may happen without bringing about the seeing of Oneness, and Oneness may be seen without there being transcendence. Transcendence is an experience, although often a very refined 'spiritual' experience. The seeing of Oneness is not an experience, because there is no one there to be having an experience.

Nevertheless, it can be a good thing to explore the transcendental aspects of our nature if we want to live satisfying lives, just as it is a good thing to explore the intellectual, emotional, social, creative and physical aspects of our nature. In fact I would say that it is difficult, for example, to fully bring about therapeutic healing of ourselves without some apprehension of the transpersonal or the transcendent. I must acknowledge, however, that there are therapists who would disagree with this.

✻

DEATH

What is death? I would very much like to believe that at death not all of me will be annihilated. But nothing I've come across in non-duality has helped me to understand death.

When it is seen that there is no person and there never has been a person, it is known that at death there is nothing to be annihilated. Then concerns about death tend to disappear. A traditional way of putting this is "What you really are was never born and so can never die."

It's all very well for the one who has seen non-duality to say "What was never born can never die." But for the one who hasn't seen non-duality, this is impossible to understand. That makes this conversation extremely paradoxical and problematic, doesn't it?

Yes, you express the paradox and the problem very well. Communication about non-duality can never get us anywhere, apart possibly to a mental understanding, which unfortunately is without value. Nevertheless, some of us are drawn to this communication like iron filings to a magnet.

❁

NEGATIVE HABITS

Recently in a sudden experience the sense of separation and any sense of seeking ended completely.

Since then the apparent 'me' has returned. In spite of this I notice a stillness underlying all my impressions. I am both confused and frustrated by this. Any sense of seeking has disappeared, but when 'me' returns I still find myself overwhelmed by my negative habits. Why do both these habits and a sense of personal identity still arise, despite this awakening?

I also notice that now I really want to be with people and at meetings where non-duality is discussed. I love anything that points to the non-existence of 'me'.

You describe a clear awakening event, in which the person suddenly falls away and Oneness is seen, but then the person returns, along with their negative habits.

This is quite common, and the mixture of stillness, confusion, frustration and the loss of a sense of seeking which you describe is also quite common. It is possible that the sense of 'me' that you still have coming and going at times may gradually fade, or that there may be another event in which it disappears. Or it's possible that neither of these may happen, because there are no rules.

Your strong desire for communication with people about non-duality indicates that your head is now in the tiger's mouth. From this, of course, there is no escape.

I don't really understand your metaphor of the tiger's mouth.

Ramana Maharshi said "Your head is in the tiger's mouth and there is no escape." This sums up very well the period which many individuals experience when a passion for non-duality has seized them but liberation is not yet seen.

❋

PRESENCE

Everything is happening of its own accord. There is no person and so there is no choice. Sometimes there's a feeling of contraction, sometimes there's a feeling of relaxation, but neither of these are happening to 'me'.

The apparent self deconstructs itself with or without self-enquiry. Past and future are a dream. Thoughts arise and fall away again out of nothing. There is no mind apart from these thoughts.

As you say, there's nowhere to go and nothing to do. Isn't that wonderful! Thank you for writing about This.

You give a very clear description. Enjoy presence.

❋

STROKES AND LIBERATION

I've recently watched a video in which Jill Bolte Taylor talks about suffering a stroke. She seems to feel that the loss of normal left brain functioning gives clearer access to right brain functioning. As a result the boundaries which make things appear to be separate disappear. Do you have any comments on this?

I've come across Jill's video. It's fascinating, but I don't recommend a stroke as a way of seeing through separation. As there are no rules governing how the separate self may drop away, having a stroke doesn't guarantee it and not having a stroke doesn't prevent it.

Nevertheless, her account is very interesting. By the way, I believe that Ram Dass (Richard Alpert) had something to say of interest about this after having a stroke, but I haven't followed it up myself.

✸

MALES, FEMALES AND BABIES

Why for babies to arise do males and females have to merge? After all, the planet with its seas and its rivers, its sun and its moon, its mountains and its valleys, simply exists.

The mind is addicted to asking 'Why' questions. This keeps the mind eternally occupied and eternally in control, which is where it likes to be. Meanwhile the wonder that is This is being missed. Any answer to your question would just be a story, which another mind could easily countermand or contradict with a different story.

✸

TIME

I have often heard non-dual speakers deny that time exists, saying that the impression that everything flows with time is an illusion.

If this is the case, how does one event follow another? Are impressions of past events really a kind of false memory?

You may have had a dream last night in which events appeared to unfold in time. But now you know that none of those events actually happened. The time in which they seemed to unfold did not exist. In liberation it is noticed that the same is true of this waking dream that we call everyday life.

Time is constructed by consciousness and events appear to succeed each other only because of consciousness. The past is a thought rising in this.

The mind can never really understand this because the mind lives in time. But in even one split second of awakening, time may be seen through and neither past nor future taken seriously again.

❋

FEAR OF DEATH

Many people, including me, fear death. Why is that?

As long as there is the sense of a separated person, it is quite natural to fear death because death threatens to bring this person to an end. This is why we make up so many religious and spiritual stories about how we may continue after death in some kind of afterlife or series of rebirths.

When the sense of separation falls away, it is seen that although there is no continuation of the separated person after death, there is no continuation of the separated person before death either, so fear of death tends to diminish or die away—although there is no necessity for this to happen because anything can arise in liberation.

The seeing in liberation of unconditional love also tends to diminish the fear of death.

❋

GRATITUDE

Why do you speak about gratitude?

There is a great enjoyment of presence here and what arises in presence, so there is gratitude for the life of this waking dream as long as it continues.

❋

NOTHING TO DO?

Is there really nothing for 'me' to do?

It would be more accurate to say that there is no one who does anything. However, if a feeling that you can do something arises and it seems a wise or pleasant thing to do, you might as well follow it.

✸

THE SENSE OF SEPARATION

Can you explain what you mean by the sense of separation? Separate from what?

The sense of separation is the sense that 'I' am separate from 'everything else'. This is what it feels like to be a person—to be separate from everyone and everything. In awakening it is seen that this separateness is an appearance. The underlying reality is that there is no separation.

✸

AM I A PERSON?

Am I a person? If I'm not, then what am I?

If you feel yourself to be a person, we might as well say that you are one until that changes. But what you really are is Oneness itself. Alternatively we could say you are Being itself, Consciousness itself, or the phrase which most appeals to me "You are the light in which everything arises."

But alas, this can only be seen when it is seen—please excuse the tautology. That happens when the sense of being a separate person dissolves or drops away.

✸

BUSINESS AS USUAL

After a strange period of seeing with 'me' being absent, now everything seems to have returned to business as usual except that it's also subtly different. Of course I realise that this is also Oneness.

How can anyone really tell that something has been seen, as there is no one there to see anything?

"Business as usual except that it's also subtly different" is a good a way to put it. We could say that nothing is changed because life simply goes on as before, yet everything is transformed because life is now going on for no one.

In Zen they say "First mountains are mountains". In everyday life everything seems ordinary.

Then they say "Then mountains are no longer mountains". In awakening the ordinary is seen to be extraordinary.

Finally they say "Then mountains are mountains again". Eventually the body-mind becomes used to awakening and so everything seems ordinary again, yet now it is subtly transformed.

One way of describing this is that everything goes on as before, yet no matter what is happening, there is a resting in stillness and silence.

Your last question is too metaphysical for me. All I can say is that stillness and silence are known by no one, even as the drama of the character in the waking dream continues. That is the best description I can give.

❁

CAN ANYTHING BE DONE?

Since there is no 'me' to bring about the seeing of non-duality, would it be accurate to say that I can do nothing? It simply happens? Is that correct?

That's correct. It simply happens. But you can't do nothing. If you try doing nothing you will find that something will always happen, except in dreamless sleep.

In the meantime, if you feel like there's a 'you' who can do things, you may as well do things that make life more comfortable or that you enjoy. For example, I used to do therapy and I used to meditate. These things made life more comfortable. Now I walk round the park and drink coffee at the lakeside café, which I enjoy.

Of course it would be more accurate to say "There is no one who can do anything."

❋

POSITIVE THINKING AND THE SHADOW

Recently I've been feeling confident and pleased with my achievements. But now I'm finding myself immersed in a lot of fear, especially about financial and health matters. This is also bringing up a lot of anger for me. I know that my friends and colleagues would be very surprised by this if they knew, as I seem very together on the surface.

All my achievements seem without value and nothing brings me any pleasure. I've never felt so negative before. The only relief I get is when I'm immersed in non-duality, either at a meeting or when I'm reading about it, although I'm still able to get some enjoyment from being in the countryside.

For some time I've been practising positive thinking techniques and trying to change my negative feelings into positive ones. However, I feel I've finally come to the end of the road with these. I've come to the conclusion that they don't work and they require great effort. Can you comment on my predicament?

I'm sorry you're having such a hard time at the moment. Many people who seem confident and together on the surface are suffering so much beneath the surface. I'm reminded of the French priest who said that one thing he had learned from a long lifetime ministering to people was that most people are a great deal more unhappy than we think.

These techniques of positive thinking have become an unhealthy modern obsession, almost a religion. When they become an obsession they can have very negative effects on us:- they can drain us of our energy; they can encourage us to beat ourselves up when we inevitably fail to master them; they may make little allowance for the healthy expression of the shadow; they can encourage us to deny how things really are for us and to turn away from what is towards a fantasy reality.

All this can lead to the opposite of acceptance, although 'the positive thinking sales force' often preaches acceptance. These techniques can also induce a lot of guilt and easily become a form of 'spiritual fascism'. I have acquaintances who suffer a lot from this.

Barbara Ehrenreich has written a book called 'Smile or Die' about the current obsession with positive thinking. You might find it interesting to read or you could look at the author's website. Another enjoyable attack on the positive thinking movement is Oliver Burkeman's 'The Antidote: Happiness For People Who Can't Stand Positive Thinking'.

A healthy way of dealing with our shadow and with uncomfortable feelings is to acknowledge them and let our attention be on them for a while, rather than to ignore them or try to force them into becoming something else. The humanistic psychologist John Rowan writes that the best way to get from where we don't want to be to where we do want to be is to stay exactly where we are, even though we don't want to be there. In other words, even though we don't like how we are feeling, we can simply acknowledge it and stay with it with as much attention as we can naturally muster without strain. This may sound counter-intuitive, because our culture teaches us that if we don't like a feeling we should try to get rid of it, but it is actually highly effective.

If we focus on the feelings in the body, rather than on the story in the head, these feelings begin to change and transform. They often uncover other feelings which we've been trying to avoid but which really need our attention. For example, underneath anxiety there may be anger, or underneath anger there may be sadness. Any combination of feelings is possible. There is quite a lot of wisdom in the humanistic saying "What you resist is what you get." So if we don't acknowledge our anger, for example, we tend to get more anger.

We don't need to worry about what to do with these feelings, other than giving them focussed time and attention. That's all they're clamouring for. I recommend doing this regularly for a few minutes at a time, or however long feels okay without strain. After that we might go and do some simple thing that we enjoy.

All of this communication has of course been from Richard the therapist. As a therapist I've rarely found anything more effective and best of all we don't have to pay a therapist to do it.

✸

PERSISTING NON-DUAL AWARENESS

I'm conducting research into mystical and non-dual states and unity consciousness. As you live in a state of persisting non-dual awareness I'm wondering whether you would be interested in participating in this research.

The description of someone who "lives in a state of persisting non-dual awareness" is not one that I'd apply to myself. Instead I'd describe myself as an ordinary chap, where Oneness is seen, but not by me.

Words about this are always paradoxical but my description of non-duality is that it can only be seen when the person has dropped away or is not there anymore. After that, life goes on in a pretty ordinary and non-dramatic way, but maybe with a certain easing of tension, a certain dropping away of stress and neurosis, and a certain ability to enjoy simple things in presence.

✸

LIBERATION IS MEANINGLESS AND JOYFUL

Thank you for your little jewel of a book.

Some time ago all searching ended for me just as it has done for you. Since then life has gone on pretty much as usual. So it seems that in the twenty-first century there's no need to retreat to the caves or the mountains.

Now everything is seen to be meaningless but gloriously joyful.

Thank you for your lovely message. You express it so well. "Meaningless but gloriously joyful" really sums it up.

❋

NOTHING HAPPENING

I've often heard non-duality speakers say "Nothing is happening". But I notice that motion is everywhere. My fingers type this message, my cat stalks through the kitchen, my chest rises and falls with every breath that I take. How can there be all this energetic motion and vitality, yet nothing is happening?

Perhaps the closest we can get to understanding this is by analogy with a night-time dream. In a night-time dream, plenty seems to be happening but when we wake up it is realised that nothing has actually taken place. The people we met, the journeys we took, the places we visited in our dream, were all unreal. They were transient apparent phenomena arising in This.

We could say that, just as with a night-time dream, this waking appearance is both real and unreal. This is only a metaphor, but it may help the mind to grapple with that which can never be grasped by the mind.

❋

IS THIS ALL THERE IS?

You have written "This is it." Tony Parsons says "This is all there is." If I am lying in my bed and I shut my eyes, does the world stop existing?

"This is it" or "This is all there is" are not philosophical statements. They are descriptions of what is seen in liberation when the dream-story of the individual is seen through. However, the mind cannot make any sense of this, because to the mind there is obviously a world out there, for example a house, road and town in which you and your bed are situated.

As the mind can make no sense of this, it might just be better to forget about it. After all, it makes no difference. The dream-story continues whether this is seen or not. But if your mind wants to wrestle with it a little longer, you might contemplate the analogy of a night-time dream. All sorts of 'realities' can appear in a night-time dream, yet when we awaken, it is known that none of them were real.

As you read these words from the liberated perspective that you have, do you experience them as words that someone else has written in some other place and time, or as meaningless chaotic energy?

Liberation has no necessary implications. Everything simply goes on as before. Nothing is changed, yet everything is transformed because now it is seen that no one is experiencing it. A cup of coffee, a walk round the park, words on a computer screen, all continue to arise as before, but now they arise for no one.

By the way, I do not have 'a liberated perspective' because I am not liberated. No one is liberated. There is no such thing as 'a liberated person'.

✻

SHARING NON-DUALITY WITH OTHERS

How often do you share your seeing of non-duality with others in your everyday life?

When I'm trying to share about this with friends I find I often end up having to fight my corner.

In my everyday life I rarely talk about non-duality to others unless they are very interested in it. I find that most people are not interested and so when I'm with them we talk about other things.

And I'm wondering why you want to fight your corner.

❋

LIBERATION—EVENT OR NO EVENT

You have described how your experience of liberation happened at a specific time and place. I assumed that this was the norm but then I heard Tony Parsons say that he had no idea when he experienced liberation. He simply realised at a certain point that liberation was the case.

Have you noticed any pattern with other people? If so, is it like yours or Tony's?

Tony describes an event. He was walking through a park, then there was just walking through a park but nobody doing it. Nathan Gill describes an event. He was riding a bicycle down a lane, then there was just riding a bicycle down a lane but nobody doing it. I describe an event. I was walking through a country town, then there was just walking through a country town but nobody doing it.

The realisation of liberation may come with that event, or later, or not at all. Or the realisation of liberation may come without any event. There are no rules to this, because liberation is all-embracing and therefore excludes no possibilities.

The trouble with hearing these stories about 'liberation events' is that they can set up an expectation that some event has to occur and this can lead to yet more searching. But if that's what happens, it's what happens. Sorry about the tautology.

Yes, some people give me descriptions of similar events. For other people there is no event, just a gentle gliding into the realisation that liberation is already the case.

❁

DIFFERENCE BETWEEN LIBERATION AND DEATH

What is the difference between liberation and death? If those two events are equivalent, what is the point in writing about liberation, or in working to see what will happen at the moment of death?

The difference between liberation when the body-mind is still alive and physical death is that in the first the story, or waking dream, continues but now it is seen to be a story or waking dream. In physical death the story ceases.

There is no point in writing about liberation or in working to see what will happen at the moment of death. There is no point in anything. But if that is what is happening, then it is what is happening. In other words, everything is exactly as it is and it cannot be any different.

❁

WHY TEACH NON-DUALITY IF EVERYTHING HAPPENS AS IT WILL?

I have heard you and other non-duality teachers say that everything happens just as it will. It cannot be any other way. So why do you and others teach non-duality? How can you or anyone else tell people what they should do or think? How can you give people advice about this?

I don't teach non-duality. I just get together sometimes with a group of people and try unsuccessfully to describe This. I don't tell people what they should do or think, or give them advice about this.

Of course I can't speak for others. You'll have to ask them directly.

❋

HELP! MY GIRLFRIEND'S INVOLVED WITH A CHANNELLER!

I'm hoping you can give me some advice. For some time I have been very interested in non-duality. At the same time, my girl-friend has been attending weekly meetings with someone who claims to channel an archangel.

The channelled messages always stress how we are totally responsible for every thought we have and every action that we take. They emphasise the absolute importance of our free will and self-responsibility, and how we can create the reality we desire through the power of positive thinking.

I'm finding that, although I do not want it to happen, these beliefs are slowly and insidiously creeping into my skull. I'm being drawn into these beliefs that I should be able to control my life through my thoughts and now I'm getting depressed at my failure to do this. This is happening even though I can recognise that these beliefs are absurd. To make matters worse, my girl-friend is preening herself under the approval of her spiritual teacher, who tells her weekly that she is 'an old soul' and 'spiritually advanced'.

Can you comment on my predicament?

The situation you describe, that of being with a partner who is following a spiritual path that fascinates them, is a common one. The story that we can receive channelled wisdom from great spiritual beings such as an archangel is highly seductive and appeals greatly to our spiritual egos. The very popular theory that we create every part of our own reality, that we are totally self-responsible, and that we can manifest anything that we desire, is also highly seductive. Put the two together and you have an almost unbeatable combination, with a channeller whose acolytes will hang on their every word.

But of course this channelled 'wisdom' is still just a story and meanwhile there is only This, presence apparently unfolding itself.

We might also notice how banal the channelled messages are, even when they are dressed up in cod medieval language as they often are.

I don't give advice, but perhaps the recognition of the seductive power of the story that your girlfriend is following and the nature of its appeal, may help you to stay grounded in presence, the actuality of what is. Then you may be able to enjoy whatever simple things appeal to you, while those around you spin the kind of fairy stories that children love to listen to.

✾

WHO ARE YOU?

I have just finished your book 'Drink Tea, Eat Cake' and I have one question. Who are you?

Sometimes I disappear, leaving only the perfect emptiness and fullness that I long for, but then I return with just a memory of that.

I am an ordinary chap. I am a character, just like you and everybody else.

Perfect emptiness and fullness as you call it are always there, although not necessarily always noticed.

Just like me? You must be kidding! I am still frantically pushing boulders up the mountain.

You say that perfect emptiness and fullness are always there but not always noticed. Do you mean that you do not always notice them?

84

Being asleep and being awake are the same thing, so there really is no difference between you and me. The problem is that in being asleep, this is not known. Instead it is believed that there is a difference. That's why searching goes on and that's the reason for all the pushing of boulders up the mountain like Sisyphus. In being awake it is known that there is nothing to search for, so pushing boulders up mountains stops.

Perfect emptiness and fullness, or silence and stillness as I usually say, are always there. Sometimes they're in the foreground, sometimes in the background. Sometimes they're noticed, sometimes not. It no longer matters which.

❋

BETWEEN AWAKENING AND LIBERATION

I like your books because you are non-compromising about non-duality. When I started to read about non-duality, a lot of my beliefs suddenly seemed to be superstitions and they dropped away. My beliefs in karma and reincarnation fell away for example. It felt wonderfully liberating just to be free of these. There were also sudden flashes of insight but after a while everything calmed down and became ordinary once more.

But now I feel stuck in quite a painful place, with lots of over-powering emotions coming up including fear and anger. I've stopped reading about non-duality as it seems to consist mostly of compromises on offer, like self-enquiry. I'm no longer seeking but I still have a strong urge to return home. Life is difficult right now.

It sounds like you are in that place between awakening and liberation. Oneness, or the non-dual nature of everything, has been seen, so the stories about meaning and purpose have dropped away. But there is still a sense of something missing, something to be found, while there is also a knowing that nothing can be done to find it. This can be very frustrating. It is like being in a desert or being stuck between an old way of being and a new way. It is one version of what the Tibetans call a bardo.

Many people go through this period. I did myself. It ends when the fullness of everything is seen as well as its emptiness. This can happen suddenly, or so gradually that it is hardly noticed until one day it may be quietly remarked "Oh. It's all over."

❀

LOCALISATION

I've followed Zen for some years, partly because like you I feel that if there is a 'truth' to be found, it has to be very simple.

Now I've started reading about non-duality. You write about an awakening event in which the person vanishes. I cannot imagine how this can be, as there must be a point of localisation, a place from which it is known that this event is happening. How can it make sense to call this 'a disappearance'?

What I describe is the complete disappearance of any kind of localisation. In this event, awareness is, as it were, seen to be 'spread out everywhere'. You are right, this cannot be imagined by the person, because they seem to occupy a specific point in space-time.

This complete disappearance of locale does not last. After a while, the sense of localisation returns. What does not return in liberation is the sense of contraction that is experienced by a person. Then it is seen that there is no person, there is only Oneness, undifferentiated being appearing as all differences.

❀

CAN WE CHANGE THE DREAM?

I recognise that this life is a dream. It is not real, yet paradoxically it is real. The great seers say that even the attainment of power over death can only happen within the dream.

Nevertheless are we able to change the dream from within the dream? For example, can we take action to avoid toothache or hardship in general?

Within the dream there is clearly cause and effect operating and it seems therefore that we can influence things. So if our teeth hurt, it is sensible to go to a dentist. If we face hardship, it is sensible to do whatever we feel we can do to ameliorate it.

But I am pointing to the possibility of seeing beyond the appearance, the possibility of seeing that there is no one who does anything, that there is only This, the immediacy of presence in which all activity and apparent doer-ship unfolds. In other words, there does not need to be a person for an appointment with a dentist to be made or for hardship to be ameliorated. Everything within the dream is simply happening, apparently.

❋

SUMMING UP NON-DUALITY

Can you sum up for me the non-dual teaching in a few short sentences?

There is no one. There is no separation. There is nothing to find and there is no one who seeks. There is only This. This is it and This is enough. There is unconditional love. This is not a teaching.

So there is only THIS and not THAT? Is that correct?

There is only Oneness but in Oneness the appearance of separation arises and therefore the appearance of THIS and THAT arises.

You sometimes refer to a separate self. Do you mean separate from all that is?

Yes, the appearance of a separate self early in life, or the appearance of self-consciousness as we might call it, creates the powerful impression that 'I' am separate from everything else that is.

I've read that this is "Nothing appearing as everything". How can nothing appear as everything? Is nothing full of everything? What would sum this up briefly?

"Oneness is Nothing appearing as Everything" is a good description. 'Everything' simply means whatever is. But I'd like to add that these words and concepts don't really matter. If I had to sum up non-duality in less than five words, I would say "There is no doer."

This stuff seems insane. Are you saying that the sense of self may just drop away of its own accord? Am I really at the whim of Oneness? Can you not give any guidance?

The mind can never understand how Nothing, or undifferentiated Oneness, can give rise to everything. The mind will always be confused by this and may very well consider it to be insane. This is why mystics are so damned impossible to understand. It can be very frustrating. But if the sense of being (or having) a separate self drops away even for an instant, it can then be seen directly that there is only Being giving rise to the appearance of everything.

That's the best I can do. I can't give any guidance about making the self drop away. It's either there or it isn't. There's either someone walking down the road, or there's just walking down the road with no one doing it.

Because the sense of self is a false sense, there is nothing it can do to make itself disappear. But if this communication doesn't appeal to you, there are many teachers out there who not only will tell you that you can do something, they will also be happy to recommend exactly what you should do. Many people are attracted to their teachings and would take no notice at all of what I am saying.

Then if there is no doer, everything that happens is supposed to happen and there is no one responsible? So what is this show? Is it a dance, a play of light without substance?

"Everything that happens is supposed to happen" is a misleading phrase because it suggests that there is a plan that is unfolding as it should do, presumably with some purpose to it. But there is no purpose to being, other than being itself. So nothing is supposed to happen.

Yes, what is here is a dance, a play of light without substance. That is a good description. But while we are caught up in the drama of being a separate person, there certainly seems to be substance. In awakening and liberation that is seen through. Then it is seen that This is both real and unreal.

❁

ON FARTING ABOUT

I've been reading someone who seems to be saying the same as you only without the recommendation to fart about.

That's nice to know, but it may turn out that farting about is the really important part!

I suppose that after awakening, everything becomes delightful and not just farting. A cup of coffee, the sound of a dog barking, the texture of the chair I'm sitting on right now. That is the real miracle.

There's a confusion over language here that needs to be cleared up. 'Farting' and 'farting about' are not the same thing. I recommend the second but not necessarily the first. I'm going to walk up to my local park now and when I'm there I'll definitely fart about, but I won't necessarily fart.

Thanks for clarifying that. So by 'farting about' you mean wasting time doing trivial things, focussing on the fun part of life.

Rather than wasting time doing trivial things, I would say that when the self has been seen through, and all the stories about important meaningful things have fallen away, then everything can be seen and enjoyed simply for what it is, the play of Oneness.

So is anything really important?

Only to the one who feels separate. When that's been seen through, farting about can become quite delightful.

I deeply long for awakening to happen. But I found life more attractive when I still believed that there was something I could do to get rid of myself. Now that it's seen that there is no hope as awakening either happens or it doesn't, the world feels emptier.

What you express is a common experience when searching has lost its attraction but the person is still there feeling a sense of separation. This is sometimes described as being in a desert. I don't give advice, but if I did it would be to spend some time doing whatever simple things you find in any way enjoyable.

Like farting about, I suppose. Thank you guruji!

❋

ABRAHAM MASLOW

I've read that Abraham Maslow's philosophy is non-dual. Do you know of him? Would you agree?

I know the work of Abraham Maslow. He was one of the fathers of Humanistic Psychology. The idea of the 'self-actualising' human was his. It's got some similarities with Jung's idea of 'individuation', which Jung saw as the goal of a well-lived life. I would see his approach as being very different to that of radical non-duality. He's full of recommendations for doing and becoming and interminable self-improvement. It's okay if you like that sort of thing, but it's quite tiring. I believe that Fritz Perls once accused him of being a spiritual fascist.

❋

SUFFERING

I am going through a lot of suffering at the moment. Although I under-stand intellectually that there is really no person who suffers, when suffering comes it overwhelms me. At these times, nothing that I know about non-duality helps me. Can you offer me some guidance?

Within this waking dream, great suffering can arise. This can even happen when non-duality or Oneness is seen. All I can suggest to anyone who is suffering is that they pursue whatever seems to offer comfort and makes the dream more comfortable. Although I can't advise anyone as to what that might be in their case, I found in the past that meditation and paying non-judgemental attention to feelings were very helpful to me. So was doing very simple undemanding things that I enjoyed, such as walking round the park. Many years ago I also found psychotherapy helpful as well as physical practices such as yoga. Now I find tai chi delightful.

❋

SUFFERING AND WHAT TO DO

Although I enjoyed your book, since reading it I have felt that there is nowhere to go. I feel hopeless and helpless and I can't find any meaning in life.

I realise that there is nothing 'I' can do because 'I' do not exist, but I want to have some advice, even while knowing that no advice is possible.

You put very well and very succinctly what people often feel when they are in touch with non-duality but haven't yet seen the full-ness of Oneness. I don't give advice, but I found that when I was feeling hopeless and helpless, I wanted to derive what pleasure I could from doing simple everyday things like walking round the park, reading a book or watching a film.

❋

SUFFERING: IS THERE ANYTHING I CAN DO?

I've been reading about non-duality. Ever since I was young I've felt that life is really a game, somehow fundamentally unreal, and now I feel that I may not be crazy after all. There are others who see life in the same way as I do!

Recently, 'I' suddenly wasn't there. This felt like the recognition of something I've always known and quite natural. It even felt normal. But once 'I' had returned, I felt terribly depressed. I was confronted with knowing how reality really is, but not living that reality. That is very painful.

I'm still able to enjoy certain things such as classical music and the countryside. I know that it's ridiculous to ask you if there's something I can do, but I can't resist. So here goes... Is there anything I can do?

I recognise what you write about very clearly. It certainly sounds as if you are in that period which can often happen after awakening, a time when the unreality of the person has been seen but the person nevertheless comes back. Many individuals report that this can be a very difficult time, a time when they still feel that they are searching for something, that there is something missing, but it is seen that there is nothing that can really be done about this. I went through such a period, which in my case lasted for about a year.

I don't give advice, but nevertheless I would suggest doing whatever simple things you find pleasurable, as it sounds like you are doing with classical music and the countryside. As you like music, perhaps you could go to a concert. As you like the countryside, perhaps you could go for a walk. If you like food, perhaps you could have a nice meal. At some point perhaps it will be seen again that there is no one who is doing any of these things.

Thank you for your very good non-advice, which I'm following by enjoying music, walking and good food. But I'd like to ask you another question, this time about my relationships with people.

I'm finding my daily contact with people very troublesome. In one way I'd like to talk to them about non-duality, but my attempts have not been a great success, to say the least. And I don't want them asking me lots of questions if they are not 'simpatico' to this. So I'm minimising my contact with people at the moment and talking about superficial things. How do you manage this?

I don't manage it, or anything else. Everything simply happens. But awakening can certainly make relationships with other people difficult, particularly because we are likely to lose our enthusiasm for so many things that might have interested us before. I've lost contact with certain people who are very committed to following spiritual paths and I tend to avoid talking about non-duality to most people that I know. But apart from that, communication with others tends to become quite easy and simple, just like everything else.

It feels like Oneness had a very healthy impulse when it decided to write to you. There's no searching going on at the moment, just a feeling of freedom from the need to change anything, especially 'myself'. And the recognition of the simplicity and beauty of the ordinary things that are going on—the cat asleep on a chair, the snow outside the window. I don't know what I'm thanking you for, but thank you.

❈

BULLSHIT, GLORY AND THE COSMIC JOKE

This morning I realised that life is bullshit. And that life is full of beauty and glory. These two thoughts seem to me to be connected.

This is a cosmic joke, isn't it? And it's at our expense.

So what is here writing this to you? Is it just this body of flesh and bones?

It is a great paradox that seeing This as meaningless or bullshit and seeing This as beautiful and glorious are inextricably mixed. For me this seeing gives rise to gratitude.

As we and the cosmos are One, the joke is not at our expense.

What is here is Oneness appearing as all phenomena—including flesh and bones.

✻

WHO IS TYPING THIS? DO POETS WRITE ABOUT THIS?

If nobody was ever born and nobody ever dies, then who or what is typing this message to you?
Are there any poets that write directly about this?

Oneness is typing this, Oneness is reading this.

People mention Hafiz and Rumi. Non-Duality Press publishes books of poems by Nicholas Czernin, 'Wasteland Words', and by John Astin, 'This Is Always Enough'. However I haven't read either of them, so I can't recommend them.

✻

WHAT IS ONENESS? WHAT SHOULD I READ ABOUT THIS?

What is Oneness? And if I were your son, and in some sense I am, what one book would you urge me to read before I die?

Any attempt to describe Oneness is futile because words can only describe separation. So all I can write is that Oneness is what is seen when the sense of being a separate person in a world of separate objects and experiences disappears. Then it is known that there is no separation and all the stories that we tell ourselves to make sense of the world are simply that, stories. There are many hints of this in the world's religions and spiritual philosophies but they are usually quite well hidden.

There is no book that I would urge my son to read, but in the area of non-duality I can't do better than recommend Tony Parsons' book, 'As It Is'.

FEAR OF DEATH

The older I get, the more I find death a fearful prospect. Why is this? Can you recommend any book about death?

Where there is the sense of a separate person, as there usually is, the continuation of that person seems to be important and its inevitable end seems to be a threat. But once it is seen that there never was a separate person, this no longer seems important.

I'd hesitate to recommend any particular book about death but I very much enjoyed Ken Wilber's autobiographical book 'Grace and Grit'. Carl Jung also wrote very insightfully about ageing and death. I might recommend his autobiography 'Memories, Dreams, Reflections' though I found it heavy-going in places. More accessibly, you might like a book about Jung. You could try Anthony Stevens 'On Jung' which has a whole section on the mid-life to death period.

Can you recommend a book that directly addresses the absence of the individual? That feels more relevant to me than Jung.

The books that I'd most recommend that directly address the absence of the individual are those written by Tony Parsons or by myself. This may not be as narcissistic as it sounds. It's not that there aren't other excellent books that do so, it's just that either I haven't read them, or if I have, I've usually not enjoyed them so I couldn't recommend them to others. However, you might also enjoy 'Awakening to the Dream' by Leo Hartong.

I'm very poor so could you recommend just one?

Tony Parsons—'All There Is', published by Open Secret Publishing.

I can't afford it.

Try Tony's 'As It Is'. It's shorter and therefore cheaper. Alternatively read the stuff on his website for free. Google 'the open secret', to find it. Good luck.

※

HOW MANY PEOPLE BECOME LIBERATED?

I've been a spiritual seeker for many years and recently I've been a teacher in a well-known spiritual organisation. The basic teachings of the 'master' are quite like yours except, like so many others, he says that we can save ourselves and the planet through our spiritual work. This seems to involve giving his organisation quite a lot of money. Like many others he gives 2012 as the 'big crunch' deadline for our efforts. (Author's note: since this message was received in about 2010, this deadline has come and gone quite uneventfully, perhaps because of the good offices of the 'master' and his followers.)

I'd like to ask you how many of the people attending your meetings have 'awakened' or become 'liberated'? Can you answer that question?

By the way, I'm quite good at farting about, as recommended (well, kind of) in your books.

I very much enjoyed reading your message. To be accurate, I'd have to answer "None" to your question because no one awakens or becomes liberated. However, in the spirit in which your question is asked, I'd give a resounding "I don't know", although the seeing of liberation seems to be happening more frequently nowadays.

I'm glad that you're quite good at farting about. So am I. In fact I've recently given up some part-time lecturing so that I have more time to pootle about, which I also enjoy a great deal. I'm off now to pootle about in the park.

I was so pleased to read your answer. I understand that no one awakens and no one is liberated. Nevertheless, there seems to be an epidemic of awakenings sweeping the world with more and more books on the subject. We will see if the 'master' is right and 2012 brings about a great change (Author's note: it didn't), *but "Don't hold your breath" as they say. It would be a shame if we destroy the planet—it's such a lovely toy.*

※

PSYCHOTHERAPY

I had started training as a psychotherapist when I unexpectedly came across non-duality. It has had a profound effect on me and now I am experiencing great doubts about whether I should go on with my training. Do you have anything to say about whether there is a conflict between psychotherapy and non-duality?

There is no conflict between psychotherapy and non-duality, unless your mind wants to create one.

You could avoid getting too caught up in any of the many different psychotherapy theories or stories. The best psychotherapists are usually the ones that know a wide variety of them and don't take any of them too seriously.

Essentially, psychotherapy is a relationship. Beyond that, everything is in doubt.

※

ARE YOU A CHARLATAN?

In my younger days I spent some time in Osho's ashram. I also read Ramana Maharshi, and once or twice saw Ram Dass. I liked them all and regarded them all as enlightened. Then I started to wonder whether they were simply self-deluded or actually charlatans. And now I find myself wondering the same thing about you.

'Charlatan', 'self-deluded' and 'enlightened' are all stories. Meanwhile This simply goes on being this.

Characters like Osho, Ramana Maharshi and Ram Dass become the targets of many of our most powerful projections, both positive and negative. This is because we live in separation and are looking outside ourselves for that which is inside ourselves. The language I am using here is rather careless but it makes the point well enough so it will do.

Jung expressed this much better than I can when he wrote that the last thing that many of us can believe is that anything good could come out of ourselves. "People will do anything, no matter how absurd, to avoid facing their own souls. They will practise Indian yoga and all its exercises, observe a strict regimen of diet, learn theosophy by heart, or mechanically repeat mystic texts from the literature of the whole world—all because they cannot get on with themselves and have not the slightest faith that anything useful could ever come out of *their* souls." (Carl Jung)

When I worked as a lecturer, I had a colleague who said "The trouble with students is that they are always at your feet or at your throat." The same could be said of devotees. My colleague's words are a wonderfully concise summary of the problem of projection.

By the way, I saw Ram Dass in Albuquerque many years ago and I liked him.

When it is seen that there is no self at the centre, then life just goes on. As they say in Zen, before liberation chop wood, after liberation chop wood. Life may get better. It may not. But it is seen that it is not 'my' life. No one is living it and no one was ever living it.

That is the revelation and that is why sometimes it is said that "Nothing is changed but everything is transformed." After that our speculations about whether so-and-so is enlightened, self-deluded or a charlatan are likely to seem quite unimportant.

❊

IS THIS LIBERATION?

Some time ago, after I had been searching for a long while, there was an awakening. There was no self or time and there were no thoughts. In spite of this, life seemed normal, almost disappointingly so. But after a few days I became aware of 'me' again and I started to search for how I could replicate what had happened.

Since then I seem to be integrating all this, but it's been quite a rocky road. There have been times of deep peace when all paths and practices seem futile and the past and future unreal. But at other times it feels like I'm in a desert, with fear and despair as my companions.

Do you have any comment on what's going on for me? By the way, when I was writing this I made an interesting typo. Instead of "There were no thoughts", I first typed "There were no oughts." Well, those disappeared as well, I guess!

From what you write, it sounds like it is probably all over for you and your head is not just in the tiger's mouth, but the tiger has bitten it off.

However, the mind may be hanging on to the idea that perhaps there should still be something else—for example that feelings of fear, despair and hopelessness should not arise in liberation. This is just a story which may simply fall away.

And congratulations on losing the 'oughts'. That alone should allow some relaxation to arise.

It's odd that so many of us visit so many teachers and spend so much time and money to discover what was always the case. We really are like fish discussing how to get more in touch with the sea.

I feel that most gurus and teachers are misleading. They can't help at least implying that there is something other than This, some secret that can be discovered, probably only through their help.

Personal enlightenment or any other kind of 'advanced spiritual state of being' is clearly an illusion when this is seen for what it is. It's a relief to give all those beliefs up.

The meetings I enjoy most about this are the simple ones, the ones without any bells and whistles.

Yes, discussions of this are exactly like fish talking about how they can get more in touch with the sea. That's a wonderful metaphor. "We are fish complaining that we are thirsty."

WEIGHT LOSS

Dear Richard, I'm re-reading your splendid 'The Book of No One'. It's Friday morning. I'm drinking tea and looking out through the window at a huge sky that is contriving to make a little weather. I laugh and scratch remarks in the margins of your book. I am fond of chuckling and laughing.

A glimpse into the possibility that one's own grave personage is in fact a fiction, lighter than air, can cause an unexpected levitation. This puts me in mind of St. Joseph of Cupertino who would bob among the rafters if not properly ballasted, or was that Teresa of Avila? No matter. The point is that I find myself occasionally weightless and bobbing around. I can only attribute this to missing baggage, or lost luggage.

It seems No One weighs almost Nothing. So it must be concluded that your book has every right to be considered a very effective means of weight loss. For selfish reasons I'd like to encourage you to write another. All the best, Rupert Peene

Dear Rupert, I love the metaphor. A third book has now been written but alas, it will only be available in German at first. An English edition should appear eventually, but the mills of publishers grind very slow. Best wishes, Richard (Author's note: it has now been published in English as *Drink Tea, Eat Cake.*)

❀

THE LAWS OF ATTRACTION

Many people are fascinated by the laws of attraction and fully believe that these determine what we experience in life. They say that if we follow these laws attentively, our lives should become smooth and fulfilling and we should obtain whatever we want.

What would you comment? Is this just another story?

The story of the laws of attraction is simply one of many that we love to entertain ourselves with to persuade ourselves that we understand the mystery of being and can be in control of something called 'my life'. It is a very seductive story and very fashionable at the moment, but like all such stories it takes us away from the simplicity of presence and focuses us on the non-existent future and past.

A superstition is an improbable belief held on insufficient evidence. You can decide for yourself whether you think the story of the laws of attraction comes under this definition.

❄

PRE-DETERMINATION

May I ask you whether, in the light of of non-duality, you think that everything is pre-determined? Or would you say that the reason events happen is pure chance?

To say that events are pre-determined, or that they are chance, or that they are fated, or that they are the result of karma, are all equally stories. There is nothing wrong with holding to any of these stories, but in liberation they are all seen through as equally meaningless.

There is no need to seek for an explanation as to why events happen and no explanation is anything more than an invented story. We could add that because there is no time, nothing is actually happening anyway. But because the mind constructs the appearance of time, there appear to be events happening and the mind would love to have an explanation for these.

In other words, the mind is always trying to solve a non-existent problem which it has itself invented. It is a bit like puzzling over whether God will be angry if we wear a hat in church, or if we do not.

I read your words "nothing is actually happening anyway" and for a while all my questions fell away. But of course after a while my mind came back again and rebelled against this statement. The thought that life is without meaning is very threatening to me from my 'non-liberated' perspective. Can you not offer me any hope or any way out?

No, there is no hope and no way out. Some individuals hear this with relief, some with despair. I don't give advice but if I did I would suggest to people that they relax and do whatever small and simple things they enjoy doing.

❋

AWAKENING OR LIBERATION?

I recognise the experience you describe in your book. Some time ago for a few days I simply wasn't there. This was a joyful time and I was quite sure that it was 'all over' for me.

But now seeking has re-asserted itself, just as you write can happen. I have some questions I'd like to put to you about this:-

1. Is this what the Buddhists call 'rigpa'?

2. Can this experience disappear? I feel that my ego has returned, but in spite of this, presence and stillness are often much more real than before. But at other times my feelings and thoughts completely overwhelm me, even more strongly than before.

3. Can you give me any advice?

1. I know only a little about Buddhism, so I can't comment much on the term 'rigpa'. Within Tibetan Buddhism, it is the word that most closely approximates to what can be described as the seeing of non-duality, or the seeing of Oneness. The form of Buddhism it relates to, Dzogchen, is the closest form in Tibetan Buddhism to radical non-duality.

2. Often there is a period of time between awakening and liberation when the self comes back and reasserts itself for a while, even though its unreality has been seen. Sometimes this can be experienced as a very painful time, a time without hope.

Moreover, sometimes even after liberation itself the mind can simply doubt that this is 'the end'. This is because even in liberation uncomfortable thoughts and feelings can still arise. However, in liberation they are seen through. They may arise but they tend not to be taken very seriously. It is difficult to comment from your description on which of these has taken place, not that it matters in any case.

3. I don't give advice.

✳

IS THERE TIME OR NOT?

For me there is quite a clear sense that there is no self, there is only Oneness. But I have a problem when Advaita teachers say that there is no time and that nothing has ever happened. I simply don't understand this. It is obvious that events are happening and have done for hundreds of thousands of years.

Perhaps I'm wasting my energy on something that doesn't really matter. I feel that for me this is the last real obstacle.

In liberation, when the person drops away, it is seen that This, presence, whatever is happening, is all that there is. It is the totality of existence. Of course there is a past, but it exists only as a thought that arises in This. Of course there is a future, but again it exists only as a thought that arises in This. Of course there seems to be continuity, which requires time, but that continuity is constructed only in consciousness which exists outside time.

The non-existence of time, like the non-existence of space, is either seen directly or it is not. The mind can never get it. As I often say in my meetings, I wouldn't worry about it. After all, what can you do with it anyway? As long as there is an apparent individual in this waking dream we call life, time and space will continue to appear and the next apparent moment will probably, though not inevitably, arise.

I think I get what you mean. At least your description makes more sense to me than anything else I've read about this. But I'm confused by your phrase 'consciousness which exists outside time'. I would describe this as 'the ever-present now in which everything is apparently happening, like waves eternally breaking on a beach.' There's no real forward progression, but time appears to flow. Do you think that gets it?

Yes, that is as good a way of effing the ineffable, or describing the indescribable, as any.

❀

A CONSTANT STATE OF CONSCIOUSNESS?

How did you attain your state of consciousness? Do you experience it as constant?

It is not a state of consciousness and I did not attain it. It is neither constant nor inconstant, because it is outside time.

The seeing of non-separation happens in spite of us, not because of us. Liberation is seen because the 'I' is no longer there blocking out the view of non-duality. I'm sorry if this sounds paradoxical or confusing but liberation is not something that can be related to any personal experience.

You wrote in your reply that liberation is not something that can be related to any personal experience. But the appeal of liberation to me is that it offers the promise of improvement to my personal experience of life. If it doesn't in fact do this, why should I or anyone else be interested in it?

Liberation is not instrumental. We cannot use it for our profit in any way. If liberation is seen, the experience of life may be improved or not, because there are no rules.

An interest in liberation either arises or it does not. If it does, that's a mystery. If it does not, that's a mystery. In either case, it has nothing to do with who we think we are.

DOES LIBERATION DEEPEN?

Dear Richard, Your interview on conscious.tv chimed with me. Some time ago, when I was out walking, I suddenly saw that everything— the sky, the moors, the stone walls—was just as much me as this body is. There was nothing external to me. I was filled with wonder at the revelation that there is no border between me and the external world. Since then I have tried to talk about this to friends but I'm met with incomprehension and disquiet, so I've learnt to stay silent.

I have one question for you. Do some aspects of liberation deepen for you as time apparently goes by and do you notice new aspects that weren't noticed before? Best wishes, Jason

Dear Jason, Thank you for your description, which I enjoyed reading. To answer your question, liberation simply is, so it does not deepen. But that which arises within liberation is constantly changing and this may involve the noticing of new aspects, or new realisations, or a deepening of certain experiences. Really this is no different to 'before' liberation, to use time-bound terms. Being asleep and being awake are the same thing.

Dear Richard, I very much relate to the experiences that you describe during awakening. But I find that I am also experiencing a lot of fear, as if this waking dream is so fragile that it could disappear at any moment. I think that I am still recovering from the initial shock of seeing that my life is only a dream.

I realise that this fear is also part of the dream and that there is nothing wrong with it, but it is very uncomfortable. Can you suggest anything which might help me with it? Best wishes, Jason

Dear Jason, I don't usually give advice or make recommendations, but the therapist in me would say that the best thing to do with the fear you are feeling is simply to pay attention to it on a visceral level. In other words, locate where it is in your body and just focus on it for as long as you are comfortably able to. This is much more effective than getting caught up in the stories in your head about what it may be about. Do this regularly and just notice what happens without trying to change anything. It may get stronger or weaker or reveal some other feeling underneath it. Just go along innocently with whatever happens. Eventually it will transform. Best wishes, Richard

✺

IS THE IDEA OF SELF AN ILLUSION?

Is the idea of the self an illusion that develops during our growing up? Could it be said that non-duality is actually our natural state? When non-duality is seen, is that a return to our natural state through the removal of delusion?

The sense that there is an autonomous individual, or self, is much more than an idea. In other words, the sense of separation that arises along with self-consciousness when we are children is more than conceptual, and this is why we cannot rid ourselves of it with the mind. As the sense of separation is so powerful for most people, I call it an appearance rather than an illusion. 'Illusion' sounds too ephemeral and suggests it would be rather easy to see through.

You are right, non-duality is a return to the natural state of being. It could be described as "the removal of delusion", but we are powerless to remove it. However, it can simply drop away.

✺

DESPAIR, GOING CRAZY AND COMPETITIVE ENLIGHTENMENT

Recently for a while I disappeared and I was just left seeing nothing, in the way that you and Tony Parsons and Nathan Gill have written about.

However, I've been reading a lot of conflicting stuff about this and I find myself becoming very fearful and despairing as a result. One so-called 'enlightened master' writes that he no longer engages with the world in any normal way. He doesn't have any relationships any more or do any normal activities. What's more, he says that this is the mark of 'absolute enlightenment', and anyone who doesn't experience it like this is not fully enlightened.

He also says there is awakening 'in' the dream and awakening 'from' the dream, and that most 'awakened beings' are not fully awakened because they are not awakened from the dream. He has lots of other very complex ideas about enlightenment, and he frightens me with all the stuff that he says we should do. A different writer that I've come across also uses the term 'absolute enlightenment' and claims it gives access to 'the fourth dimension'.

However, when I read you, Tony, Nathan and a few others, you all sound much more relaxed about enlightenment. I like this but it leaves me feeling very confused. So is enlightenment some spectacular state involving the fourth dimension, whatever that is, or are these stories simply misleading?

Do I have to go mad to see Oneness?

I wouldn't describe awakening as 'I' seeing nothing. I would describe it as the seeing of nothing because 'I' am not there anymore. In awakening 'I' comes back afterwards. In liberation, 'I' leaves the stage and doesn't come back.

Liberation doesn't lead to despair because in liberation the fullness of nothing is seen, the fullness that is unconditional love. But awakening can lead to despair because in awakening only the emptiness of nothing is seen. The person who comes back after that seeing often feels helpless and hopeless.

You certainly don't have to go mad to see Oneness because seeing Oneness has nothing to do with you, whether mad or sane. Seeing Oneness happens in spite of you, not because of anything you do or anything you are.

It sounds to me like the 'enlightened master' you refer to is peddling competitive enlightenment. Liberation is simply the seeing of the emptiness and the fullness of nothing. Everything else is just stuff happening. If liberation is seen, it doesn't matter whether there's still an engagement with the normal activities of the world and relationships or not. Whatever happens, happens. The world may very much still be enjoyed as play. In fact a delight in whatever is present often occurs in liberation.

Remember that detachment, which can be developed through techniques by a person, is often mistaken for enlightenment. Detachment is cold, empty and sterile. It has no value. Non-attachment, on the other hand, may make life flow more easily.

Awakening 'from' the dream is physical death. Awakening 'to' the dream is liberation while the body-mind is still alive. You might like to look at Leo Hartong's book, 'Awakening to the Dream', on this point.

I feel that I am opening up gradually to this, although my mind still wants a special event to happen. The seeing of nothing or emptiness that happened seems to me to be grace. Perhaps I am already mad but I don't feel this is the case.

Yes, you are right, awakening and liberation are grace. And yes, you are right, awakening and liberation can happen gradually. There are no rules about this at all.

If you don't feel you are mad, then you are probably not. When the fullness of liberation is seen as well as its emptiness, that is the end of all searching.

Thank you for that. I've been searching for enlightenment for a long time, and now for the first time I'm beginning to realise that maybe I don't have to become enlightened.

Yes, that's really important. You don't have to become enlightened. In fact you cannot become enlightened. Liberation can only be seen when you are not there. That is the core of this.

DIFFERENT VERSIONS OF NON-DUALITY

A book on non-duality that I've read recently says that 'consciousness' exists and that we can become enlightened if we become increasingly aware of consciousness. This seems to be a method that the writer prescribes.

You and Tony Parsons seem to see things differently. You write that there simply is no one and no self. I'm very drawn to your message that there is no method and no right or wrong. I also like it that you say that from the standpoint of liberation everything is meaningless and without purpose.

Would you agree that there are very different versions of non-duality out there in the 'enlightenment market place'?

Oh yes, of course there are different versions of non-duality out there, just as there are different versions of Christianity, Islam, Buddhism, psychoanalysis and Marxism. The disputatious mind will always create different versions in all matters and there's no reason why non-duality would be any different.

Dennis Waite gives a summary of what he sees as the three main strands in non-duality. He calls them 'traditional Advaita', 'neo-Advaita' and 'pseudo-Advaita'. A brief outline of his model is that in traditional Advaita there is liberation and a path to liberation, in neo-Advaita there is liberation but no path to liberation, and in pseudo-Advaita there is neither liberation nor a path to liberation.

> "In traditional Advaita there is something to be realised and a path or practices that can lead to this, in neo-Advaita there is something to be realised but no path or practices that can lead to this, and in pseudo-Advaita there is neither something to be realised nor any path or practices."

According to his own description, Dennis would fall clearly into the traditional Advaita camp and Tony Parsons and I would fall clearly into the neo-Advaita camp. Of course none of this has any importance at all, but it can sometimes be very entertaining. And it's amusing to consider that there might be three different kinds of Oneness.

In case you are not confused enough already, I recently saw a book on non-duality which, while rejecting paths and practices, promised nevertheless that it contained '*detailed* instructions' for 'a *practiceless* practice'. So as with religion, there is never any end to the sophisticated madness that our mischievous monkey minds can produce.

❋

GRADUAL AWAKENING

Can awakening happen slowly bit by bit? Some years ago there was a kind of awakening for me, but after that everything went on as before for a long time. Then a little while ago there was a subtle emotional change. I'm not so upset by events now and there is a profound feeling of peace inside me. Sometimes I seem to be observing myself as if I were a robot, or as if everything's happening in my absence. I also have a much stronger impulse to be alone than I've ever had before.

Yes, awakening can definitely happen slowly. I know someone who had a very clear awakening when she was seven. It was a long time before any further realisation. The recent changes that you write about—not being so upset by events, peacefulness and an impulse to be alone—are common characteristics of awakening. I know of many other individuals who experience them. Your description of observing yourself as if you were a robot reminds me of another common characteristic of awakening, the seeing that although events happen, there is no doer.

❋

THE PAST AND DEPRESSION

I have had a very troubled life. I am often overwhelmed by the thought that I have ruined my life through making a lot of bad decisions. This makes me depressed. Although I know that there are no bad or good decisions from the ultimate standpoint of non-duality, I haven't really accepted this on a deep level and so I still suffer. Have you any comment?

Many individuals feel as you do. They miss the moment, or presence, or This so often because they are lost in regrets about an imagined past. But as you say, there were no good or bad decisions and, more importantly, there was never anyone to make them. There was also no past to make them in.

When this is directly seen, regret is likely to fall away or to be seen through or at the very least to diminish. Even the mental understanding of this can sometimes bring relief. Apart from that, it is a question of making the apparent prison more comfortable and that can be done in a variety of ways.

I didn't quite understand what you meant at the end of your reply. Did you mean that I can decide to have more comfortable thoughts?

I would not say that you can decide to have more comfortable thoughts. Nevertheless, an inclination might arise to do things that tend to produce more comfortable thoughts and feelings. For example, doing simple things that we enjoy, spending time in green places, taking exercise, being kind to people and animals, have all been shown to alleviate depressive thoughts and feelings to some extent. Some people also find meditation or mindfulness helpful.

Of course none of this has anything to do with seeing non-duality. Ultimately it may be seen that there is no one who has depressive thoughts or who spends time in green places or who is mindful.

My depression is compounded because I seem to have had a lot of bad luck. To me this seems inexplicable. Is everything that has happened to me coincidence or was it predestined?

I'll try to give you an answer, but the problem is that the mind always deals in stories. So if I say that neither of those stories are true, the mind simply looks for another one. I can say that it is a waste of time looking for explanations for that which is unknowable, but the mind won't accept this.

'Coincidence' and 'predestination' are each equally stories to explain the inexplicable. You touch on this when you use the word 'inexplicable' yourself. Why something happened to you can never be known. All explanations are stories, invented by the mind because it hates uncertainty. Meanwhile, there is just This, just Oneness and whatever is arising in Oneness. Or we could say that there is just whatever Oneness is arising as.

The only important thing, I suppose, is to attain liberation. But it's not possible for me to force this to happen, is it?
    Did 'Oneness' plan the ruin of my life?

You are right. Liberation has nothing to do with us so we cannot force it to happen.

As soon as we ask a question like "Did Oneness plan the ruin of my life?" we are back in a story, adding an invented meaning to whatever is happening. It's natural for a person to do this and if it's happening it cannot be helped. But as long as we are lost in these stories, there isn't the simple seeing of This.

Some of my depression is because I feel I have ruined myself finan-cially through making stupid decisions. I feel that I can never forgive myself for this. How can non-duality help me with this?

There's little I can add to what's already been said. It may be seen that there never was anyone who made decisions, whether stupid or wise. It may be seen that there is no one who requires forgiveness or who could forgive. There is no way that anything can be different to what it is. Sometimes the realisation of this can bring relief and diminish or put an end to regret.

I have never said that non-duality can help anyone in any way. Non-duality is entirely non-instrumental.

You've been very patient with me—thank you. I understand non-duality intellectually but I know that this is not much help. I guess it's only possible to relax into the inexplicable when the person has disappeared and liberation has actually been seen.

You express it so well. The inexplicable can really only be accepted when the person has disappeared. This is why it so difficult to communicate about this. Nevertheless, some people find some relief in communicating about non-duality, although others do not.

❋

ARE RELATIONSHIPS AND LOVE POSSIBLE AFTER LIBERATION?

My boyfriend and I are very much in love. We have shared our spiritual search as friends as well as lovers and now we are both becoming hooked on non-duality.

But I am frightened that if liberation is seen, we will no longer have a relationship and we will lose each other. Is it possible to have a relationship and a normal family life when liberation is seen?

One of the reasons I'm asking you this is because I read a book about non-duality recently in which the author's description of liberation sounded cold, empty and lonely. But your description and Tony Parsons' description sound much nicer than this.

That author's description may be applied to awakening but not to liberation. In awakening only the emptiness of Oneness is seen. That is why it can seem cold and lonely. But in liberation unconditional love, or the fullness of Oneness, is also seen. Don't worry about the mind understanding this—it can't. But when it is seen, it is simply incontrovertible.

So there is no need to worry about what may happen in liberation.

A relationship is an entity composed of ideas and as such is seen through in liberation. But relating is a process which can continue and may grow deeper in liberation. This is because much of the neurosis that belongs to a person may fall away when liberation is seen, and neurosis makes our behaviour with our lovers very problematic.

We could even say that it is only in liberation that real ungrasping love can flourish. When all the stories that are attached to being a separate person drop away, what is left may be the simplicity of love, the lover and the beloved.

❀

DESPAIR AND AWAKENING

Ever since I was a young man I've devoted myself to spiritual seeking. But then my world was turned upside down when I fell passionately in love. For a while this was wonderful, but I experienced extreme jealousy and because of this my girlfriend eventually left me.

I now feel almost suicidally depressed and that my life has no meaning. I'm wondering whether this has been a kind of awakening and whether this kind of intense romantic love has something in common with the unconditional love that you write about. Could you comment on this?

Awakening is a temporary dropping away of the person, sometimes for only a split second. Liberation is the permanent dropping away of the person. You will probably know if that temporary dropping away of the person has happened, but not necessarily, because it is possible for awakening to happen without any conscious recognition.

Certainly awakening can sometimes plunge the individual into the kind of crisis that you describe. A great romantic love for another person followed by a rejection can also be a shattering experience. The initial stages of romantic love can have something in common with the unconditional love which is seen in liberation, but romantic love usually becomes conditional very quickly.

An approach that some individuals find helpful in this kind of crisis is to stay as much as possible with the visceral experience of what is happening, rather than getting caught up in the story of it in their head. It may also be helpful to seek out some appropriate therapy or healing. Although this can't in itself bring about the seeing of liberation, it may help the person who is seeking liberation to feel less troubled and more comfortable in themselves.

As to suicide, I don't recommend it. There is so much beauty in the world, even in the sight and sound of leaves rustling in the wind. I feel it's a shame to miss this. I wish you well.

❀

IS THERE CAUSATION AND TIME?

Dear Richard, I have been very taken with the sincerity and obvious first-hand experience in your books.

I have been fascinated by questions about time and causation for many years since reading Kurt Vonnegut's wonderful book 'Slaughter House Five'. In this the hero, Billy Pilgrim, comes unstuck in time. He finds that all the moments of time are like the beads on a necklace, that every bead has always existed, and that despite everyone's experience to the contrary, it is consciousness that moves and not time.

I have recently been reading the book by Leo Hartong which you recommended. He has this to say about time:

"Clearly, the timeless does not start later on, nor is the ever-present on its way, scheduled for arrival at some point in the future. It is present right here and right now. When I say 'here and now' I do not mean the fleeting moment between past and future, but the

eternal present, which contains the apparent flux of time. Now, in this moment, I am writing these words; and now, in this moment, you are reading them."

I am trying to understand what Leo means. He wrote those words at a moment which was now and I am reading them in another moment which also qualifies as now. Between those two moments of now, there is no break. In fact, it would seem that there are no breaks anywhere in all the moments which qualify as now. I should like to know how you view the connection between those two apparently separate moments in which Leo typed those words and I read them. Best wishes, Allan

Dear Allan, I like Leo's description very much. Of course all descriptions are simply attempts to "eff the ineffable" as Alan Watts put it.

Causation can only exist in time. But there is no time and therefore there is no causation, except as a thought arising in This. There is only This. And in This, thoughts of writing and reading words in other apparent times arise.

Another way of putting this is to say that time can only arise in consciousness.

The mind loves to wrestle with questions such as this. But we might also notice that as long as the mind is doing this, the miracle of presence—the taste of a cup of coffee, the sound of a car driving past, the texture of cat's fur, whatever is appearing in and as consciousness—is being missed. Best wishes, Richard

✻

ENJOYMENT AND MAKING CHOICES

Now that you have realised non-duality, do you still enjoy doing certain things, such as being in nature? And how do you make choices?

I have not realised non-duality. No one realises non-duality. Non-duality is only realised when there is no one there to realise it. Sorry about the paradox.

Enjoyment still goes on. By and large, there's a preference for quite a simple life here. Yes, being in nature is enjoyable. So is being in the city.

There is no need to make choices. There never was any need to make choices. There is no one who could make a choice. Life simply happens.

❋

FEAR OF DEATH

I fear death and loss, particularly the possibility of losing my children. Who would it be good to read or listen to about death?

It is quite natural for a person to fear death, the loss of loved ones and the loss of their own individuality. Religions exploit this natural fear of death mercilessly.

However, when non-separation is seen, there's a tendency for death no longer to cause concern. As there never was an individual who was born, there is no individual who can die. In presence concern with death is likely to collapse because it is about the future—the non-existent future, we might add.

The only reading that I know of to recommend are the usual suspects. That would include Tony Parsons, Nathan Gill, Leo Hartong and of course myself.

❋

I'M SAD THAT THERE'S NO MEANING

I've been reading about Advaita for a while. I also go to the meetings of various speakers including yours.

When I notice that there is no doer, I feel a definite sense of peace. But the lack of a meaning to the world, and the recognition that I can't do anything because 'I' am an illusion and life is just a dream, make me feel sad. I can't stop seeking even though I know that there's nothing to find and I can't do anything to make myself wake up. My mind is baffled by this.

Being spiritual seems to offer a kind of false happiness to people. Spiritual people feel that they can help to heal others, save the planet and usher in the coming Age of Enlightenment. They channel messages from great astral beings or become 'light workers'. But I feel unhappy and isolated because I can't believe in any of this anymore.

So what can I do? Can you offer me some comment?

You sum up very clearly the dilemma that many seekers find themselves in. What do we do when the hopelessness of seeking has been seen, but the person who cannot help searching is still there?

All I can suggest to this is, if you can, relax and do things that you enjoy doing. You can leave the saving of the planet, the bringing of messages from great astral beings and the light work to those who believe that all of that is important.

❈

MYSTERY, QUESTIONS AND UNDERSTANDING

Whether there has been awakening or not, the world is utterly amazing even though it is transitory. But it is also a great mystery. So when the individual has dissolved, is the mystery clarified? Does the individual then understand the relationship between the author, the creator and the director?

Do questions end because the mystery has finally been understood or is it because of some more ineffable reason?

Questions drop away because the stories that they relate to are seen through, so there is no need to ask them any more. Beyond that, everything is seen as a mystery so questions become futile.

Awakening and liberation are a fall into a great unknowing, so the mystery of this astonishing manifestation deepens rather than being clarified. In presence, questions about this mystery can still arise but they tend not to be taken seriously anymore. This is because it is now known that there is no possibility of an answer that will finally satisfy the mind.

Remember that liberation is a loss—the loss of the person. One of the things that is lost in liberation is much of what the person thought they knew.

There is no author, creator or director.

❋

IS NON-DUALITY JUST ANOTHER STORY?

I love non-duality, but whenever I have followed any path I have ended up having doubts about it. Now I am torturing myself with the thought that non-duality also might just be another story.

Although I know that there is no possibility of proof that will satisfy my mind, I still want to have it! What a paradox! I want to know the reality of non-duality but I guess that's only possible through direct seeing.

Anything that can be put into words or that exists as thoughts is a story. So yes, non-duality is also a story. But it is the story which most clearly describes reality. All the other stories, such as the world religions or philosophies, add either fantastical or philosophical decorations to what is. Non-duality simply attempts to describe what is. That is why I call it 'the mother of all stories'.

Of course you will never know the reality of non-duality. That will only be known when you aren't there. Good luck with your disappearance.

*

SELF-ENQUIRY

Many teachers of Advaita insist that it is necessary to do self-enquiry. I've noticed this particularly with teachers influenced by Bob Adamson and Papaji (H. W. L. Poonja). But I think there's a paradox in expecting non-doers who don't have a self to do self-enquiry.

I have done self-enquiry and my experience of it is that it simply reinforces the sense of separation. When I've asked teachers about this, they've said that this is because I am not pursuing self-enquiry with enough determination and sincerity. Essentially they are saying that I'm not asking "Who am I?" or "What am I?" with enough earnestness.

Now I have come to feel that nothing works. As you say, either non-duality is seen or it isn't. But I find this very frustrating and in this state everything certainly doesn't seem to be full of unconditional love. Nevertheless, I have a lot of resonance with your books. Could you give me your opinion of self-enquiry?

As it is a person who is self-enquiring, it will not lead anywhere except perhaps to the reinforcement of the sense that there is a person. When the person drops away, there is no need to self-enquire, because then it just becomes obvious that there is no one.

I don't make recommendations, but if I did it would be to stop torturing ourselves with techniques, relax and enjoy whatever small thing we are able to. For me it might be a walk round the park and a nice meal.

The problem with your reply is that, as long as there is the sense of separation, relaxation does not seem possible. And it also seems impossible not to seek.

Rather than relaxation, I often feel contraction. So I guess the best thing to do is to try to relax by making the prison more comfortable. Do you think the usual self-improvement techniques help with that?

Or would it be better to chant your mantra "Hopeless, helpless, meaningless"? It's definitely the best mantra I've come across.

Nevertheless, since I've come across non-duality I've felt more relaxed and less neurotic. But what can I do about the continuing feeling that this still isn't it?

Seeking continues until it stops. Relaxation happens or it does not. In the meantime, we may as well make the prison more comfortable by doing whatever we like doing. If self-improvement appeals, then do that. If walking round the park and having a meal appeals, then do that. If all of those appeal, do all of them.

I like one phrase from your books in particular: "We are in a hopeless case". I'm fed up with teachers who insist that it is only through dedicated and committed investigation that we can discover non-duality. Having tried that for a long time, I'm now faced with teachers who tell me that I haven't become free because I'm lazy and uncommitted. I think that's bullshit! I like to think that it happens through grace.

This is a common trick of spiritual teachers, to tell you when things don't improve that it's your fault for not trying hard enough. Of course, if things do improve, they take the credit.

Indeed, what bullshit. After you've taken a Bachelor of Science (Bull Shit) in non-duality and a Master of Science (More Shit), you can do the Ph.D (Piled high and Deep).

❀

CAUGHT HALF WAY

I keep trying to see my own absence. My belief in the validity of the self seems to be fading gradually away but that's the only progress I'm making. Tony and you both seem to suggest that we relax and enjoy whatever is happening and that seems to suit me.

Could you comment on this feeling that I have that I'm stuck half way? Sometimes I'm a person, sometimes I'm not.

The feeling that you have of being stuck half way is a common one. Sometimes there can be a sudden event in which the person is gone and it's simply all over. But sometimes there is a more gradual thinning of the person over a period of time and sometimes there are two separate events, between which the person seems to be coming and going. Either of these can give rise to the feeling of being stuck which you describe.

Remember that however much we try, we cannot see our own absence. When we aren't there, then our absence is simply obvious.

Thanks for your reply, Richard. Tony also says that this is common. Liberation is probably more natural than I tend to think. It's difficult for me to get rid of the idea that path and practice are necessary to bring about awakening. But I'm beginning to get that they are irrelevant. I really appreciate your clarity.

✺

A FLASH OF AWAKENING

The sense of being a separate person still comes and goes here, but some time ago the energy of seeking was suddenly switched off. In an instant, although nothing changed, the sense of an inside and an outside vanished. At the same 'time' there was an absolute knowing that it was impossible to understand this. Somehow, the attempt to understand could only arise from the sense of a separated person.

That's a great description. Nothing changes, yet even if the person returns after an event like this, it is forever transformed.

✺

FEAR

A lot of the time I feel quite peaceful, but suddenly I'll feel anxious, fearful or even terrified. At these times I wonder whether I'm going mad. I cope at these times by doing everyday things. For example I like taking my dog for a walk. But often the fear returns.

It may help to stay innocently with the fear, or whatever other uncomfortable feeling is arising, wherever it's noticed in the body. Simply pay attention to the feeling in the body rather than the thoughts going through the mind. Do this for a few minutes at a time—maybe up to about ten or twenty minutes. Then go and do something else, preferably something that you enjoy—a walk in the park, a cup of coffee, taking your dog for a walk if that's what appeals to you. Go back to paying attention to the uncomfortable feeling in the body frequently, a few times a day or at least a few times a week. Notice what shifts come.

※

DEVELOPING LOVE AND COMPASSION

I've heard you say that the individual cannot derive any advantage from enlightenment. Something about hearing this enabled me to relax considerably. Before that I had put a lot of effort into becoming enlightened and increasing my compassion.

You and Tony say that after liberation it is simply seen that there is unconditional love. So is it of any benefit to try to enhance our compassion towards others within the story, perhaps by doing a loving kindness meditation practice?

Does it matter whether we increase our compassion or not?

There may be benefit to the individual in doing some kind of loving kindness practice. Enhanced compassion sometimes makes life flow more easily for the person practising it. There is scientific evidence that both giving and receiving acts of kindness increase our levels of oxytocin, which is a 'feel good' hormone. You can read more about this if you want to in Dr. David Hamilton's book, 'Why Kindness Is Good For You'. It is probably for this reason that some Buddhists recommend performing 'random acts of kindness'.

Nevertheless, remember that any practice which is 'forced' is likely eventually to increase rather than decrease stress.

What I am pointing to, however, is the realisation that there is no one who practises loving kindness. Loving kindness is simply practised or it is not. Another way to put this is that, if an interest in the practice of loving kindness arises, it's quite likely that it will be pursued. If not, not.

Ultimately, the practice of loving kindness is as meaningless as everything else. Everything is already whole and adequate. Everything is already Oneness doing its own thing, apparently. Nothing needs any added meaning to justify it, except to a person living in a story.

❀

YOU ARE THE LIGHT IN WHICH
EVERYTHING ARISES

You and some others have written something that I find very puzzling. Your way of putting it is "What is sitting there, although it might feel like a person, is the light in which everything arises."

I can't make any sense of this. I am an individual with my own identity, which other people with their own identities recognise. I might not be able to pin-point where my point of view is precisely located in space, but it is 'somewhere'. If I have a pain in my shoulder, it is I who feel it, not you. If you have a pain in your shoulder, you feel it, I do not.

An analogy might be a character in a film who acts as if they have a pain but doesn't really have one. But they are not the light in which the film is appearing. They are just a character and if they disappear from the film, the film still continues. Their disappearance makes no difference to the film. So the words "You are the light in which everything arises" puzzle me very much.

I suspect that discussing this won't get me anywhere, but I feel impelled to ask whether you can cast any more light on it. Perhaps I need a blue pill.

When I say you are the light in which everything arises, I do not mean 'you the character' or even 'you the person'. The phenomena associated with 'you the character' are simply phenomena. This includes the sense of separation, if that is still there.

The light in which everything arises is Consciousness, or Being, or Oneness. We could say that it is this which gives rise to all phenomena, or in which all phenomena arise. It is this which you really are.

The experiences you associate with being a person are froth on the surface of the ocean. You are the ocean itself.

Nathan Gill's way of expressing this is that there is 'awareness and the content of awareness'. In these terms, you mistake yourself for the content of awareness, but actually you are awareness itself. Of course these are not actually separate, so it would be more accurate to say that the content of awareness *is* awareness arising as its own content. That, however, may sound more difficult to grasp.

This probably doesn't help, as words rarely do.

Sorry, I haven't got a blue pill to give you. However, my favourite line from 'The Matrix' is "Follow the white rabbit."

❋

THE EGO

I've always liked Ronald Laing and I've been discussing him recently with a friend. We've also been reading your book 'The Book of No One'. In this you write "Ego is not the person." Could you explain a bit more what you mean by this?

Like many others, I was influenced by R. D. Laing in the seventies and eighties. When I was training counsellors, I used to show them the wonderful documentary about him, 'Did You Used To Be R.D. Laing?'

Let me address your question about my remark that "the ego is not the person". The word ego is used to mean different things by different people. However, these meanings often come down to one of two or three. Ego is often used to mean selfishness or arrogance, as in "He has a very big ego." It is also used to mean the central organising principle, as in Freud's definition of the ego as the arbiter between the superego, or morality principle, and the id, or pleasure principle. And sometimes it is used to mean the sense of selfhood, or the sense of being a separate person.

In saying that the ego is not the person I am making two points. Firstly I am saying that reducing our level of selfishness or arrogance or our level of personal egotism will not bring about the seeing of liberation. However, this is erroneously suggested in many spiritual traditions.

Secondly I am saying that the sense of being a person consists of more than Freud's conscious organising principle. Even if we can somehow see through this principle, that will not bring about the seeing of liberation, because the sense of selfhood comes about through an energetic contraction. This cannot be dissipated through any kind of purely mental insight.

We can also consider this from the other way round. Seeing liberation will not necessarily reduce an arrogant person's level of arrogance or an egotistical person's level of egotism. Nor will it necessarily change the way the character's organising principle operates. Again, spiritual traditions often erroneously suggest that these will happen.

The seeing of liberation is completely impersonal and therefore has no necessary implications for the character and may have no effects on the character at all. Having said that, I have observed in both myself and others that there are certain characteristics that tend to change after the seeing of liberation. However these are only tendencies. There is no necessity for them to happen.

❈

COMING TO TEA

Instead of trying to explain non-duality to people, I just give them your 'Die' book, so that's been really helpful to me. Some years ago it happened to 'me' and swept away years of searching. That's been replaced by stillness. Maybe I'll drop by for tea one day. I wonder whether like me you use loose tea and a cosy?

Yes, come for tea if you're nearby. I use tea bags but the choice will include Earl Grey.

✻

AM I STUCK?

There has recently been an awakening experience. Everything I believed has been turned upside down, including all my beliefs about life, death and purpose. Now everything has settled down again and seems normal. The idea of 'me' seems to have come back. But there remains a change. It's difficult to describe but things seem a bit translucent and there's no real belief in the past anymore. However, I still feel somewhat neurotic, with some of the old feelings of inadequacy still here. But there's no impulse at all to search anymore.

It seems to me that "the story of me" will continue to express the conditioning that this body and mind has been subjected to. It may go on responding to situations in its habitual conditioned way. But it's finally getting that This is it.

Does it sound to you like I'm stuck between awakening and liberation?

If thoughts or feelings of being stuck arise, that's just what's happening in This. There is no one who can avoid them or prevent them.

If there is no further impulse to search, then probably what has been seen is complete. However, there may still be an expectation in you that certain feelings, such as being stuck, should no longer arise. But this is just a thought, like any other thought.

In liberation, any phenomena can continue to arise. It is simply seen that they no longer arise for a person.

❉

WHY BOTHER DOING ANYTHING?

I haven't had a dramatic awakening, but I know that I don't exist, that in a way I'm a fictional character. I can't take seriously the things that I do anymore now that I know that separation is an illusion. I know now that this is a dream.

But I have a problem. I contemplate doing something and then the thought comes in "Why bother? Everything's unreal anyway." I can't help this, even though I know that there is no free will and whatever happens will happen regardless. Life unfolds as it does and there is no one to do anything about that. I suppose I might as well smile and acknowledge that I have no answers. I don't think I even know what the questions are anymore! Can you comment on all this for me?

You answer your own question as well as I could do. 'Bothering' happens or it doesn't. Thoughts that this is a dream happen or they don't. Seeing that 'I' am a fictional character happens or it doesn't.

There's always something happening, except in dreamless sleep. We either resist it or we do not, and that is also simply what is happening.

❉

ON NARCISSISM AND BEHAVING LIKE AN ASS

Until two years ago I was searching. But more recently there have been some significant changes. My sense of having a self got thinner and then more or less disappeared. Then I felt like I was falling into darkness— it seemed like the abyss you describe as sometimes being between awakening and liberation. And then suddenly there was a complete disappearance and what remained was just non-localised awareness.

I was reading your 'The Avatar of the Single Malt' again recently, which in my view is comedy gold. It's brought to mind a problem I'm feeling. I tend to be quite narcissistic, big-headed and generally prone to behaving like an ass. And this still seems to go on. Is it the same for you? Are you big-headed about the things you've done, such as writing your books? Is it okay for the self to still be there in this way?

Awakening and liberation have no necessary implications. Any phenomena that arose before can still arise. It is simply seen that they do not arise for anyone. So being big-headed about writing books could arise, and so could being narcissistic and behaving like an ass.

Thinking that there might be something wrong with any of that, or that it might mean that the self is back in the frame, is simply the mind's way of trying to draw us back into the story of "There's something incomplete here. There's still something to find." This is simply another thought, in other words another phenomenon happening in this.

❁

IS LIBERATION TERRIFYING?

I've heard and read several people communicating about non-duality. Some of them, particularly U.G. Krishnamurti and Suzanne Segal, make liberation sound terrifying. My concepts about spirituality have been blown apart. Have you found liberation terrifying?

The seeing of liberation here hasn't been terrifying. But it certainly has nothing to do with most people's concepts of spirituality. In a way spirituality can be regarded as another entertainment in the funfair of life, whilst there's nothing particularly entertaining about liberation.

Here life simply goes on, with no Suzanne Segal style traumas.

❁

HAVE YOU A QUESTION FOR ME WHILE I DRINK SAKE?

Dear Richard, I'm re-reading your lovely books. They continually delight me, but I don't know why. Every night at 10.30 I get into my bed (it's a very fine bed by the way), pour myself a little cold sake and read. It's delightful.

I have no complaints whatsoever.

I wish I had a question to pose so I'd have an excuse to contact you. But I don't.

If by any chance you have a question for me I would be glad to answer it.

Regards, Rupert Peene

Hi Rupert, Thank you for your message. I really appreciate it and I'm glad you enjoy the books.

The sake probably helps.

No, no questions from me either. Best wishes, Richard

❋

AWAKENING

Dear Richard, I've just finished reading 'I Hope You Die Soon'. Some time ago I had my own little 'train station' experience, although it was actually in a hotel lobby. It left me pretty confused.

I was presented with this wonderful experience that gave me the certainty that I'm not separate. But my arthritis still hurt, my bills were still due, my kids were still fighting. I thought "How come?" Now your book has enabled me to relax.

It is what it is and that's it. You understand what I mean, don't you?

Well, thank you. I can't say that I'm fully at peace but I'm certainly taking things more easily now. Take care, Karin.

Dear Karin, Thank you for your very interesting message. Train station, hotel lobby—it's all the same thing, isn't it? You express both the realisation and the aftermath very clearly. Best wishes Richard

Hi Richard, Sometimes I still feel frustration or even despair about this. In Portuguese we have a saying: "Se correr o bicho pega, se ficar o bicho mata." This translates as "If you run, the beast hunts you down. If you stay where you are, it kills you." It means that it doesn't matter what you do, the outcome is always the same. Karin

Hi Karin, I love your Portuguese saying. It's such a wonderful encapsulation of the futility of thinking that we are in control of anything, or even that there is a 'we' who could be in control of anything. It reminds me of an American expression: "Sometimes you get the bear. Sometimes the bear gets you." Best wishes, Richard

✷

ENERGETIC TRANSMISSION

The title of your book 'I Hope You Die Soon' reminds me of Rumi's invitation to us to "die before we die".

Can there be a transmission of energy from the one who speaks about non-duality to the one who listens? I've sat in meetings with Tony Parsons and his open empty presence seems to resonate with me and others. Does this facilitate the dropping of the self? Or is there no point in listening to anyone speaking about this?

I enjoy going to Tony's meetings very much myself. I certainly feel that there is a very enjoyable energy there. However, I don't want to suggest that this in any way implies that there is a method for finding liberation, which of course the mind is always interested in discovering.

Rather I'd suggest that there is no one who chooses to go to Tony's meetings. An impulse arises to go there or not but there is no one who owns that impulse. Seen in this way, a question such as "Will this do me some good?" becomes irrelevant.

In other words, when Tony holds a meeting, you will either be there or not. However, you will not have made a decision leading to that because there is no you.

❋

WILL LIBERATION BRING FULFILMENT?

Now that I am quite elderly I find that I have never felt so much joy as I do at present. Should I now seek liberation? It seems to me that even if I found it in the future, it wouldn't guarantee me the joy I currently feel. Maybe liberation would deprive me of that?

Your way of liberation doesn't seem to guarantee me fulfilment. I've read your book and although I relate to a lot of what you write I'm very confused by other parts of it. I get that there is really no person, but as I haven't yet achieved a liberated state, I'm still relating to the world as a person. Can you cast any light on this?

The joy that you are now experiencing is liberation. It is liberation expressing itself as joy felt by you.

I have no "way of liberation" so it will not guarantee you fulfilment. There's no need to worry that your presently felt joy will disappear if you achieve a liberated state in the future. Liberation is not a state, you cannot achieve it and there is no future.

I'm still confused. You write that after we attain liberation there is no change as we may still experience sorrow, fear, anger and so on. I know I'm paraphrasing roughly.

For me there is so much joy and everything changes.

"So much joy" sounds good to me.

When liberation is seen any feeling may still arise. Joy, sadness, happiness, unhappiness can all still arise. But these feelings are seen to belong to no one because there is no one.

Please don't think I'm nit-picking if I add that "we" do not "attain liberation". This is a most fundamental point.

❊

DOES LIBERATION BECOME PERMANENT?

Having had an awakening event, everything in your book resonates with me. As you say, it's impossible to put such an event into words so I won't even try.

But I still find myself powerfully identified with my character including what I call its faults. I still suffer from anxiety, guilt, pride and jealousy among other feelings. I feel that I am in the desert that you describe.

Did there come a time for you when the underlying seeing of presence became permanent so that it was the basis for all your experience? If so, is this what you call liberation?

After the second event that I describe, all remaining questions dropped away and the seeing of This, the seeing that there was nothing left to search for, remained. This is what I describe as liberation. We could say that it is liberation from searching.

Liberation is a term that is often misunderstood. It contains no promise of a necessarily better life for us. It simply reveals that there is no one who has a life. Any phenomenon that arose before liberation was seen can arise afterwards as well, including experiences and feelings that we find uncomfortable. But there can be no more searching when liberation is seen, because it is known that there is nothing to search for. Of course thoughts of searching can still arise, but they are seen through.

❊

ON THINKING AND THE MIND

There are several enlightened masters who state that thinking stops after liberation. They say that after this, thinking only happens for practical reasons, for example when planning to cook a meal.

However, others say that the mind never becomes completely silent and even after liberation it is inclined to chunter on. What do you think?

There is no such thing as a mind. The mind is simply the process of thought. Thinking is Oneness thinking. When liberation is seen it's possible that the energy of thinking may lessen or dissipate but it's also possible that it may not. But in either case it's no longer a problem because it's seen through.

There's also no such thing as an enlightened master.

❄

DIFFICULTIES AFTER AWAKENING

A while ago I had a brief instant of awakening. Since then I've read your books and they've helped me to understand what's going on for me.

But life has been quite tough since then. I have a family, a job and a very busy life, but I've been really obsessed with non-duality since this awakening. I find it difficult to get up much interest in anything else. And I'm worried about the possible effects of liberation on my family and friends. Sometimes I think it would be better if it doesn't happen. Can you comment on this for me?

It's common that after awakening there can be an obsession with non-duality and a loss of interest in almost anything else. But in liberation, life often becomes quite simple. Then there can be a great enthusiasm for the ordinary and the everyday.

I hope the final seeing of liberation occurs for you. When it happens, life tends to go on as before, but it is seen that everything is simply happening of its own accord. So hopefully it will be okay with your family and friends.

However, liberation tends to bring about the collapse of all the stories of meaning and purpose, such as the religious and the spiritual stories. So if members of your family or your friends have a heavy investment in one of these stories, this could cause a problem. In that case, I suggest that you try to be understanding. It can be a shock for family and friends when someone close to them sees non-duality and loses interest in their old ideas and viewpoints.

❀

THE STRANGEST BOOK

Hello Richard, yours is the strangest book I have ever read in my old life. It's the one I keep beside the fire at night with my booze. Seamus Gilroy

Hello Seamus and thank you. I'm glad it's by the fire and not in the fire. Best wishes, Richard

❀

GREAT DIFFICULTIES AFTER AWAKENING

I feel that after an awakening event, I am now lost in what you call the desert and it's very painful. I'm feeling increasingly depressed and anxious, and I long for the completion that seems to come after the seeing of unconditional love in liberation.

I've lost all sense of purpose and meaning and consequently there are aspects of my life which are frankly falling apart. Seeing every-thing as at least partially unreal is very difficult for me. One of the strangest aspects of this is that my family and friends do not seem to have noticed any change in me.

In a way I wish I'd never come across the term 'enlightenment'. Can I ask you whether you experienced anything like the suffering I'm going through?

There is some familiarity here with what you are writing about, although in my case it was in a less dramatic form. After awakening there was a period which I describe as being in the desert, in which the hopelessness of my searching was apparent but there was still a feeling of separation and wanting to find liberation. After about a year there was another dropping away of the person, in which the fullness of Nothing was seen as well as its emptiness. This fullness consists in the seeing of unconditional love. After that there was no more searching and no more separation. Now life simply goes on as before. It is just seen that there is no one living it.

❀

ONENESS

What is this Oneness?

Oneness is Nothing appearing as everything. As the Christian mystic Marguerite Porete* wrote, "Now this soul has fallen…into nothingness, and without such nothingness she cannot be All."

*Marguerite Porete was burnt to death as a heretic by the Catholic Church at the beginning of the fourteenth century.

❀

PSYCHOTHERAPY

After a recent awakening I've found myself reconsidering my plans to train as a psychotherapist.

I've heard Tony Parsons say that a teaching that suggests to an apparent individual that they can arrive at enlightenment through a progressive path is a teaching of imprisonment.

I've also heard you in an interview talk about your professional involvement with therapy. Do you think that some forms of psychotherapy address non-duality and are not built around the ignorant belief that there is a self?

Psychotherapy should never be "a teaching that suggests to an apparent individual that they can arrive at enlightenment through a progressive path." When he uses this phrase, I'm pretty sure that Tony is addressing not psychotherapy but the myriad spiritual and New Age paths. I would consider at least some of these paths to be 'anti-psychotherapeutic' in their effects.

On psychotherapy directly I have heard Tony say that he considers it to be one of the most intelligent things that a person can do. I would agree with this. In other words, as long as we perceive ourself to be a separate person in a prison, doing some form of psychotherapy may be one of the most effective ways of making ourself feel more at ease.

For me, the core of any psychotherapeutic encounter is the being of the psychotherapist. My own preference, as I have often said, would be for a psychotherapist who is not there. In other words I would prefer a psychotherapist who has directly seen the unreality of the self.

There are some forms of psychotherapy that are at least to some degree informed by the non-existence of the self. You could take a look at what's happening in Third Wave Cognitive Behavioural Therapy, particularly as it is informed by Acceptance and Commitment Therapy (ACT) and mindfulness.

If you go ahead with your training, I wish you well with it.

❀

DEPENDENCE ON MEN

I don't feel remotely liberated. Instead, I feel very dependent, particularly on the men that I have relationships with. Consequently my life is full of emotional pain. I am able to enjoy very little because of my insecurities in this area.

Would you recommend psychotherapy as a way for me to overcome my insecurity? In addition, do you think that my insecurity is a block to the unfoldment of liberation? In other words, do I need to deal with it for liberation to be seen?

It's possible that psychotherapy might help you to free yourself of your dependency on relationships, so that you could relate to men in a freer and more spontaneous way. If you're drawn to this, then I recommend it. But it won't be relevant to the seeing of liberation because nothing that we do as a person is relevant to that.

So your insecurity is not a block to liberation. In other words, you don't have to deal with your issues as a person to realise that you are not a person.

❀

WHAT ONE THING WOULD YOU SAY?

What one thing would you say to this character to get it to see This?

Alas, I could not get that character or any character to see This, not by saying one thing or a thousand things. Nevertheless, it might be seen suddenly that there is no one asking the question.

❀

ORIGINAL SIN, RELIGION AND NON-DUALITY

From a non-dual perspective, I would say that the notion of original sin in Christianity represents the appearance of duality. I believe that the earliest definition of 'sin' was 'illusion'.

Do you agree with me that most religions are at their heart non-dual and that it is only the difficulties of communication that have obscured this?

An alternative meaning of 'sin' that I like very much is 'error'. I believe that this is from the Greek 'hamartia', meaning 'missing the mark', like an archer who takes aim and misses the target. The implications of this are less punitive and guilt-inducing than the usual translation of 'sin'. Thus "Go and sin no more" (John 8:11) becomes "Go and make no more errors."

At the root of many religious traditions there may have been the realisation that All Is One. But this has become much obscured. Once a concept of a God who is irredeemably separate from humankind develops, as in most forms of the Abrahamic religions, we have entered into a completely dualistic cosmology. From then on, the best that can be hoped for is that we may approach closer to him-her-it and worship him-her-it. This is of course a metaphor for eternal separation.

❊

THE LAST IMPEDIMENT TO SEEING LIBERATION?

When I first read your book, I thought it was about me! I'm really glad to have finally found someone who can explain the experience that I had.

The only difference for me was that what you describe as two events were both experienced simultaneously. There was the sudden seeing that there was no person, no inside or outside, and that just as I was in everything, so everything was in me. I'm trying to describe it, but as you've written yourself, it is beyond words.

In its absolute fullness, this event lasted a few days. Since then my thinking has become much slower and there is little impulse to think about the future. The past and the future are seen to be a story. There's absolutely no more searching.

Nevertheless, it now feels as if in some way 'I' have come back. Normal life goes on. In some ways it's even more normal than before. So I want to ask you whether 'Richard' has also come back. Are you living with the memory of having seen liberation, or have 'you' simply not returned?

Now I am really on the planet and I know that there can be no other life and no better life.

As you say "This is it." I hope you will write another book for the lucky illumined ones.

For many individuals, as for you, there can be the complete loss of separated awareness and a merging with everything. Thus there may be walking but no one walking, seeing but no one seeing, hearing but no one hearing. In this event both the emptiness and the fullness of everything is seen but by no one.

This total merging does not last permanently. Eventually there is a return to a sense of awareness being located in a specific place, 'here' rather than 'there'. However, if it is all over for the separated person, the sense of contraction that was previously felt disappears for good. That is what is sometimes called liberation, although really it is the seeing that there is no such thing as liberation because there is no one who could become liberated.

After that, any thought, feeling or experience can still happen but it is seen through. It is seen to be part of a waking dream which, because it is known to be without purpose, can really be enjoyed. As you say "Now I am really on the planet and I know that there can be no other life and no better life." That is a beautiful way of putting it.

However, sometimes there is a trap. The individual for whom the sense of location has returned may feel that they have lost something because of this. Then it is possible that searching can resume. This does not matter of course, but it can make life more uncomfortable than it needs to be. Often it only takes the realisation that liberation contains all possible experiences, including ones we may find uncomfortable, for this last 'impediment' to fall away.

From what you write, I would say that there is nothing more to be seen and realised than what 'you' have seen and realised.

❋

AWAKENING AND LIBERATION

I very much relate to what you say about appreciating the ordinary experiences of life, such as the smell of coffee, walking in the park, listening to the wind in the trees.

Some time ago when I was feeling quite exhausted I suddenly disappeared, leaving just exhaustion. There was no doubt at that point that separation was an illusion. It was both extraordinary and ordinary at the same time, and also in an obvious way the 'normal' way of being.

After a time 'I' or 'my mind' came back. Since then there have been various changes. For example I just don't respond to many things in my old habitual way. I also take much greater enjoyment in simple things. But I miss that complete disappearance, so what has also returned is my searching as I try to get back to that event. All the things that I thought I knew have been replaced by 'not-knowing' and there's a kind of hopelessness about this. This isn't unpleasant, it's just a certainty about the impossibility of knowing anything.

It feels like I'm in the desert that you describe. I'm wondering whether I have some kind of fear about liberation and this stops liberation from being seen. Nevertheless, there's a profound relaxation into the knowledge that whatever happens is simply happening and there's no one to do anything about it.

I very much enjoyed reading your very clear account of awakening.

Although there are no absolute rules about awakening, many people seem to go through an event such as you describe. The absolute non-existence of the person and the emptiness of everything may be seen, but the person comes back afterwards and continues searching.

Later there can be another seeing in which this impulse to search simply ends. This is because it is fully seen that there is nothing any longer to search for (although actually, of course, there never was).

Or sometimes this sense that seeing is not yet complete can simply fade away over time.

I call awakening seeing that everything is empty and liberation seeing that everything is also full.

Remember that even in liberation everything may simply continue as before. It is simply seen that it is not continuing for anyone. Sometimes I talk to an individual and get the impression that everything that there is to be seen has been seen, in its fullness. Nevertheless, an idea continues for that individual that "This still isn't it" because life continues in its ordinary way.

In other words, what sometimes needs to be let go of is just an idea, or an illusion, that life seen in liberation should in some way be different to and better than the life that was lived before. But remember, "Being asleep and being awake are the same thing" or as they say in Zen, "Before liberation, chop wood. After liberation, chop wood."

Yes, I do think that I still have an idea of what liberation should be like but I'm pretty sure that this is becoming fainter now.

One thing still puzzles me. During the awakening event there was no person experiencing or interpreting that event. There was only direct experience itself, direct perception itself. But now the person is back, although not in exactly the same way as before, and that direct felt-sense of there being no one has disappeared.

I'm not even sure that I'd be able to function at all if that complete disappearance remained permanently. I don't know if I'd even get out of bed in the morning!

Nevertheless, after the event there remains a powerful understanding that there really is no person.

So what is liberation? Is it the permanent experience of the complete absence that was seen in the event? Or is it the experience of whatever phenomena are arising, including sometimes feeling like a person and sometimes not? Or is liberation simply the understanding that there is no person that remains after an event, even though the person has come back?

Is it simply this constant directness, right here, right now, that seems to result from this plunge into not-knowing?

I like your clear no-nonsense communication about non-duality. I've noticed that there's a lot of diversity among those who write or talk about it. Some seem to think they have something to teach, others not. Is this because the individual will always interpret this in their own way?

I draw a distinction between what I call 'contraction' and 'localisation'. In an awakening or a liberation event (let's settle for those misleading words) all sense of both contraction and localisation can disappear. This is what you describe.

However, this complete disappearance does not last. There is then either a return of contraction, in which the person has returned from awakening still feeling separate and still searching, or a return only of a sense of localisation. This simply means that 'awareness' is once again located within the frame of an apparent individual but all seeking has ended. Now it is known that no matter what is happening in the drama of life, This is it, This is all there is, and This is sufficient.

"This constant directness, right here, right now," is it. It has always been it. There was never any possibility of it not being it. And that is either seen or it is not seen. As it is put in the Upanishads "The lightning strikes, the eye blinks. Then? You have either seen or you have not seen. If you have not seen, too bad!"

And yes, liberation is a plunge into not-knowing, as all the stories we once believed in fall away.

When this is communicated, it always has the flavour of the personality of the communicator. In addition many communicators of non-duality have an agenda. Usually this agenda is to help people have the experience of liberation, even though this is not possible because liberation is not an experience.

Thank you! I've got it!

✵

SADHANA

What's the point of sadhana (spiritual practice) as practised in ashram communities? It seems to be very much emphasised as an important aspect of a spiritual path.

The main point of sadhana in an ashram is to keep the ashramites busy so that they don't get up to too much monkey business.

If this sounds unduly sceptical, here is a quotation from Michael Graham's book about Muktananda and the Siddha Yoga community:- "[In a letter] Muktananda emphasised the fact that we were already God if only we knew it, and that there was nothing to be done. Sadhana (spiritual practice) was just a constructive way of filling in the time between life and death."

Interestingly, Michael Graham also quotes Muktananda in the same letter as saying "Please release me from your love." Make of that what you will.

✵

EXISTENTIAL QUESTIONS

What am I? Does anything really matter? Can you recommend anything to read about this?

You may think you are a person who has responsibility and acts autonomously in the world. To this person, many things are likely to matter.

What you actually are is Oneness. When this is seen, you might say that nothing truly matters, or you might say that everything matters simply for what it is—every leaf, every ant, every delicious sip of coffee.

I'll tout my own market stall—you could read any of my books. Apart from those, I recommend the books of Tony Parsons. There's also a book called 'The Telling Stones' published by Non-Duality Press (now out of print). It contains a section called 'The Mad Bastard's Guide to Enlightenment' which has some good stuff in it. I also like Leo Hartong's book 'Awakening to the Dream' or you could try Nathan Gill's book 'Already Awake'.

❋

UNCONDITIONAL LOVE

It's not obvious to the mind that everything is unconditional love, but I agree with you that once it's seen, it's seen. Then it's known that everything is allowed in this play. It makes no difference whether the mind judges it as 'good' or 'bad'. Love is eternally present and eternally non-judging.

You're right. Everything is allowed and unconditional love does not judge it. That's really the bottom line. It's tough for the discriminating mind to understand, though.

No, not tough. 'Impossible' is the right word.

❋

EMPTINESS

What do you mean by 'emptiness'?

In awakening it is seen that all phenomena are empty. We could say that they arise out of emptiness. In liberation it is seen that emptiness is also full, however paradoxical that may sound. The nature of this fullness is unconditional love.

Emptiness is silent and still, and from it arise the sound and movement of duality. Although this may make no sense to the mind even after years of puzzling over it, it is seen directly in a moment of awakening.

Hints of this reality are there in many traditions, although they are usually misunderstood or ignored or drowned out by the clamour of much louder and more insistent messages.

✻

NO SELF AND RELATIONSHIPS

When there is no longer an identification with the self, does this bring about changes in relationships?

There are no necessary implications of seeing through the self, so anything can happen. However, there are tendencies for certain things to change.

A certain amount of neurotic energy tends to dissipate in the seeing of non-duality. Because of this, the process of relating usually becomes easier and less tainted by our projections. Another way of putting this is that we tend to see others more as they actually are and less through the veil of our own imaginings about them.

In some cases, however, the loss of interest in previously shared stories of meaning and purpose may cause a relationship to break down.

✻

TIME

Do you see time as a construct? Is it simply a concept, as it were?

Yes, time is a construct, an aspect of this waking dream. In the seeing of non-duality, time is seen through.

Nevertheless, the character who remains still lives in this waking dream and in that sense is still subject to time. Ramesh Balsekar was said to insist on getting to airports extremely early when he was travelling. I am much the same with both airports and railway stations. You see, this character values a relaxed way of life, and getting to airports and railway stations in plenty of time tends to increase relaxation.

※

FEAR OF THE UNKNOWN

What is it that drives us to know liberation? Is it fear of the unknown? Or is it fear of death?

Rather than fear being the origin of our wanting to know liberation, we are fuelled in our searching by a sense that there is something missing. We could call this a sense of loss, except that we don't know what it is that we have lost.

So we search and we search and we continue searching. We may find many things, until eventually wholeness or unity is found. If that is really seen, all searching ends.

※

DIFFERENT VERSIONS OF NON-DUALITY

Dear Richard, I notice from browsing the internet that there are a lot of different versions of non-duality around. For example, some websites link non-duality to the Laws of Attraction and other New Age philosophies. Some link non-duality to the modern cult of Positive Thinking and never allowing yourself to have a negative thought. To me this smells strongly of denying the shadow.

These so-called non-duality philosophies say that on the one hand everything is perfect as it is, but on the other hand that there is something which needs to be fixed. They hold that somehow, unlike the rest of nature, we are separate and able to control the universe.

I think there's a lot of spiritual crap out there. What do you think? Best wishes, Brett

Dear Brett, Non-duality is very simple but the mind is very complicated. So the mind wants to graft on to non-duality other stories that seem more exciting and that give it something to do.

As a result, on the internet you'll find a lot of 'non-duality plus'. This will include 'non-duality plus amateur psychotherapy', 'non-duality plus the Laws of Attraction', 'non-duality plus the Cosmic Ordering Service', 'non-duality plus purification through yoga' and many other ingenious concoctions. The search for 'an impossible state of constant bliss through non-duality' is very popular. So is its close cousin, the search for 'an impossible non-dual state in which no anger, sorrow or fear can possibly arise'.

All of this is very good for maintaining an on-going sense of inadequacy and failure in the seeker, as the realities of life fail to live up to these expectations. Three large spoonfuls of Denial a day should be enough to cope with this and keep the search going.

It is all good fun, though probably more so if we can maintain a bit of detachment from it and not get caught up in web-rage on the forums. Best wishes, Richard

Dear Richard, I relate very much to your reply to me. Recently I attended a weekend retreat which was supposedly on non-duality. The opening talk seemed to be devoted to an insistence that Oneness can contain nothing but 'light' and that we should rid ourselves of any 'darkness' such as anger. I talked about how the Buddha's life had a lot of pain and conflict in it, about how his cousin wanted to kill him and about how he died a painful death, probably from being poisoned. As you can imagine this didn't go down well at all. For the rest of the day people were encouraged to talk about their mothers. I couldn't bear it and left at the end of the day.

Life isn't just gentle. Mother Nature is bountiful in her expression but she also eats her young. In the past there were symbols that

reflected this—dark, powerful, mysterious figures like Shiva and Kali. Nowadays we seem to emphasise love and peace as the true nature of existence and everything else as some kind of defilement. This isn't a very good preparation for life as it actually is. The full and natural expression of life's dance includes both the light and the dark. Best wishes, Brett

Dear Brett, The thought of a day during which everyone talks about their mother and we are all encouraged to deny our anger doesn't fill me with delight.

If we pretend that we can become beings of light only, with no acknowledgment of the dark side of our being, we create dangers both for ourselves and others. When we deny the shadow it tends to leap out and grab us by the throat and also leap out and grab others by the throat. As Jung wrote, it sets both my house and my neighbour's house on fire. He also wrote "The brighter the light, the darker the shadow."

It is the very acceptance of our shadow, our willingness to be open about it and to own it, that can help others to accept theirs. "She who bears her own shadow liberates the collective." (Sylvia Brinton Perera)

Much of the detail of the Buddha's life that you mention is in Stephen Batchelor's excellent book 'Confession of a Buddhist Atheist'. The Buddha's life is quite instructive but the details are hard to unearth because they have been buried under the weight of so much spiritual projection. All credit to Stephen Batchelor and others for doing the difficult scholarly spadework and making it accessible in popular form.

The point you make about the inclusion of figures such as Kali and Shiva, which represent aspects of the shadow in the mythology of India, is very important. There's an interesting comparison with Christianity here. In Hinduism the shadow side is acknowledged as part of the necessary cycle of creation and destruction. In Christianity we are invited to reject the shadow in the figure of the Satan. This rejection leads to all kinds of unfortunate shenanigans.

"That there is a devil
There is no doubt,
But is he trying to get in
Or is he trying to get out?"

Best wishes, Richard

❀

QUANTUM PHYSICS AND NON-DUALITY

I know a yoga teacher who says that non-duality is the same as quantum physics. I have a faint memory that in one of your books you may have said that this is not the case. Have I remembered this correctly?

Quantum physics' view of the ultimate nature of reality is very similar to the view that non-duality reveals. But it is not identical. For example, no physicist working at the Large Hadron Collider has noticed yet that the nature of nothing and everything is unconditional love.

It is at least a little bit interesting that twentieth and twenty-first century physics has come to a view of reality that is very close to that of the ancient seers of India.

Quantum physics challenges our concepts of time and of cause and effect. Seeing non-duality simply blows these apart. However, I am not a scientist and I understand no formulae, so I had better not comment any further. When individuals like me with a liberal arts background comment on quantum physics, we usually make fools of ourselves pretty quickly.

So up to a point I would agree with your yoga teacher.

❀

150

SUFFERING ON AWAKENING

I spent years painfully walking a spiritual path. Since an awakening event recently my life seems to have become drenched in suffering, even more so than before. Worst of all is all the time, effort and money I spent with those guru-teachers. It all seems such a waste now.

The situation you describe yourself as being in is a common one, especially for those who have for a long period of time been "walking a spiritual path". I certainly relate to the pain that can be felt when disillusion with the guru sets in. I hope you are able now to find some of the enjoyment that can be had from simple things.

❋

PSYCHOTHERAPISTS

After taking medication for some time because of psychological difficulties, I started to see a variety of psychotherapists. Then I got interested in non-duality and the psychotherapists started to annoy me.

I think this was because I felt they were full of 'person' and they made assumptions about 'being a person' that I no longer accepted. This is true of the ones I saw, anyway.

I wonder whether it would be better for me just to go and do something that makes me feel better. I know that some non-dual teachers say we should "stay in the nothingness" so maybe I should search for nothingness so that I can relax. Have you any comment on this?

The sentence of yours that most strikes a chord with me is "I wonder whether it would be better for me just to go and do something that makes me feel better." Although I don't give advice, it always seems to me to be a good idea to do something that makes us feel better if we find ourself drawn to something. For myself, this is usually something simple, like a walk round the park, a cup of coffee or a tai chi class, but for others it might be many other things.

I have no idea what is meant by "stay in the nothingness" nor how you would do that. I don't know how you would "search for nothingness" either. I know that many individuals find it helpful to stay with whatever they are feeling on a visceral level, especially when those feelings are uncomfortable. Again, that is not advice. We each have to experiment and find what works best for us.

It is possible that you were unlucky with the psychotherapists that you saw. Some psychotherapists are indeed "full of person" but some are nicely emptied out and know that there is no self at the centre.

❀

WEI WU WEI

There are not many authors on non-duality that I like. But you are one of them and Wei Wu Wei is another. I can't remember his exact words, but he wrote something like "The seeker is the sought and there is no one. All else is bondage." Could you comment on this?

I've read very little of Wei Wu Wei, but that's a great quote. The shock that is often felt in awakening comes from the seeing that we have always been the very thing that we sought—which is both Nothing and Everything.

❀

WHAT AM I?

When I die, nothing matters. Correct? So what is this thing called John?

Correct. But of course that is not how it seems to the person who is searching. As to "What is this thing called John?" we could answer in many ways, all of them metaphors. One answer is that

152

John is a process rather than an entity, an ever-changing flow of thoughts, feelings, perceptions and sensations. Some neuroscientists call this the 'bundle theory' of the person, and it is pretty close to how Buddhism has described the person for over two thousand years.

The essential seeing in non-duality is that, whatever you consider yourself to be, there is no self at your centre, only emptiness. So you are an arising out of nothing and a falling away into nothing.

❀

ANXIETY

I have been a seeker for many years. I've followed Eastern visionaries and I've been in Western personal development groups. After reading Krishnamurti, Osho and Nisargadatta I did a retreat with Tony Parsons. I found him particularly impressive. I've also practised mindfulness for some time.

But throughout my seeking I've been afflicted with anxiety and depression. At times I've been prescribed anti-depressants. Now I'm considering seeing a psychotherapist, probably one who practises Cognitive Behavioural Therapy.

I've read your books and I like your suggestion to 'relax' and the fact that you have a background in psychology and therapy. Can you suggest anything for me? Do you think CBT is a good idea?

I'm not really in as bad a state as this may make it sound. One thing I've learned over the years is not to take any of it too seriously.

After many years of involvement with therapy, I feel that one of the most effective and simplest long-term ways to deal with anxiety and other uncomfortable feelings is to spend some time paying attention to the feeling in the body in an innocent way. This means attending to it without trying to change it, but allowing it to change of its own accord if it does so. This is very different to listening to the 'story of anxiety' in the mind.

This paying attention to feelings can be done each day, often to very good effect. A technique like Focusing may be an effective way of learning how to do this but if you have already practised mindfulness you are probably able to do it naturally.

CBT can also be very helpful for anxiety and depression. It has been clinically shown to be as effective or more effective than pharmaceutical intervention in some cases. If you decide to give CBT a try, I hope that you find it helpful.

✸

PRACTICES

For a while I practised a meditation technique in a group. The teacher was very insistent that only his method would work. But then I had a sudden awakening and I realised that it had nothing to do with the practice that I was doing. It revealed that the 'separated me' is the one who wants to do all these techniques. It became obvious that liberation has nothing to do with anybody bringing it about through meditative or any other kind of practices.

I hope to come to one of your meetings soon, but it will have to be in secret as my partner gets worked up when I mention non-duality.

I would describe the lack of a relationship between practices and awakening in the same way that you do. Many others also describe it in this way.

I hope you get to a meeting eventually. The difficulty with partners is quite common. Good luck with it. I have a vision of people creeping off to non-duality meetings in secret, much as others might creep off to betting shops, opium dens or brothels.

Well, you can lose something in all three of the places you mention: your money, your mind or your virginity.

✸

LACK OF CONTROL

It's increasingly obvious to me that I have no control over events. Nevertheless, something in me continues to try to exert an influence over them so that I can somehow get something from them. Ironically, when I do this I don't even know what it is that I want.

It is like a car running down a hill with its engine switched off. Even though the cylinders are no longer firing, the wheels are still going round and round.

That's an excellent metaphor. Another one that occurs to me is that it's like a hamster wheel that's still spinning after the hamster has got off.

Even when Oneness is seen there usually remains some level of neurotic 'machinery' in the organism which tends to gradually unwind and play itself out. This may take a long time or a short time and it doesn't matter which.

So feelings of trying to influence things or get something from them may continue to occur. Or they may gradually or suddenly die away. That also does not matter.

By the way, it's not that you have no control over events. It's that there is no 'you'. Events happen. Or they don't.

❋

MYSTICAL EXPERIENCES AND AWAKENING

It seems to me that mystical experiences are different to awakening. I've had mystical experiences in which there was a feeling of pure unbounded love but somehow 'I' was still there experiencing this, even though I felt kind of 'transparent'.

But in awakening 'I' wasn't there at all. There was just a free-fall into nothing—no one there, no reference points, nothing to grasp onto. There was just knowing but no knower. After that there was a certain amount of fear but also wonder.

Does anything in my description sound familiar to you?

I agree with you that there can be mystical, or transpersonal, experiences but that these are rather different to awakening. The clue is in the word 'experience' and the difference is that there is still someone there, no matter how rarified and translucent, who is having the experience.

An awakening event can happen with or without the seeing of unbounded love.

The bottom line is the simple recognition that This is it, This has always been it, and This will always be it. It is this recognition that brings an end to searching. After that life goes on in its ordinary way. Wood is still chopped, water is still drawn. But it is realised that there is no one doing it.

❋

DEATH

You write in your book "The false self may drop away while the individual is still alive but it need be of no concern if it does not, because at the death of the body there is only liberation in any case".

I can't share your sense that there need be no concern about death! And I note that you seemed to be pretty desperate at the point that Tony Parsons said to you "I hope you die soon."

What does it mean that at death there is liberation? Does this mean that both death and liberation are nothing? Is being liberated like being dead in a way?

I'm still waiting for the tiger to bite my head off so I'm hoping you can comment on this while I'm waiting. Perhaps it will help to pass the (timeless) time.

More than anything else, my words about liberation are an attempt at a description. They do not offer a philosophy, a metaphysic, an interpretation or even a rational argument.

As a matter of description, it is reported here and by others that when separation is seen through, death ceases to be of concern. That is partly because in liberation it is seen that what we really are was never born and so can never die.

But even in saying this we have gone into interpretation and away from description. We could conjecture many other things about death and they would all be stories.

As to Tony's remark "I hope you die soon", that was said to a person who was in the desert and feeling the despair of still being separate, while knowing there was nothing he could do about that.

❋

OUT OF THE BODY EXPERIENCES AND FEAR

I sometimes have out of the body experiences when I'm going to sleep. I feel that if I could just let myself go at these times, the 'I' would finally fall away. But then I always panic and with that fear I find myself back in the body.

Suzanne Segal writes about experiencing a lot of fear in her book 'Collision With The Infinite'. I'm wondering whether you've experienced something similar.

I've read 'Collision With The Infinite'. The degree of fear that Suzanne Segal experienced on awakening is unusual and I did not experience anything like that. However, I did experience a great deal of despair between what in the story of time is sometimes called awakening and liberation.

The experiences you describe having are fairly common. Others report similar events, particularly, like you, in the hypnagogic and hypnopompic states just before falling asleep or on waking up. Whether you let go or panic is not in your hands. What happens is simply an automatic energetic response of the body-mind system.

You may be interested in reading Susan Blackmore's book on OBE's, 'Beyond The Body'.

AWAKENING AND EMOTIONAL SUFFERING

I'm beginning to recognise that emotional suffering gets stronger after awakening. Others that I've talked to about this say the same. So even though I see life now as a kind of dream in some ways, in other ways it is more vivid than before. If I have an argument with my girl-friend, I feel angrier and more upset than I used to do. Every feeling is simply allowed to be what it is, raw and natural, with no holding back. Instead of being retained in the body it's fully felt or expressed. It feels like this is the natural way of being after awakening.

My mind is also completely shot. Is this common in awakening? And is the mind the same thing as the person?

Tony Parsons says that this ruins your life. I feel I know what he means by that now. Yet in a way everything stays the same, except there are some subtle changes that I notice. For example life just unfolds of its own accord in an easier and more effective way. And my sense of responsibility and guilt have more or less disappeared.

Nowadays I live a very simple life. I used to think so many things were important in my life but most of this sense of importance has disappeared. In a way it's a relief but in another way I almost feel nostalgic for my old way of being.

You describe aspects of seeing non-duality very clearly. Yes, life is seen to be a kind of waking dream and yet more vivid and real than before, because now the many projections and neuroses of the person no longer get in the way of experiencing it directly.

Before liberation, we tend to project a great deal of our own psychic material onto reality, rendering it dull and colourless. After liberation we tend to see life itself. And yes, because every-thing becomes more immediate, suffering may actually increase, or become more raw as you say. But it also tends to pass more quickly than for the neurotic person.

The mind is almost synonymous with the person. You write that the mind is shot. My way of putting this is that in liberation it is seen that there is no mind, there is simply a flow of thoughts, feelings, sensations and perceptions arising. Before liberation these create the impression that there is a mind from which they come, but in liberation this is seen through. It is seen that there are thoughts but there is no thinker, just as there are actions but there is no doer. This is partly why guilt and responsibility tend to fall away.

By the way, when I first wrote this I made a typo and it came out as "the mind is shit." That will do just as well as a description of the mind.

I agree with Tony that this ruins our life, or we could say that it ruins what we thought was our life. But it brings the gift of simplicity and a falling in love with the ordinary.

※

AWAKENING AND THE VOID

I get the impression that more and more people are becoming awakened. But many of them are encountering a common problem. The initial experience of being without a self is followed by a sense of a complete void, an emptiness, a desert. That's what it's like for me. This can be very painful and very difficult to deal with.

Do you recognise my description? Do you know of others who are going through it? Did you go through it? If you did, how did you cope with it?

'The desert' is a commonly used term for the state that you describe. It is a stage that is often experienced between awakening and liberation. Non-duality is seen, but after that initial seeing the sense of being a separate person returns, bringing with it a sense of emptiness or despair. This is partly because there is still a sense of separation but now it is known that there is no one who can do anything about it.

Yes, I know of many others who go through this. Yes, I went through it myself. I coped by doing simple things, such as going for walks and reading books and deriving from them what enjoyment I could.

❋

TEACHERS AND PRACTICES

Who are the teachers of awakening and non-duality that you would recommend? Which practices do you think are the most effective?

It is not possible to teach awakening or non-duality and no practice will give rise to awakening. The attempt to teach awakening is simply misguided so I'm unable to recommend anyone who does this.

❋

MAKING AN EFFORT

Although I know intellectually that there is no person, I still find that thoughts and feelings of a disturbing nature come up for me. Should I be making an effort to rid myself of these or should I just wait patiently?

Whether you make an effort or wait patiently, what I am trying to communicate is that there is no one who does either of these things. In other words ultimately it may be seen that everything is unfolding of its own accord.

Do you know Osho's dynamic meditation, the one where you make a huge effort to jump up and down, shake, roar and express whatever feeling is in your body, especially anger? Have you ever done it?

I've been doing it even though I find that I don't like it. Although I don't seem to be getting anything from it, I'm wondering if I should simply make more effort at it.

I have a lot of problematic feelings that I think I need to get rid of. I don't know whether I should just relax with them or make more of an effort. I've been given a lot of different and confusing advice.

And can I ask you what 'effort' is in any case? If there is nobody, why should we have to make an effort?

And while I've got your attention, what is 'will'?

Long ago I did Osho's dynamic meditation for a very short while. I hated it and felt I got nothing from it. But I did a relaxed sitting meditation for many years and loved it. Now I do Tai Chi, which I also love. The point I'm trying to make is that different things feel appropriate at different times to different people so there is really no point in trying to force anything.

Many people find that an effective way to deal with problematic feelings is simply to put their attention on the feeling in a relaxed way wherever it manifests in the body. Then they follow it with their attention, noticing whatever happens to it.

If this appeals to you, you could try it for a little while. Then you could do some small simple thing that you enjoy. This is neither a recommendation nor advice. I simply notice that many people find it effective so it might be worth a try.

I associate the word 'effort' with strain. It is often uncomfortable and so perhaps best avoided when possible. As to 'will', the person living in separation often considers that they own a possession called 'will' or 'will-power'. When separation is seen through, it is seen that we do not own any such thing, because there is nobody who owns anything.

So how can I awaken? Without effort and will, surely I cannot do anything to achieve realisation.

And what do I do about my life?

Seeing through separation reveals not that you "cannot do anything" but rather that there is no one who does anything. That is quite different.

Meanwhile, as you may have noticed, stuff keeps on happening. It might also be possible to notice that this stuff keeps on happening of its own accord. However, the sense of separation makes us feel that we are doing it.

You can't do anything about your life because you don't have a life.

What do you mean by "this stuff keeps on happening of its own accord" and "you don't have a life"?

The heart of awakening and liberation is the seeing that everything is appearing of its own accord and that there is no self which runs our life. This is what Buddhists mean when they refer to 'empty phenomena rolling by'. I know this is baffling for the mind. I'm sorry that there is nothing more that I can say to make it clearer.

Although I understand what you write intellectually, I don't really 'get it'. Both making an effort and being passive seem like traps to me.
   There's a lot of emotional suffering in my life. I also have disturbing physical symptoms. I very much hope to be happy one of these days.

Yes, intellectual understanding is not the same as seeing through separation. Neither effort nor passivity are relevant here but it may be recognised that there is no person who either makes an effort or is passive.

   As to the emotional suffering and physical symptoms that you mention, it is sensible for any person who is suffering to seek whatever help they may be drawn to, for example healing or therapy or medical advice. Because I am writing about the absolute I do not give advice but there are many people who can give good advice about the relative events that cause us suffering.

   I hope you will be happy too and send you my best wishes.

❋

TIME

After periods when I've thought "This is liberation" my mind has raised its voice again and confused me. Then I've ended up thinking "There must be more still to find, maybe piece by piece. Or perhaps I'll keep disappearing one bit at a time." Sometimes it seems to me that I'll never stop waiting for liberation.

Then I remember hearing Tony Parsons say "You cannot have less and less of nothing."

I've also heard Tony say "Being is not in the least interested in seeing or not seeing."

I once asked you how it's possible for liberation to happen either suddenly or gradually when time does not exist. As far as I remember, you said "Time is in the appearance." For some reason, this really shocked me. So what is time?

When only the emptiness of Everything and Nothing is seen, that tends to leave searching still going on. But when the fullness of Everything and Nothing is seen as well, searching tends to end.

Even after that, in the appearance there may still seem to be a process going on as remaining neurosis gradually drops away. But as Tony points out, Oneness isn't the least bit interested in this, or in whether seeing through duality takes place or not, because This is all Oneness anyway and ultimately being asleep and being awake are the same thing.

Everything in the relative world, the world of the appearance, including an apparent journey towards liberation, can only unfold within the appearance of time. The absolute is timeless. Finally, in liberation, the relative and the absolute are seen to be the same.

❀

DEATH

Why do I have so much fear of death? Do you have any advice about this?

Have you made friends with death?

Where there is a sense of being a separate autonomous person it is natural to fear death, because death seems to threaten the end of our separate existence. But when separation is seen through, it is known that what we really are is Oneness itself 'pretending' to be a separate person. By the way, that's only a metaphor.

What we really are was never born, and so can never die.

I would not say that I have "made friends with death." It is simply noticed that once separation has been seen through, concerns about death and interest in death tend to fall away. That has been noticed here and in other individuals.

This lack of concern about death has nothing to do with the mind and cannot be produced by anything the mind may think about death.

❋

FEELINGS, DRUGS AND LOSING LIBERATION

Some time ago you suggested to me that I relax into my feelings. I did this and the disturbance I was feeling then has diminished. Somehow as I relaxed into the feelings, the feelings themselves relaxed too. One of our core problems, I think, is that we tend to focus obsessively on our problems and this feeds more energy into them.

May I ask you another question now? If liberation has been seen, can that seeing be lost again because of circumstances? For example if you take a lot of drugs or drink heavily, can you lose presence?

When we focus on a problem in our mind, it often tends to stay stuck. When we're mindful of how the problem feels in our body, the energy behind the problem tends to release. Be aware that this can be a gradual process that takes place over a long time.

Liberation is the simple seeing that there is no person, that everything arises from Nothing, and that the nature of Nothing is unconditional love. In that, anything can arise, including the taking of drugs or alcohol. However, the impulse to take drugs and alcohol is often neurotic and neurosis tends to decrease when liberation is seen. So it's reasonable to expect that in that case the impulse to take drugs and alcohol may reduce in liberation.

But remember, there are no absolute rules. You cannot tie Oneness down or put it in any box, including one labelled 'No Drugs Or Alcohol Here'.

You cannot own presence, so you cannot lose it.

I AM IN THE SPACE

I am aware of the space around me and I notice that I am in the space.

Recently I experienced a sudden flash. It was as if there was a total depersonalisation. Everything became me and I became everything. The buildings were in me and I in them. This felt very stable and powerful, but then suddenly it was gone and I was back.

Rather than you are in the space, I would say the space is in you. Actually, you and the space are one. The 'flash' you describe is an awakening event.

❈

ADVICE

I've heard you say "This is it and this is sufficient". But I still own the added piece of software that Tony Parsons calls "me". This causes a deep and never-ending nagging inside, which makes it impossible for me to see This as "it" and "sufficient".

There is still a programme running inside me which constantly searches for meaning. Although I do what you suggest and drink tea and eat cake, I feel frustration a lot of the time.

You often say that you don't give advice. Nevertheless you have suggested that we relax. But for someone who can't relax, what can they do?

I feel stuck with no one to talk to. On the one hand I don't trust advice from those who haven't seen liberation. On the other hand those who have seen liberation don't care anymore about anyone's apparent story. But heigh ho, maybe you'll write to me anyway.

It is frustrating, both for the one who asks for advice and the one who is asked for advice, to see that no advice about the Ultimate is possible. Once the game of giving and receiving advice about liberation is known to be useless it tends to die.

Nevertheless, there are obviously things that the seeker can do to make their apparent life more comfortable.

Years ago I used to phone Tony for advice. He might suggest that I go for a drive in the car or have a nice meal. At the time I found this very frustrating. However, now I can see the wisdom in it, because when separation is seen through, what is left is the simplicity of presence and the enjoyment of simple things.

I wouldn't say that I don't care anymore about anyone's apparent story. Empathy still arises here, but there is also the knowing that where liberation is concerned, all I can do is give a description. I cannot suggest any path or practice.

For some reason I just love to be around communication about non-duality—this attempt to express the inexpressible. Like you I have a background in psychology and following gurus and spiritual paths.

I know that no real help with this can be expected. Nevertheless, I've heard Tony Parsons say that his talks are really an excuse for something else to happen—an energetic shift in which the boundless may be recognised. Do you have any comment on this?

I feel very frustrated because I recognise that there can be no real end to neurosis and psychological suffering except through liberation, but I know that I cannot do anything to bring this about. And I 'get' that even recognising Oneness is a kind of illusion as it's never really been lost. What a joke it is to know all this intellectually yet still be caught up in the appearance of duality! Oh well, I suppose it's the little joke of Lila that it will go on until it doesn't.

It sounds like your head is well and truly in the tiger's mouth—in which case there is nothing to do but wait and see whether the tiger bites your head off.

I agree with Tony that this energetic shift can happen. But of course there are no rules about whether it does or not.

Perhaps it is possible to notice the simple and obvious fact that whatever is happening is happening. There is no possibility of it being any other way. If we are sitting with Tony, either experiencing or not experiencing an energetic shift, that is what is happening. If we are sitting in a bar, experiencing or not experiencing a pint of lager, that is what is happening. This is always It and this is always What Is Happening.

It's part of the frustration of seeking that intellectual knowledge makes no difference.

I found your first sentence, with its reminder of my helplessness, strangely comforting.

I suppose the constant invitation of Oneness is to notice that whatever is happening is happening. When things are going well, this is easy. But when there's a lot of suffering it's difficult to hold on to this insight. I have an expectation that after liberation the suffering may decrease but that may be the last illusory hope of the seeker.

There are no rules, so all expectations are false. Remember the Zen story of the monk who said "Now I'm enlightened, I'm just as miserable as ever." But I know individuals who would say something different—so no expectations!

❀

SEPARATION

You write "There is no separation." What do you mean? Separation from what?

I mean separation from all and every phenomena. I mean separation from objects, from people, from everything that arises in This. I mean separation between 'I' the subject and 'it' the object.

These are not metaphors or poetic forms of expression. In an awakening or liberation event it is seen that there is literally no separation between that which is experienced subjectively as 'me' and that which is experienced objectively as 'other'.

❀

THERAPY AND NON-DUALITY

I have been reading your books, as I hope you will be pleased to hear.

You have written that if you were ever to visit a psychotherapist again, you would prefer one who is not there. In other words, you'd prefer to go to one who has seen liberation.

I feel intuitively that I agree with you. Could you comment further?

I hope you've not only been reading my books but also enjoying them.

Yes, I would prefer a psychotherapist who at least knew about non-duality, or even better, one who wasn't there. I feel this is particularly important if the client perceives their experiences as having to do with awakening.

When presented with experiences of awakening, psychotherapists who are unfamiliar with these can assume that the client is suffering from psychosis or disassociation. This is of course profoundly unhelpful.

A psychotherapist who is not there is less likely consciously or unconsciously to impose their own agendas on the client. They are more likely to have seen through their own stories, including the particular stories that an interest in psychotherapy tends to develop. This may create a space in which it becomes more likely that the client will see through their own stories, without this becoming yet another agenda of the psychotherapeutic sessions.

✷

SEEKING

A month ago I went on one of Tony Parsons' retreats. It was not my first and I absolutely loved it, as I have in the past.

While I was there I noticed a recurring pattern that I have. Even before it was over I was planning to attend the next residential in a few months time. I'm always looking to the future, it seems, even though I understand that there is nothing to seek!

I'm beginning to realise that, as long as no great shift has occurred for me, I'm stuck with the feeling that "something else has to happen". It seems to me that this very belief is sustaining my seeking.

I have had quite a few flashes of "no one here" but they have all been very brief. I have the feeling that something longer has to happen to convince me that seeing is complete.

Do you relate to this? Was it like this for you after awakening?

The sense that the energy of seeking is still going on, even when it's been understood that there is nothing to seek for, is frustrating for many people.

Here there were two distinct events. After awakening, when the absolute emptiness of everything was seen, the energy of seeking went on even though it was known that there was no way to seek. Some people call this period being in a desert. It can be a period of despair.

After liberation, when the absolute fullness of everything was seen, the energy of seeking ended. Now life goes on and it is known that everything is simply what it is.

❋

CHOICE OR NO CHOICE. WILL OR NO WILL.

I've heard you on a video tell the story of a friend of yours who believed that the universe would always support him. As a result he decided to give up the job that he didn't like very much. Eventually when he had used up all his savings, he couldn't pay his rent, lost his house and was on his way to live in a tent in the park.

What I hear in this is that he is exercising his 'personal will'. So who is it that is choosing to allow the universe to take care of him? Did he choose this, and if so, was it his choice that led subsequently to his financial disaster?

The anecdote that you refer to was about someone I had not met, but who had phoned me a number of times from America. Each phone call chronicled his further decline in fortune until he was facing homelessness and about to move into 'tent city'. That was the last phone call I received from him so I can only guess at what happened next.

Of course what happens is simply what happens. The sensation that there may be 'personal will' exercised and someone who is making a choice is exactly that—simply a sensation. One way of putting this is to say that there was an apparent choice, or an apparent decision, but there was no 'self' making that choice or decision. Let me be absolutely unambiguous: I am not saying that there is no choice, I am saying that there is no one who makes any choice, which is quite different.

In this waking dream, there are actions which appear to lead to consequences. In our night-time dreams there are also actions which appear to lead to consequences, but when we wake up in the morning this is seen through. Then it is known that both the actions and the consequences are unreal. In liberation, that is known about this waking dream. That is why it can be said that this is both real and unreal.

Thank you for your reply. For me that expresses the subtle difference that the mind refuses to recognise.

❈

ABIDING SAHAJA NIRVIKALPA SAMADHI

Has your realisation continued and become a steady abiding? And do you consider this state as more akin to savikalpa, *as I would expect, or* sahaja nirvikalpa samadhi? *Is this the state others you know are in, such as Tony Parsons? Does* nirvikalpa samadhi *appear at all for you or for anyone that you know?*

I myself have been in this state, as well as in savikalpa samadhi. *My breath was suspended for at least half an hour. I was dead to the world but peacefully and blissfully super-conscious with no sense of I at all.*

I am signing this in my spiritual name.

I know almost nothing of the terminology of traditional advaita so I cannot comment on the specifics of your questions. Nevertheless, I am occasionally drawn to the sayings of some of the Christian mystics. I also very much like some of Nisargadatta's sayings in his well-known book 'I Am That'. I am probably paraphrasing but I find myself quoting his "Seeing I am nothing is wisdom. Seeing I am everything is love".

As to what happened here, I can't do any better than refer you to my first book for a description. I also like Nathan Gill's description very much. Again this is probably a paraphrase: "First there's someone cycling down a country lane. Then there's no one cycling down a country lane yet cycling down a country lane is still happening."

By the way, the seeing of non-duality has nothing especially to do with bliss, peace, the suspension of breath, super-consciousness or being dead to the world. These are all states and as such cannot abide. Seeing non-duality is seeing that out of which all states arise.

❋

UNCOMFORTABLE FEELINGS AND THOUGHTS

I appreciate the way you don't make the slightest concession to dualism in what you communicate about non-duality, so I'd like to ask you a question.

Whenever we feel bad or downcast, our every thought seems to be related to that feeling. This almost invariably increases the pain we feel. Why is this? Do thoughts have their own kind of power?

Sometimes thoughts precede feelings, sometimes feelings precede thoughts. An angry thought, for example, can clearly generate angry feelings. It is not quite so obvious that an angry feeling can colour whatever thought comes into the mind, so that it will be an angry thought.

This is well-known among teachers of meditation. It is why they warn meditators not to act immediately on a thought that may come to them in meditation.

When I taught meditation, I would tell my students that if they came out of meditation wanting to phone their boss and shout abuse at them (as sometimes does happen), they should wait for twenty-four hours before deciding whether to act on this or not. If they still wanted to do it after that time, then fair enough. They could have their fun and start looking for a new job.

It is natural that uncomfortable thoughts and feelings increase the suffering that an individual experiences. We might even say that this is what suffering consists of. But I would not describe this as thoughts having power. It is simply the nature of whatever is arising in This. Out of Nothing arises the appearance of everything, including uncomfortable thoughts and feelings.

Remember that in reality there is no such thing as 'a thought' or 'a feeling' because a thought and a feeling are not entities. They are processes, just as you are not an entity but a process. So there is only the process of thinking and the process of feeling.

Equally we could say that you are Oneness manifesting the process of 'William-ing'.

❈

LIBERATION, FREE-WILL AND DEPRESSION

There was an awakening event for 'me' a few months ago. It was confusing and this glimpse of my 'death' left me feeling depressed. Nevertheless, what I had recognised seemed profoundly familiar.

Prior to this I had the usual amateur career as a seeker. I had done many self-development courses, much psychotherapy and some self-enquiry.

Since the awakening event I've read Stephen Pinker's 'How the Mind Works'. He puts the view that all of our experiences are the result of natural selection and that any beliefs that there is a benevolent deity are simply the result of electro-chemical reactions in our brains. Of course he holds that free will is an illusion.

This all adds to my depression.

So I want to ask you whether liberation is simply the seeing that 'we' are the result of blindly evolving physical processes. If not, what is it?

Let me start by saying that in liberation it is also seen that the nature of Oneness is unconditional love.

Evolutionary theory has huge explanatory power. Of the three great thinkers who influenced late nineteenth and twentieth century thought so powerfully, Marx and Freud have been somewhat discredited but Darwin marches on triumphantly as the theory of natural selection and adaptation explains more and more about our world and about our selves.

Stephen Pinker is one of several interesting writers in this field and in the field of neuroscience. What he and others are describing is analagous to but most definitely not the same as what is seen in liberation.

These writers claim with good reason that there is no such thing as free will. However, in liberation it is seen that there is *no person or central self* who could exercise free will. This is substantially different. In his excellent book 'Free Will' even Sam Harris shies away from overtly recognising the non-existence of the person, although he demonstrates the fallacy of free will very clearly. And Sam Harris is one of the most open-minded of the scientists writing about consciousness, neuroscience and free will. This is possibly because like Susan Blackmore, another open-minded scientist, he has a background in Zen.

There is a world of difference between thinking that you are a person who has no free will, a kind of automaton, on the one hand, and recognising that you are Oneness doing its thing on the other. We could say that you are Oneness doing its 'David' thing.

The prevailing paradigm in science is material realism, sometimes known as 'physicalism'. This holds that physical reality is primary and that consciousness arises only as a secondary phenomenon, or epiphenomenon, of the physical. Indeed it can be professionally damaging for any scientist to challenge this orthodoxy. What is seen in liberation is sometimes held to be the opposite of this—that consciousness is primary and gives rise to the physical manifestation. It is more accurate to say that consciousness and the physical manifestation co-arise. By the way, I am using the word 'consciousness' to mean simply the perceiving of phenomena. I am not implying that there is some kind of subtle 'consciousness effluvia' or 'mind stuff' wafting about the cosmos like a London fog.

Scientists won't be able to describe reality accurately until they see that everything arises from unconditional love. If they see this they will be confronted with the impossibility of describing it anyway. That is why, if you want to know about ultimate reality, you have to go to a mystic, not a scientist.

When Oneness is finally seen in its fullness, our own emptiness is not seen as depressing. Instead, freedom from the self is seen to be the ultimate and the only real freedom.

How do you know that there is unconditional love? Can you verify this? Is not this claim itself a kind of dogma like any other religious dogma?

There are no satisfactory answers for the mind to your questions. Ultimately all that can be said is "When this is seen, it is seen." This is because what is being given here is a description and no understanding or knowledge has any bearing on this.

As an analogy, think of the taste of an orange. No amount of conceptual knowledge about oranges, including an analysis of their chemical constituents, can convey the flavour. But with one bite of an orange, the flavour is known even if there is no conceptual knowledge at all.

As to whether this is just another dogma or not, I would say that where there is a dogma, there is always an agenda. In other words, the person with the dogma wants you to get something.

Or just as likely, they want to get something from you. But there is no agenda here. There is no one here who cares whether anyone gets this or not. There is just a character who finds it interesting sometimes to communicate about this.

❀

EVOLUTION

I have heard you talk about evolution at a meeting that I attended. But you also say that there is no time. If there is no time, how can there be evolution?

In this waking dream there is the appearance of time and there are numerous phenomena. When seeking to understand these phenomena, evolutionary theory has a great deal of explanatory power. In fact at the moment for many of them it's the only game in town.

Analogously, in a night-time dream, all sorts of events unfold in time. But the time in which they unfold is not real. Or it might be more accurate to say that it is in a way both real and unreal.

❀

REBIRTH

You have said that rebirth is a story which the mind finds attractive because the separate self feels itself to be threatened by death.

I have recently read a book about awakening which includes this short passage: "Everything disappeared and then what arose was an image of what seemed like an infinite number of past incarnations, as if heads were lined up behind one another as far back as I could see."

This book seems to be giving a genuine account of awakening. So is Oneness appearing as an apparent series of rebirths before awakening, perhaps as a kind of game?

Questions such as "Is there rebirth?" or "What happens after death?" resolve themselves in liberation, not because they are answered but because it is seen that they are unanswerable in any way that would satisfy the mind. Then an interest in them tends to die and the energy that the mind invested in them fades away, leaving a simple resting in This.

No teacher and no answer could finally satisfy the mind which asks these questions. No matter how long the guru's beard, how magnificent their hat, how beautiful their garlands of flowers or how many their prostrate devotees, the mind would eventually start doubting what they said.

From your description, the author you quote is describing an inner experience, albeit a transpersonal and rather extraordinary one. Inner experiences are of course subjective. If we are ruthlessly honest it cannot be known what the nature of this or any other inner experience is, other than that it is what it is, a subjective event. This author is quite open about this. He says that what arose was an *image* which *seemed like* past incarnations *as if* heads were lined up

Let me relate this to my own experience. Many years ago I was involved in transpersonal and humanistic psychology and psychotherapy. As part of this involvement I had many sessions of past-life regression and I 'experienced' many 'past lives'. Later on I led groups through past-life regression processes. It is in fact very easy to invoke these experiences in many people.

At the time, because I was convinced of the story of rebirth and had invested time, money and belief in it, I was inclined to think that these were in some way real memories. Now that there is no investment remaining in the story of rebirth, it is quite clear that this could not be known. As a result any interest that I once had in such experiences has died.

In liberation it is seen that what you really are, Oneness itself, was never born and therefore can never die. This is another reason why any interest in questions about the death and rebirth of the person tends to end in liberation.

In liberation it is seen that only This, emptiness arising as whatever is manifesting in presence, is known. Everything else is unknown. The mind, because of its nature, tends to give rise to endless speculation in its attempts to know the unknown.

❀

PREPARING FOR DEATH

Is there anything I can do to prepare for death?

Death is quite able to take care of itself, with no need for us to make preparations for it.

However our feelings about death may be a different matter. For those who find these feelings disturbing, there may be things we can do to lessen our disturbance by way of therapy or healing or even simply through reading.

❀

DOES ANYTHING EXIST EXCEPT IN MY THOUGHTS?

I am alone in my garden and there is no one else around. Does the world beyond my garden and other people exist except in my thoughts?

Your question starts from the idea that you exist as person, and everyone else may only exist in your thoughts. But this is not what I am saying. It is you yourself that only seems to exist.

Awakening and liberation consist of the recognition that the central self that seems to be Catherine is an appearance that can disappear. When this is recognised it is seen that there is only Oneness, there is no Catherine in whom Oneness appears. Therefore there is no Catherine in whom others appear.

Awakening and liberation tend to reconfigure the psyche. Then there is an absolute recognition of what can be known and what cannot be known. What can be known is This, whatever is arising out of emptiness in presence. Everything else is unknown.

It is very natural for the mind to ask questions like yours. In liberation this questioning tends to cease, not because the questions are answered, but because it is seen that they are unanswerable. In other words, the mind, rather than being satisfied, simply gives up.

❋

RAMANA MAHARSHI

Ramana Maharshi said that there was nothing to be gained from looking for body consciousness. What is the difference between body consciousness and awareness?

I don't use the term 'body consciousness' myself and I use the term 'awareness' only rarely and with caveats. I am therefore reluctant to comment on what Ramana Maharshi may have meant by this.

Some people use the term 'awareness' to mean personal awareness. That leads to the popular idea that we can become liberated by developing our personal awareness. This is highly misleading.

The only sense that I can make of the term 'body consciousness' is awareness of what is going on in the body. Developing this can have considerable therapeutic benefits but it is irrelevant to liberation.

To me, the terms Oneness, Non-separation, Non-duality, Being and Consciousness are synonymous.

What did Ramana Maharshi mean by "You have to find out who you are"?

If there is no one, what is it that we are really seeking? Are we seeking the simple recognition that we do not exist?

I cannot comment on what Ramana may have meant. What you really are is Oneness but that will not be realised until you are no longer there.

As long as there is a state of separation, seeking is the human condition. You are right, we are seeking the recognition that we do not exist, but that can't be seen until there's no one there to see it.

Does the subconscious exist or is it a myth?

Considering the subconscious to exist as an entity is an example of what some psychologists call 'reification'. This means regarding an idea as if it were a real thing.

The subconscious is an idea, or a set of ideas, which can be very helpful in explaining why people behave as they do. It can be a useful map. It can have a lot of explanatory power and it can help us to understand our own and other people's psyches. However in saying this we risk another reification. We risk reifying the psyche.

Another way of putting this is to say that the subconscious and the psyche are both processes rather than objects. Indeed, the same is true of you and I. We are processes, not things.

So the subconscious does not exist as a thing, but neither is it a myth. It is an explanatory story which can help us to make sense of our own behaviour and the behaviour of others.

We should bear in mind that some of our stories about the subconscious can also mislead us and render our psyches and behaviours even more mysterious.

❊

IS THERE ONLY THE PRESENT?

Is there really only the present moment?

Yes, there is only the present moment. Or rather there is only presence. But in separation there also seems to be the past and the future, which are often attached to feelings of fear, regret, anxiety, guilt, nostalgia and hope. These feelings all make the past and the future seem very real.

When separation is seen through, there is only This. Then the importance of the stories of the past and the future diminishes, as do all other stories.

❉

UNDERSTANDING IS NO HELP

I understand enlightenment but I know that this understanding is of no help. The large sums of money that I've spent on psychotherapy have not been any help either. I hoped non-duality would make my problems disappear but it's only been of some help mentally. Now I feel hopeless. Can you offer me some advice?

All I can do is attempt to describe this state, which is not actually a state, that is sometimes called awakening and liberation. I am not able to offer any advice about either reaching it or dealing with it, because it arises spontaneously and is 'experienced' by each individual differently.

However, I am quite often contacted by other individuals who are experiencing hopelessness about liberation as you are. There are groups to be found via the internet if you wish to share with others about this. For example there are several non-duality Meetup groups. I wish you well.

❉

DOUBTS

I have been to meetings with Tony Parsons, whom I like very much. My own sense is of a deep resonance with non-duality.

It's been quite clear for some time now that no one is living 'my' life and that in fact this life only seems to be mine. But I still experience doubts about whether liberation is really being lived. I feel a resonance yet I ask myself whether this is really it.

Can you send me some words which might help this character to die?

Doubts arise naturally. They are simply thoughts arising and falling away. They are themselves liberation expressing itself as doubts as to whether this is liberation.

These thoughts can still arise even when separation is seen through, but they are usually not given much attention anymore. This is because there is no one inside listening to them. Because of this they tend to fall away quite quickly.

✳

ENJOYMENT AND DISGUST

Is the body-mind organism's tendency to avoid pain and to seek out pleasure natural? Or is it something we learn? Is there anything wrong with the enjoyment we experience when eating a lovely piece of cake, or with the disgust we feel at seeing a filthy toilet?

Some pleasure and pain responses are learned but many are Darwinian imperatives and are necessary for our survival. Attraction to food and sex and disgust at rotting matter which might spread disease are obvious examples of these.

Of course there is nothing wrong with either enjoying a piece of cake or feeling disgust at a filthy toilet.

Any foolish ideas that are picked up on the spiritual path that we must rise above both pleasure and pain, regarding all phenomena with the same bland equanimity, are simply that— foolish ideas.

That's why I'm going off now to have a lovely cup of tea in a nice clean cup.

✳

JUST WATCHING THE FILM

Two days ago I vanished, as I have heard Tony, you and others describe. It didn't seem a particularly special event. It was as if the watcher of this film wasn't there for a few seconds and there was just watching the film. Then 'I' was back and in charge again.

Is there anything that I can do or should do about this now? As I write these words to you, something inside me knows that your answer will be "No".

You describe an awakening event very well and, as you have indicated yourself, there is nothing to do now. You will know whether it is all over for you if searching has stopped.

Searching tends to stop when it is seen that everything is full, rather than when it is seen only that everything is empty. The fullness that is seen consists of unconditional love.

Seeing unconditional love can feel blissful for a while. This bliss almost always fades after a time. That does not mean that the self has come back. If searching has ended then it is all over for the self. Then the nature of what is arising becomes less important, whether it is pleasure or pain, or happiness or sorrow, because it is not arising for anyone.

❋

UNHAPPINESS AND TENSION

There seems to me to be a great freedom in knowing that there is no self and no free will. But I tend only to feel this when I am happy. When I'm miserable I may be able to go on trusting the universe intellectually, but I feel downcast and tense.

There's quite a cult of advising us that in difficult circumstances we should stay positive. But I think it may be better to do nothing and accept our tension. Then I think "But we can't do nothing! Even doing nothing is really doing something!"

Can you advise me or comment on this?

It's a common experience that when there's unhappiness we are likely to feel more of a sense of separation. I don't make recommendations but if I did it would be to find some simple thing that you enjoy doing and do it at these times. And if tension arises, it will probably be less troublesome if it's accepted rather than if it's fought against.

As you point out, we can't do nothing. If we try to do nothing, something will always happen. Knowing this, it might be possible to relax.

❋

LIBERATION EVENTS

Tony Parsons, Nathan Gill, you and others have 'experienced liberation'.

I understand that there is no self but I have not experienced this. Do I need to? Is this experience necessary for everyone? And why is the experience of no self important anyway?

Understanding liberation and seeing liberation have no connection. There can be understanding without seeing, seeing without understanding, both or neither.

The kind of event that some individuals describe is not necessary. The seeing of liberation can arise with no specific event being noticeable.

Seeing that there is no self is not important. However, this seeing tends to re-configure the psyche of the individual so that the life that is lived from then on is usually somewhat different from the life that was lived before.

Is not "seeing that there is no self" what the seeker longs for?

The seeker searches for an end to their dissatisfaction. They may long to see that there is no self but can have no idea of what this really means until the self disappears. Until then 'seeing that there is no self' can only remain a thought.

Are those who teach traditional Advaita not right to stress the importance of seeking and of a method to give rise to seeing?

No. These teachings are stories to satisfy the mind of the seeker.

Can the psyche be reconfigured with only an intellectual understanding of Advaita? If not, why not?

No, intellectual understanding is simply intellectual understanding. It does not produce 'seeing'. The taking on of different views, opinions or ideas about liberation has no relevance here. Seeing liberation is an energetic shift which 'we' are unable to bring about because 'we' are an illusion.

I cannot understand how something with no meaning attached to it can affect the psyche and produce a shift into liberation. Ramana Maharshi, Wayne Liquorman, Nathan Gill and others searched for the meaning of liberation before they experienced the shift.

Your failure to understand is probably because you cannot help thinking of liberation as a mental shift. It is not. The psyche is not simply a set of ideas, and the ideas that it contains are in any case irrelevant to liberation.

Individuals such as Ramana, Wayne, Nathan or even myself may search for the meaning of liberation before it occurs or they may not. But this has no importance except as part of a story.

❁

LIFE AND DEATH

I'm still recovering from reading your book 'Drink Tea, Eat Cake'. Wow!

I fear death. Ironically I also don't know what to do with my life. Can you offer any advice?

I hope it's obvious why I never offer advice, although I do sometimes say that if I did, it would be to relax and find something simple that you enjoy doing and do it.

184

You say that you fear death and do not know what to do with your life. In liberation fear of death tends to fall away and it is seen that we do not have a life. Life simply unfolds.

Apart from that I can only suggest the same as other individuals might. There might be books to read or people to talk to that might help you to deal with these issues.

❋

FEAR OF ONENESS

I have been to meetings with Tony Parsons and with you. I find a stillness and humour at both that I value. But I have a question.

I experience a fear of merging with Oneness, even though I have a powerful wish to lose myself. It seems clear to me that my ego is afraid to die, so what part of me is it that longs for unity?

Although the ego may think that it desires liberation as a way of ending its unhappiness, in reality the person can have no idea of what liberation is, nor that liberation entails its own disappearance. This is why there is often a tension between the desire for liberation and the fear of it. We could say that the ego is afraid to die, but nevertheless Oneness wants to re-discover itself.

❋

RUINING OUR LIVES WITH SPIRITUAL SEARCHING

I find your books very calming and very funny. In one of them you speak about how certain people can ruin their lives by following a spiritual path.

I'm puzzled by this because I understood that this message states that there is no choice. In that case, how can it be said that a person can make a decision that ruins their life?

I know that you could answer my question by simply saying "There is no person." But please don't do that. My question is about what happens in the play.

Language is a poor medium for conveying ideas about non-duality, but it's all we have got. If we always wrote with maximum clarity and lack of ambiguity, our writing would become unreadable. So much of the time it has to be understood that phrases that seem to be about personal choice and responsibility are actually not about these.

When I write of people who have ruined their lives, I mean that in this play of consciousness such things appear to happen. As long as the sense of being an autonomous person is still present, this is tantamount to saying that, in the individual's experience, such things do happen. It is only in retrospect, when the self has been seen through, that it is realised that no one ever made a decision that ruined their life.

In writing about people who ruin their lives, for example by abandoning their partner, children, home and profession to follow some guru, I am simply emphasising a certain psychological trait that some of us fall prey to in the name of spiritual development. This highlights one of the dangers that can arise when we are seduced by one of the many stories about gurus and enlightenment.

❋

CAUSE AND EFFECT IN SEEING LIBERATION

Can you explain to me how attending Tony Parsons' meetings helped you to see liberation? Is there cause and effect where this is concerned or not?

Perhaps the best thing for me to do would be to attend your satsangs?

I have never written that going to Tony's meetings helped the seeing of liberation. I have never said that anything helps the seeing of liberation. Nevertheless, in the dream of time, an enthusiasm for listening to Tony arose here, and then 'awakening' occurred and later 'liberation' was seen. There is no implication of anything instrumental in any of that and yet gratitude to Tony arises. How strange is that!

In actuality I find all the heated discussion that is generated around questions of cause and effect and choice rather vapid. In practice what happens is that either an energy to do a particular thing arises or it does not. If it does arise then it may happen, although of course it's also possible that it may not.

So if an enthusiasm for attending satsang happens for you, you may find yourself attending satsang. There is no need to add a story to this about cause and effect or choice or reason or meaning.

※

DISSOLVING SUBTLE ELEMENTS OF THE WITNESS AFTER LIBERATION

I had been a spiritual seeker for a long time when out of nowhere the realisation that there is no separate self appeared. Now life goes on but it is no longer 'my' life. The illusion of 'me' at the centre has been seen through.

I have heard some teachers say that, even after the separate self has been seen through, subtle aspects of the witness still need to be dissolved away.

Do you agree with this?

The suggestion that anything needs to be done, such as dissolving away subtle elements of the witness, is based on ignorance because everything is simply happening (apparently) of its own accord.

Just as nothing needed to be done before seeing This, nothing needs to be done after seeing This.

Who is there in any case who could do anything or dissolve anything?

Nevertheless, some minds are attracted to striving for a goal which they imagine can be achieved. For myself, I prefer to walk round my local park and have a cup of tea at the lakeside café.

❀

DOES OVER-INTELLECTUALISING PREVENT LIBERATION?

A teacher has told me that until I stop over-intellectualising about all my experiences, I will never realise liberation. Do you think this is true?

Nothing can help and nothing can hinder the seeing of liberation. The mind may see too much intellectualising as a problem, but that's just the mind doing its sweet old confusing thing. Liberation may be seen whether we over-intellectualise or whether we do not.

Some teachers tell students to stop intellectualising as a way of putting an end to challenging questions that they have difficulty answering. Docile and compliant students are sometimes seen as a great blessing by teachers.

❀

AWAKENING AND LIBERATION EVENTS

You seem to suggest that awakening and liberation do not necessarily have to take place at the same time. Am I right about this?

There are no rules about the seeing of liberation. If there were it would not be liberation, it would be imprisonment.

Sometimes there are two separate events, which for convenience we could call awakening and liberation. Sometimes there is simply one event. Sometimes there is no event, but a gradual shift into this seeing. And sometimes the sense of separation doesn't arise in childhood and there is just living in This.

IS THIS LIBERATION?

During a serious illness recently the freedom of liberation arose for several days. There was no ego present at all, just freedom. Then this faded and left me with only an intellectual memory of it. What do you think happened to me?

It is possible that all there is to be seen has been seen, but there is still an idea hanging on that "This isn't it". Such an idea can seem very powerful, but it is still only an idea.

This is fairly common. It usually happens when the individual is still clinging to a story which goes "If this is liberation, it should be better than this."

At this point it might be good to remember some Zen anecdotes. There is the story of a monk who said "Now that I'm enlightened, I'm just as miserable as ever." There was also a master who asked a student "Why do you want enlightenment? How do you know you'd like it?"

Another well-known Zen saying is "Before enlightenment, chop wood. After enlightenment, chop wood." In other words, liberation is simply the seeing that there is no central self. It has no other necessary implications. Afterwards life goes on but it is seen that there is no one living it.

❀

OBSESSION WITH READING ABOUT NON-DUALITY

For months now I've been obsessed with reading about non-duality. I don't want to do anything else in my spare time—it's really become an addiction.

Can I take this as a sign that I'm getting close to enlightenment? Or might it even be an impediment?

Nothing holds anyone back and nothing advances anyone. If there is an obsession with reading about this, that is simply what is happening in This. Nevertheless such an obsession is relatively common and quite often arises suddenly. It may indicate that your head is in the tiger's mouth.

Remember that, paradoxically and perhaps annoyingly, being asleep and being awake are the same thing. However, this cannot be seen while we are asleep. I once wrote "There's no such thing as liberation, but this cannot be seen until there is liberation." It is the ultimate paradox, but it is blindingly obvious when it is seen.

❉

PRACTICE OR NO PRACTICE

For many years I did a variety of spiritual practices because of my desire to grow spiritually. Now I seem to have lost that desire some-where—I don't know where.

What's left of me seems to be gradually disappearing. There's a character here going through the motions—going to work, drinking in the pub with friends and so on. It's as if I'm an observer of what I used to think was my life.

I'm stunned to realise that everything is going on without a God or anything else running the show. And I'm hoping that the rest of me might dissolve eventually. Can you comment on any of this?

You give a very good description of what quite often happens. Tony Parsons refers to a period of the self coming and going. He calls this 'me-ing' and 'be-ing'.

An interest in spiritual practices may arise or it may not. If it does, it may be followed by the seeing of liberation or it may not. Alternatively no interest in spiritual practices may arise and that too may be followed by liberation or it may not. There are many examples where each of these possibilities has happened. So the only thing I would say about this with absolute certainty is that there are no rules. How could there be? if there were rules this would be imprisonment, not liberation.

This seems to me to be a dream. Sometimes I think of it as God's imaginings. What is your definition of liberation?

You call this "a dream" or "God's imaginings". For me "a waking dream" is the best metaphor for This. A dream is utterly convincing until there is a waking up. Then it is seen to be unreal. Of course, this waking dream is both unreal and real. Watching a movie or a play also works quite well as a metaphor for This.

Liberation is the seeing that there is no self. This apparent person at the centre of experience is in fact empty and this appearance is an outpouring from Nothing of unconditional love.

Some individuals object to that last phrase. But it captures well the difference between awakening and liberation. That is what Nisargadatta is referring to when he says "Seeing I am nothing is wisdom. Seeing I am everything is love."

❀

DO OTHER PEOPLE'S PERSPECTIVES EXIST?

You write that what is happening is all that there is. In that case, do other people's perspectives exist or is my perspective the only one?

Of course I can't know directly whether other people's perspectives exist or not. But if they don't, wouldn't you agree that this places me in an unfeasibly privileged position?

No answer to your question will satisfy the mind. So here is my unsatisfactory answer.

It is a misunderstanding that what I am saying is "There is only your perspective." That is not it at all. Rather I am saying that there is no actual personal perspective.

This is because the person that feels themself to be perceiving this is itself unreal.

There is no person. There is no central self. Therefore there is no one having this or any other experience. In liberation it is seen that This is simply arising out of nothing for no one.

There is experience but there is no one who experiences. The apparent experiencer is simply experience itself.

In other words I am not saying solipsistically that no one other than you exists. I am saying that you do not exist, at least not as the separate autonomous entity that you may feel yourself to be.

A further problem with answering your question is that "All there is is This" or "This is it" are not philosophical statements. They are instead attempts to get as close as language can to describing what is seen in awakening and liberation. As descriptions, they may clash with logic, with reason and with personal experience. Alas, that cannot be helped.

Remember that in any case none of this matters. "All there is is This" is either seen or it is not seen and it is of no importance which.

To put it another way, being asleep and being awake are the same thing, except that while sleeping they are believed to be different, while in waking they are known to be the same.

❋

OBSERVING

I am experiencing more observing of whatever is happening than I used to.

Nevertheless, I still feel very restless and anxious about the future.

What you describe as going on for you is fairly common. There is sometimes a growing sense of observing life, which paradoxically can also involve a greater appreciation of the simple aspects of life.

Meanwhile the psyche can continue to do its own thing, so we may continue to feel restless and anxious. Remember that even when Oneness is seen in its completeness, any feeling can still arise. It is simply seen that it arises for no one.

✹

SOLAR STORMS

Some scientists are predicting major solar storms soon. They claim that these may well have the potential to harm human life. I am anxious about this, more for my children's sake than for my own. Do you have anxieties of this nature?

I don't have any information about solar storms. But to answer your question, no I don't have anxieties of this nature.

There have always been so many stories of great change, involving either terrible catastrophe or wonderful transformation, that it is exhausting to pay them much attention. Meanwhile, This goes on being what it is and here a simple life is led. One more cup of tea…

✹

MIND AND BRAIN

I have had the experience of a period of time when there was great peace on all levels. But in retrospect, that feels like an experience which has ended, just like every experience must end.

But since then some important changes have taken place. There is still some abiding sense of peace and nothing seems to matter very much now, even things that I used to consider very important. I can't really take anything very seriously anymore.

Nevertheless, I still have to earn a living, look after my family and get along with friends. I feel kind of stuck. I've seen for a little while what it means to be free of the self and I've had a heightened experience of life. But 'me' is back and I have no idea what to do about it.

Is it not true that this experience, like all other thoughts, perceptions and communication, come from the mind? And in essence wouldn't you agree that this means that it comes from the brain? I've read about 'witness consciousness' and 'awareness that is aware of itself'. Surely this too is simply a function of the brain? Isn't the very awareness that there is no one to be aware itself another kind of brain function or another function of the mind?

You give a good description of an apparent process which sometimes goes on for individuals after awakening. A loss of normal motivation and a heightened sense of awareness are often reported.

As to your questions, I am not sure that I've grasped them. They seem too abstract for me to get to grips with. Nevertheless I would comment that of course for there to be human perceptions, there has to be a human sensory system. So anything which is experienced or communicated about has to come from there.

This includes the seeing of non-duality. As Alan Watts said we are trying to "eff the ineffable", which is of course impossible. If you feel I've missed the point of your question, perhaps you might like to get back to me.

Nice try, but yes, I'm going to attempt to put it another way.

Whether someone is aware of awareness, or whether awareness is aware of itself, surely it must be the brain that enables that both to occur and to be recognised?

If I understand your question properly, the simple answer is "Yes". Every experience that arises for an individual is mediated by or through the brain. In fact, that is simply a description of what it is to be an embodied human being.

✺

THE SOUL DESCENDING

The way I describe what you write about is that the soul has to descend to its very roots in order to rediscover what it once had and has now lost. Only in doing that can it find the great silence and stillness which are the only characteristics of enlightenment spoken of in some traditions.

I tend to avoid using the word 'soul' as it carries so much baggage in Western religious and spiritual thought. There is also the problem that what we are talking about is ineffable, so any attempt to describe why or how it happens is bound to fail.

Although I would avoid it myself, your metaphor of the descent of the soul is a powerful one. It reminds me of Robert Bly's book 'Iron John' and also certain aspects of Jungian psychology, in which it is acknowledged that to be psychologically healthy we need to 'bucket out our well' or 'shovel our shit'. In other words we need to acknowledge and deal with our shadow.

There is a German film called 'Into Great Silence'. Perhaps you've seen it. However we explain it, seeing liberation certainly involves recognising great silence and stillness, although of course it is not 'we' who recognise it.

Stillness and silence are the only two characteristics that we can ascribe to liberation. Yet liberation has no characteristics. So here we are, stuck with the effing ineffable.

❀

AWAKENING AND LIMBO

Do people often feel uncomfortable after awakening? I find myself missing the excitement of my spiritual search. I've also lost all motivation where my work is concerned. As if this weren't bad enough, I can't even touch base with family and friends anymore. We seem to be living on different planets now. I feel like I'm in some kind of limbo.

The simple answer to your question is "Yes". Many individuals have described similar experiences after awakening. The inability to find comfort any longer in the practices and belief systems of any kind of spiritual or religious path is especially common.

Also common is a feeling of isolation from friends and family. They are usually unable to empathise with or understand what the awakening individual is going through. At an extreme, this may lead to an unwelcome referral to a psychiatrist.

Lack of motivation both in work and in life in general is often reported as well.

These generalities are very common, though of course the specifics may vary greatly in different cases.

❋

SOME NOTES FROM THE TRENCHES OF AWAKENING

There seem to be some pretty extreme stories of awakening about. I'm thinking particularly of Suzanne Segal and U.G. Krishnamurti.

In my case, on the other hand, nothing particularly extreme has happened. I simply recognise that I know less and less as almost everything becomes seen as mystery.

I couldn't even say whether 'I' or 'my self' ('myself'?) is still here or not. Thinking still goes on, especially when I see a particularly stunning woman and contemplate asking her out. I'm sure I feel like a person when I'm feeling anxiety or physical discomfort. And yet somehow all of this is also impersonal.

There have been one or two specific realisations. I've lost my fear of death, but the thought of dying still freaks me out. I find relating to other people sometimes becoming difficult because I just don't know what to talk about anymore. In general I've quietened down and often don't have much to say about many of the topics that my friends talk about.

Suzanne Segal and U.G. Krishnamurti are two well-known cases of extreme occurrences in awakening. However, I wouldn't pay their stories too much attention as there are no rules about this in any case.

After communicating with many individuals about this and from what is seen here, I would say that some common characteristics of the seeing of liberation are an end to searching, the recognition of the mystery and unknowable nature of almost everything, and a sense of gratitude though to no one. Any thought or feeling can still arise, including lust for a beautiful woman—thank 'god'! And yes, suffering of any kind can tend to increase any feeling of contraction. But that is simply Oneness feeling contracted.

Fear of death tends to end with liberation. Fear of dying may go on. That's quite natural.

There is a tendency for many individuals to say less when this has been seen. This is partly because strongly held opinions may decrease.

❊

POETRY

Is there a poet who describes what you describe?

Synchronistically, someone sent me the e e cummings poem 'Seeker of Truth' this week.

You could also look at T.S. Eliot's 'Four Quartets' or Hafiz among others.

❊

TRYING TO CATCH THIS

There are flashes of this, but whenever I try to catch it, it disappears.

Yes, trying to catch this has no effect on holding on to it.

❊

WHO'S GOT THIS?

How many 'entities' have got this? And can you recommend some reading?

Many 'entities' have got this. I've met and talked to quite a few of them myself.

You could try reading Tony Parsons, Jan Kersschott, Nathan Gill, Leo Hartong or myself. I'm sure there are many others but as I don't read much about this it's difficult for me to recommend other writers.

❋

SPIRITUAL EXPERIENCES

I have had experiences which seem to me to come under the heading of 'spiritual'. These have mostly occurred during meditation. There was a kind of dissolution of the edges where 'I' normally end, accompanied by an undramatic but deep feeling of joy. Is this the same as what you are describing?

I love your description and would say that I remember similar experiences in meditation. However if the experiencer remains, ultimately this is still about a person experiencing the relative, albeit the very refined levels of the relative.

Transpersonal experiences still belong to the realm of the personal, even when the person becomes translucent.

Seeing liberation has nothing to do with these refined and translucent experiences. Seeing liberation is seeing that there is no one. This brings a recognition of both the emptiness and the fullness of everything. After that, there is a great unknowing. There may also be gratitude.

❋

COMPASSION AND OVERCOMING THE EGO

You write that the strength of the ego is not an impediment to liberation in a moralistic sense.

But you also write that an egotistical person has no space to be compassionate to others. Does this not imply that the ego is in fact an impediment to liberation?

I can't remember writing that "an egotistical person has no space to be compassionate to others". However that sounds right to me on a psychological and emotional level. If you could quote me chapter and verse about this I could comment further.

But I can clarify one thing. As far as I am concerned, ego is not an impediment to seeing liberation. This is because seeing liberation has nothing to do with 'me' or my ego.

Much unnecessary misery has been caused by people believing that they somehow have to overcome their ego in order to reach liberation. Sometimes this kind of message results in self-flagellation amongst students and devotees. Sometimes it results in 'poisonous pedagogy' from teachers and gurus.

Yes, I think I mis-quoted you.

The closer I get to death, the more aware of separation I seem to become and the more obsessed with the wish for liberation. I want to 'die' before my body does. Nothing else seems to hold any attraction for me. Everything else seems dull and uninteresting in comparison.

Paradoxically, when the self is full of its own sense of being a separated person, then This, whatever is arising in presence, seems empty and unsatisfying. When the self is seen to be empty, then This is seen to be full and satisfying.

Seeing liberation is seeing that This is it and that This is enough. That is why seeking stops in liberation. Once This is seen to be enough, there can't be anything to seek for.

It sounds like your head is in the tiger's mouth.

I have always considered myself to be a compassionate person. However, after an awakening I'm struck by how much deeper this has become. Seeing suffering or acts of kindness or even great beauty is now capable of bringing me to tears.

Although I'm wary of assigning any characteristics to awakening and liberation (because there are no necessary implications to awakening and liberation), increased feelings of compassion, kindness and empathy are often present. This relates to the seeing, in liberation, of the nature of everything as an outpouring of unconditional love.

It is also difficult for us to feel kindly or empathic when we are highly neurotic. Neurosis tends to reduce in liberation so our natural tendency to feel and express kindness may be more to the fore.

What kinds of therapy did you train in? Did your training in psychological therapies have anything to do with awakening?

My training was mainly humanistic and transpersonal. It included a lot of Gestalt, some Rogerian stuff, quite a bit of Transactional Analysis, some Psychosynthesis, some Regression Therapy and a little N.L.P. After that I was a trainer rather than a practitioner. The proper word for what I did was 'psycho-education' rather than therapy, but it is not a word that has caught on much.

My training neither did nor did not have anything to do with awakening. Sorry for the paradox. What happens is simply what happens. Looking at the past to determine cause and effect where awakening is concerned is a mug's game.

I have been practising a Buddhist loving kindness meditation for a while. I don't know if it's having any effect on others, but I feel more peaceful. Do you have any direct experience of this kind of practice? Does increasing our feelings of empathy or compassion increase the chances of awakening?

Many years ago I practised Metta Bhavana meditation with the Friends of The Western Buddhist Order. Later on I was taught a similar 'happiness' meditation from the Tibetan Buddhist tradition.

Recently there have been some interesting books on the neuroscience of 'kindness'. Both giving and receiving acts of kindness releases oxytocin. Oxytocin is sometimes known as the 'empathy' or 'love' hormone. It enhances feelings of well-being in both the giver and the receiver of an act of kindness. Perhaps this is why Buddhists sometimes recommend "performing acts of random kindness" as a practice. It is good for us to do these, in that we feel better for doing them.

It is not surprising that seeing liberation may enhance our feelings of empathy and compassion, because the energy shift that is involved tends to reduce our level of neurosis. Neurosis can be a great destroyer of empathy because it focusses our attention rather uncomfortably on ourself and makes us self-obsessed.

So seeing liberation may enhance compassion. But we cannot say that enhancing compassion will lead to liberation. Because liberation is non-instrumental, we cannot use anything to reach it.

In practice this makes no difference. As exercising compassion enhances our sense of well-being, we may as well do it whether it leads to liberation or not. Of course actually compassion either arises or it does not.

One of the things I like about this aspect of the new neuro-science is that it takes considerations of morality and concepts of 'selfishness' and 'selflessness' out of the picture. We don't need to consider these slippery concepts, once it is recognised that giving and receiving acts of kindness increases the production of oxyto-cin, which enhances feelings of well-being.

I agree with you that practices are not the route to liberation. I am a good example of this as I have done many practices for many years.

But I remember reading an impressive book, 'Zen and the Art of Archery'. It is true that the author realised enlightenment suddenly, but this was only after he had mastered archery after long practice. Although the enlightenment was not produced by the practice, never-theless it probably would not have happened without it. Three years of practice had surely prepared him for Grace to occur. What do you think?

I read 'Zen and the Art of Archery' many years ago and remem-ber liking it a lot. As to commenting on preparation, practice and liberation, actually concepts about this do not matter, because what happens is simply what happens. Nothing could be any dif-ferent to what it is in any way. So if there is a history of practice, that cannot be changed. If there is not a history of practice, that cannot be changed.

Sometimes when there has been much practice, there is no seeing of liberation. Sometimes when there has been no practice, there is the seeing of liberation. So we can make no necessary connection between practice and the seeing of liberation. This can be very annoying and can seem very unjust to the seeking mind.

I have read that there are times in life when you might ask for something and then get what you wish for, only to discover that you don't really want it at all.

Recently, I have been experiencing almost unbearable emotional pain. But instead of fighting it, I've been allowing it to be there and "have its say". I've noticed that over time the pain dissolves.

I've been hoping for a long time to attain self-realisation or liberation. I want to lose my self so I can see Truth. But I've recently read a book by Jed McKenna in which he strongly advises against seeking liberation unless you really understand what it is that you are looking for. He says:

"Most (people) have bought into or been sold on the whole sweetness-and-light spirituality thing. They want to become better people, more open, more loving, happier, closer to God, and they want to achieve spiritual enlightenment because, as everybody knows, that's where the spiritual path leads. The yellow brick road may be a trip, but it's all about Oz, baby.... I encourage my students to at least consider the possibility that the world is up to its neck in caterpillars who quite successfully convince themselves and others they are actually butterflies."

McKenna thinks that people are seeking exciting experiences rather than Truth. He suggests that in order to find Truth we usually have to go through living hell.

I have found that, ever since I started to meditate regularly, I have been assailed by anxiety, guilt, fear of death and confusion, especially at night. I had been warned by my meditation teachers that something like this might happen as meditation would probably bring up my shadow or my dark side. Now I think I understand what McKenna means.

Eckhart Tolle seems to agree with McKenna. In 'The Power of Now' he suggests that many people who seek realisation will go through very negative experiences, although in his case they apparently only lasted for one night.

Yes, "Beware of what you wish for" is a well-known saying with good reason.

I would describe your own response to your suffering as 'natural mindfulness'. This is probably the healthiest possible way to respond to what you are experiencing. Whatever the nature of the emotional suffering we are going through, paying attention in this mindful way is often the fastest and the simplest way to process it or get through it. It represents the razor's edge between suppression and distraction on the one hand, for example through alcohol and other drugs, and wallowing in our feelings on the other.

As to what you report that Jed McKenna and Eckhart Tolle write, all I would say is that there are no rules. So not everyone suffers in awakening. However, I know that many people do. You may be aware of Suzanne Segal? Her autobiographical book 'Collision With The Infinite' is one testimony to the extreme suffering that may occasionally be involved.

Your meditation teachers are right. Meditation often brings up repressed material of a very dark nature so it can be processed. To this I would simply say "Better out than in."

I've noticed that when the self collapses, all sorts of very ordinary things become delightful.

Yes, it's astonishing how life can appear once the self gets out of the way of looking at it. The most ordinary aspect is seen as so alive, so extra-ordinary.

I've come across a Zen saying which I like very much: "Before enlightenment, fetch water, chop wood. After enlightenment, fetch water, chop wood." *I think this means that everything stays the same except the point of view, which changes. That's what makes the difference.*

If I'm right, awakening makes the ordinary extraordinary. And there's the realisation that it could always have been seen that way.

"Nothing is changed but everything is transformed" also sums it up very well. Nothing is changed, because everything goes on just as before. But everything is transformed, because now it is going on for no one.

In Zen they also say "At first mountains are mountains. Then mountains are not mountains. Finally mountains are mountains again." In awakening and liberation, everything can seem strange and new, but eventually everything simply settles down and becomes ordinary again. But now the ordinary is also recognised as extraordinary.

I know of a Zen teacher who writes that after awakening a process still carries on. He says that psychological problems can continue and that liberation can take time to become established. What do you think about this?

Awakening and liberation can involve a huge energy shift. In this, there is a tendency for a lot of neurosis to drop away and consequently for the psyche to be reconfigured. However, some neurosis may remain. This remaining neurosis may then unwind and dissipate over a period of time. This happens partly because there is no one inside anymore listening to it and paying it attention. Eventually it can get bored with its own babbling and give up.

So Zen teachers are right when they talk about a process continuing and that this may involve psychological problems. But although the re-configuring of the psyche that can continue even after liberation may be interesting, it is not especially significant.

Awakening is simply seeing that everything is empty. Liberation is simply seeing that everything is full. Everything else, including psychological problems continuing, is just stuff happening.

From a non-dual perspective, what is love? Could it be considered a mistake to desire love and seek for it?

Do you feel 'in love' with life? Do you have moments of loneliness like most people?

What great questions! Though if we want a communication about love, it may be better to go to the arts rather than to philosophy or psychology.

In practice most individuals know what love is, each in our own way through a variety of different possible experiences. It might be love of a partner, love of nature, love of friends, love of a child, love of a pet, love of a craft, skill or art. We could compile a pretty long list.

But 'unconditional love' which is spoken of in non-duality is beyond experience and can't be understood by the mind, because it embraces both the positive and the negative.

Unconditional love is beyond the feeling of love. It does not come and go, and it is untouched by any feelings, which are of course always transitory. At root, the desire or yearning for love cannot be finally satisfied until separation is seen through. Then, when the self is seen to be empty, This is seen to be full of unconditional love.

It is neither a mistake nor not a mistake to seek for love. Seeking love is simply something that often arises in the incompleteness of separation.

I do not feel 'in love' with life, but being in love with life arises here.

Any feeling is possible when separation has been seen through, but as a matter of fact loneliness does not arise here, although many other feelings do, for example both joy and sorrow.

❀

FEARS ABOUT DEATH

Some writers on Advaita that I have read say that a kind of mental self can survive death and be reborn, even though from an absolute point of view there is no karma or rebirth. They offer the analogy of sleeping at night, when there is just nothing, but when the person wakes up in the morning, they are back in their suffering. In a similar way, after death there could be a new birth in which suffering occurs again.

I am terrified by the possibility that I could find myself in hell or another world where there is terrible suffering. The fear of this paralyses me. Can you help me in any way with this?

I am sorry that you are so disturbed by these stories about death. When separation is seen through and liberation is seen, questions about death are resolved. Notice that I write 'resolved' and not 'answered'.

In liberation, questions about death are resolved for the following reasons. Firstly it is seen that what you really are was never born and so can never die. Secondly it is seen that This is an outpouring of unconditional love. Thirdly, and from your point of view most importantly, it is seen that all the stories about death such as the ones that you mention are exactly that—they are *just stories*. It can never be known by anyone, no matter how long their beard, how piercing their eyes or how patriarchal or patronising their manner, that these stories are anything other than imaginings. When this is absolutely seen, the mind simply loses interest in them. They are recognised as unknowable and therefore as uninteresting. The phrase 'baseless speculation' fits them well.

Meanwhile those who wish to speculate about death, mainly the religiously and the spiritually inclined, can continue to do so. It is so much hot air and not worth paying attention to. Teachers who speculate in this way often have an agenda, which is to control or influence us through fear. The other side of this coin is the offering of a story about salvation or personal enlightenment which is designed to seduce us with promises of some marvellous reward.

With my 'non-duality hat' on, I do not give advice. But on this occasion I am going to put my 'psychologist's hat' on and make a few suggestions. If you want to deal with the fear that you are experiencing, first recognise that it is a part of yourself that you have not yet integrated. In other words it is an aspect of your own shadow. One of the most effective ways of integrating this may be through mindfulness of it. Simply pay non-judgmental attention to the fear when you become aware of it. If you are able to, pay particular attention to where it arises in your body without getting caught up in all the stories in the head that others disseminate to disturb you with. If you find this difficult to do on your own, you might like to find a teacher or therapist who is able to help you. Or you can look for information about a technique like 'Focusing' on the internet.

If you want to feel more comfortable in everyday life, instead of paying so much attention to these unknowable stories, you could find some simple thing that you enjoy doing and do it. Both neuroscience and our own experience also demonstrate that giving and receiving acts of kindness and spending time in green spaces improve our sense of well-being. I wish you well.

❁

AWARENESS, DUALITY AND NON-DUALITY

Advaitists claim that the appearance of subject and object is a construction of the mind. In actuality there is no duality, no knower who is separate from what is known.

But they also claim that there is Awareness and everything which arises in it. Surely this is contradictory. Is this not a fundamental statement of duality, in which there is Awareness on the one hand and everything which arises in it on the other?

The very nature of language is dualistic, so whenever we try to describe the Absolute we cannot help creating the impression of duality. Even using the terms 'Absolute' and 'Relative' misleadingly implies duality.

There is no 'Awareness' and separately 'everything which arises in it'. There is only seamless Oneness arising as This, apparently.

As to your specific question, and *only as a metaphor*, it might help to think of 'Awareness' as one of the characteristics of nonduality. You might consider the others to be 'Energy' and 'Love'. You might recognise this description as similar in meaning to the traditional description of *satchitananda*.

This does not mean that you now have the duality of three separate entities. Still only as a metaphor, consider an orange. It has the characteristics of having a certain flavour, a certain texture and a certain colour. But these are not separate entities, rather they are simply a description of its 'orangeness'. Now consider Non-Duality. Sat, chit and ananda are simply a description of its Oneness.

If none of this helps, throw it out. It's meaningless and it doesn't matter.

❀

A GENTLE HUG

Dear Richard, After coming across non-duality I stopped meditating, although I realise that was just because of concepts. Then there were two powerful events and I realised that I am in everything and all there is is life. These events opened the door to another reality but the memory of them faded after a while.

Recently I've been experiencing a deep peace that is beyond the mind. The story of the personality seems to continue as before but it is seen somehow that this is all illusory and has nothing to do with the real me. There is a vast peaceful space that contains everything and everything contains this space. There is no fear or suffering in it, although both of those can arise within it. No matter how troubled and restless the mind seems to be, this vast peace prevails, even though the mind sometimes thinks it's lost it.

You said that in liberation emptiness is full of love. To me it feels like a gentle hug that accepts and embraces everything that arises.

There is a feeling now of having arrived. There is no 'I' in this space and the I or the mind could never have achieved this kind of peace, because it is beyond the mind, effortless and always there. The story of me still continues and I still get lost in thoughts and sometimes feel unhappy, but now this does not seem to matter. I can't make sense of it. Perhaps I never will.

I would be grateful for any thoughts you may have. Kind regards, Thorsten

Dear Thorsten, Thank you for your message. It sounds like a lovely opening into awakening and liberation has happened. "A gentle hug" does very well as a description rather than "unconditional love". All the words miss it anyway.

Thoughts and feelings continue to arise. That does not matter. And making sense of it may happen in time. Writing about this sometimes helps that process. And if it doesn't, that doesn't matter either, but you've already given some very good descriptions here.

In awakening, the emptiness of all phenomena is seen. In liberation, it is seen that this emptiness is also full. Of what? Of love. This is what finally brings an end to searching. Best wishes, Richard

Dear Richard, Yes, it doesn't matter whether it all makes sense one day or not. It's just the mind that wants to understand that which cannot be understood. For the first time in my life, I'm satisfied with not-knowing.

Could you briefly explain what you mean by fullness? Emptiness seems obvious but fullness is not so easy to grasp.

For me fullness would be seeing the aliveness of all life-forms unfolding in nothingness. Because nothing is rejected, everything is perfect the way it is. This is unconditional love—the seeing that

everything is perfect the way it is and nothing needs to be changed. There are no boundaries and everything is allowed to be as it is.

Does this make sense? I'm still trying to find the right words. Best wishes, Thorsten

Dear Thorsten, You give a very good description. What we are trying to write about is in any case ineffable, so any words we use can only approximate to it and any description will be problematic in some way or other.

I like to use the word 'love', which is nevertheless both approximate and problematic. I have also heard the description 'a certain kindness' and 'a gentle wow'. Your own words 'a gentle hug' are very good. Some individuals speak of 'joy' or 'causeless joy' and some of 'gratitude'. And yes, in This "everything is allowed to be as it is."

If this has been seen, I doubt that there is anything left to see. Of course questions and doubts can still arise from old patterns of thinking, but they will probably fall away again quite quickly and may re-appear less often as time goes by. Long-held neuroses can persist for a long time but in liberation it is simply seen that this does not matter. Best wishes, Richard

Hello again Richard, Although I don't have doubts anymore and questions seem meaningless, something seems to be missing still.

Actually of course nothing is missing. But the mind seems to be very powerful at times and can create the impression that something is missing or something still needs to fall away.

There is the understanding that this pure peaceful space which is our true timeless nature does not need any deepening. Nor of course could anything strengthen or weaken it. It just is. Yet the mind quite convincingly and very subtly still wants certain things about the personality to change.

Of course it doesn't matter whether in the story the personality changes over time or not. Nevertheless, the desire for change seems quite deep in certain circumstances.

210

Outside of those circumstances, the pure timeless space of nothing-ness is always dominant and it is also clearly seen that nothing has ever happened. I guess you understand what I am trying to describe here. Best wishes, Thorsten

Dear Thorsten, Thank you for your very clear description of what is going on. What you describe is very common. If there are impulses to change the personality in certain ways, then that of course is fine and change may or may not come about.

Yes, the mind can be very powerful. Yet underneath all of its babblings This remains still and silent. Best wishes, Richard.

❋

THE PARANORMAL

I had an awakening similar to that which you describe when I was a student. I knew that I and everything were one, that every-thing was perfect and that in a mysterious way all knowledge was already known.

Then I began to develop paranormal skills. I enjoyed these at first. I enjoyed people asking me for help and treating me with more respect than they had ever done before. But eventually I got bored with it and a bit overwhelmed with the responsibility so I stopped responding to people's requests for 'readings'.

Now I find that I'm becoming more sensitive to paranormal phe-nomena than ever and I'm unhappy with this. I don't want to be involved with this or any other 'spiritual' way of being. I'm fed up with being around people who chatter on endlessly about chakras, karma, their higher purpose and their connection to the Divine. To be frank, it all makes me want to throw up!

And most of all, I definitely do not want to talk to the dead!

Do you have any experience of how to get rid of these 'powers'? If I simply ignore them they seem to get stronger.

I feel very much in alignment with your attitude to the paranormal, chakras and other esoteric fairground rides.

As for talking to the dead, I find it difficult enough to talk to the living.

Alas, many people want to develop 'paranormal awareness' further, though to me this seems not just a back-water, but a very boring one too.

These days I get very impatient with these phenomena. Unfortunately I cannot offer you any specific advice about how to get rid of 'paranormal powers' as I am probably one of the least psychic individuals you could meet. I suppose you could try simply telling the spirits to fuck off.

Thank you for your reply. I guess I didn't really expect that you'd be able to help me. Nevertheless I really like the fact that you are so straight about the subject.

❊

CONTROL AND DECISION

According to my understanding, Advaita Vedanta describes us as never controlling anything because there is no separate 'self' which can exercise control.

I understand that in the ultimate sense we have no control because everything including 'me' is God. But I feel that within the narrative of 'our' lives, we are the creators because we are God. Therefore we are able to create apparent realities. For example I have many choices I can make. I can choose to travel or to look for a new job or to leave my partner or to do many other things. Do you agree with me?

I recognise that nothing is really true, and that this includes Advaita Vedanta. God is of course beyond comprehension and every time we think we have understood it we are wrong.

I do not usually use the word 'God', as it carries too much misleading baggage, especially in the West.

I would not say that "we are the creators" or that "we are able to create apparent realities". What happens is simply what happens, and in that the sensation that 'I' decide to look for a new job or to leave my partner may arise. But this sensation has no importance and eventually it will be seen through.

I agree with you that 'truth' is not a useful concept. An understanding of Advaita has no value where seeing non-duality is concerned.

I understand why you don't use the word 'God'. Bob Adamson talks about 'pure intelligence-energy' and Leo Hartong uses the term 'Pure Awareness'.

I think I get what you are getting at. There is no separate 'I', so there is no one controlling anything. Life is simply doing what it is doing, even though it may seem as if 'I' am deciding stuff.

❋

WATCHING THE NEWS

Has your experience of or interest in watching the news changed now that Oneness is seen?

Before liberation, chop wood and watch the news. After liberation, chop wood and watch the news. Seeing This makes no difference. Liberation is SO ordinary. It is said that Muktananda once told some of his most devoted followers "You are going to be very angry with me when you get this."

However, I used to be very interested in current affairs and social matters. Now some of that interest has diminished. But some of it continues.

❋

FEAR OF DEATH

Dear Richard, You and Tony Parsons are the only persons I can listen to about the loss of being a separate self and joy without any cause. It leaves me in a field of relaxed clarity which feels good. The joy of simply sitting in a train, walking home at dusk, feeling the wind on my skin, are all experienced so intensely. All the little things have become important again now that the stories have lost their importance. Nevertheless, like many others, I am still expecting an event to happen.

I also still sometimes experience a powerful fear of death. I fear extinction, I fear nothingness. And your analogy about deep sleep is no comfort to me!

I've written to you before about this and last time you replied "Don't worry. It will be alright." That still makes me smile and does give me some relaxation. Best wishes, Michael

Dear Michael, First I want to emphasise the distinction, which is sometimes lost, between fear of dying and fear of death. They are very different phenomena.

There does not have to be a noticeable event of awakening and liberation. Sometimes there is simply a gentle sliding into seeing This. And whether there is an event or not, some neurotic thought patterns can remain and may take time to erode. So it is not surprising if fear of death still comes up for you as it does for many people. Eventually this tends to resolve itself, for two reasons.

Firstly, the mind finally really gets it that questions about death are unanswerable except with fantasy stories. Once it realises that death belongs to the unknowable, the mind tends to get bored with it and these questions simply no longer arise. Secondly, when it is realised that what we really are was never born and so can never die, death becomes uninteresting. Best wishes, Richard

❀

SELF-ENQUIRY AND ULTIMATE FULFILMENT

I would like to ask you two questions. Firstly, in your opinion can self-enquiry bring about awakening? Secondly, is self-realisation the ultimate fulfilment that is possible? In self-realisation, does all sense of psychological incompleteness end?

Sometimes there is self-enquiry and no awakening, sometimes there is self-enquiry and awakening. Sometimes there is no self-enquiry and no awakening, sometimes there is no self-enquiry and awakening. So the answer to your first question is "No."

Self-realisation, or the seeing of non-duality, is the ultimate fulfilment as it includes everything. If there were anything beyond non-duality, it would still be non-duality.

However, your second question seems to be about the psyche of an individual. This continues until physical death with whatever quirkiness it may contain. Neurotic tendencies may continue and all kinds of other psychological and emotional tendencies may also continue. But in liberation it is seen that there is no one who owns these tendencies, so they tend to lose their grip, their bite and their sting.

One of the greatest misconceptions about liberation is that it confers a blessed state in which no uncomfortable thought or feeling could possibly arise. Out of this misconception comes the idealisation of gurus. Once this has occurred, the guru has to keep well away from his followers except in satsang, so that he is never seen by them when he is being impatient or grumpy or throwing video cassettes irritably at his girlfriend.

❋

FALSE GOLD AND SACRED COWS

Dear Richard, Being at one of your meetings is like panning for gold. You point out and rule out so many nuggets of glittering false gold.

And shoot a good few sacred cows in the process! And point out the signposts to dead-ends that wait to tempt the seeker. All the best, Cha

Thank you, Cha. I'm glad you appreciate the meetings. Instead of shooting the sacred cows perhaps we could just herd them into retirement. Best wishes, Richard

❀

SUGAR-ON-SHIT

I feel that letting go to the reality of whatever is, must involve us being spontaneous. This might include any kind of reaction to events. Therefore if I'm feeling anger at someone, I might behave angrily. I don't feel that there is anything wrong with such behaviour.

But many people who consider themselves to be spiritual say that we should only ever act in a kindly and peaceful way to others. Do you agree with them?

There are many misconceptions about spirituality. One of the most damaging is that we need to behave in some specifically spiritual way. This often leads to a denial of the shadow and therefore a failure to deal with it. This is why some spiritual people seem so irritable under their veneer of peace, gentleness and love. Eva Chapman calls this 'sugar-on-shit'. Carl Jung said of his parents "[My father] did a great deal of good—far too much— and as a result was usually irritable. Both parents made great efforts to live devout lives, with the result that there were angry scenes between them only too frequently." (Carl Jung 'Memories, Dreams, Reflections')

Although there are no rules about what happens when non-duality is seen, there is often more spontaneity, because both neurosis and beliefs about how we 'should' behave tend to decrease or fall away.

❀

NON-DUALITY TROLLS

I notice that there is a lot of vilification on some internet sites and forums of virtually all the living non-duality teachers, including yourself. Some of the comments are highly abusive. What do you think of these non-duality trolls? Do you ever respond to them and their comments?

I love your phrase 'non-duality trolls'.

Most of the really offensive comments are put on websites and forums anonymously. It is a good principle never to respond to anonymous comments on the internet. My identity and contact details are open to anyone who wants to know them. People can write to me, phone me or come to my home town and take me out for cake and coffee—especially the latter. If others want to post comments without being equally open about their identity, they are best ignored.

Road-rage and web-rage are closely aligned. In each case, the relative anonymity of the situation makes some people feel it is safe to give vent to their shadow in violent and explosive ways. So whether on the road or on the internet, some will express their shadow in ways that they would not dare to do if they met you walking down the street.

By the way, being remarkably offensive about views on Advaita is nothing new. Certain followers of Madhva (approx 788 CE to 820 CE), had this to say about Shankara:- "He's a non-dualist because he's so stupid he can only count up to one."

❀

AWAKENING EVENTS AND SEPARATION

Over many years I have done a lot of spiritual practices and also experienced a lot of suffering. But now I am very contented with life. One of the things that has contributed to this is that my beliefs about life have disappeared. This has been extremely beneficial and conducive to a much more relaxed life.

But now I have the problem that there is no problem. I had always assumed that if there were no more problems, happiness would follow. But although there is contentment and life is going pretty well, I still have the feeling that there must be more to life than this.

In essence it seems to me therefore that I still have not fully realised that there is no separation, in spite of having had many awakenings. So here I am, with everything just hunky dory, yet still feeling that I must be in prison.

On several occasions I have completely lost the sense of being located in a body which is fixed in space and time. But this has not continued and here I am back in the body. Why is this? Why do I still feel myself to be a separate organism?

I have practised self-enquiry with Mooji, but I just ended up more confused than ever. Now I feel that I am just a hair's breadth away from full realisation but I cannot get away from this sense of physical separation. Can you help?

The sense of not being located in the body, of awareness being everywhere rather than centred where the body is, only arises in awakening or liberation events. Such events may last for a short period of time or for a long period of time, but they always end. Then the sense of what I call 'localisation' returns, even where liberation has been seen.

What ends permanently in liberation is not localisation, but contraction. This happens when the fullness of everything is seen, as well as its emptiness. When contraction ends, so does the restless energy of seeking. Then all the stories of seeking are seen through and we are freed from their hypnotic grip.

From your account, it sounds as if there is probably nothing more for you to see. The only problem seems to be that you are hanging on to the idea that "If this is liberation it should be better than this". But liberation embraces everything and in liberation ordinary life goes on. It is simply seen that it is going on of its own accord, that nobody is doing it.

As to self-enquiry, the problem is that it is a separated person who is self-enquiring, so it is unlikely to be helpful.

To sum up, it sounds like the only problem is that you think there is a problem.

Thank you. That's cleared up some misconceptions I had about localisation and contraction. I realise that contraction has been over for me for a while and I haven't really felt like a 'person' since then.

I find that all the stories that I used to pay attention to have tended to disappear. If they do appear, they are quickly seen for what they are, just stories—or rumblings that the mind still mutters to itself occasionally.

I'm finally done with spiritual practices! Thank you so much.

❋

DEPRESSION AND AWAKENING

I have been experiencing a lot of depression. Can the deep suffering that this causes be used to awaken to the realisation that there is actually no one who suffers? I know that it is absurd to be a person seeking not to be a person.

Awakening occurs when it occurs. It may be preceded by depression or not, because there are no rules where awakening is concerned. As you hint at, the false self cannot use any method to see that it is itself false. Its attempts to do so simply reinforce the idea that there is a person who can discover that they are not a person.

As to depression itself, many people find that one of the most helpful things to do when experiencing any kind of emotional discomfort, is simply to pay attention to the feeling or sensation wherever it emerges in the body for short but regular periods of time. It's best if this can be done without self-judgement or self-criticism and without expectations about what might occur. If possible, it is also good to spend some time doing small simple things that bring even slight enjoyment. Of course professional help can also be sought if there's a feeling that it could be useful.

IS THIS LIBERATION?

I like the phrase "Your head is in the tiger's mouth." It applies to me. And I've found your book comforting as it reminds me that everything is actually okay even when it seems like shit. I also like your (non) recommendation to relax.

I had a dramatic awakening some years ago and since then there seems to have been a kind of gentle slipping into the seeing of liberation. My previous life, with all its dramas, years of meditation and mountains of cash spent on psychotherapy, seems like a huge joke.

There was a period when I felt I had come home. It was clear that there was no one running the show. Instead there was unconditional love and causeless joy.

Later on the person seemed to come back, just as you say can happen. I felt frustrated and began to feel that non-duality was just another spiritual trip. But I have to acknowledge that some kind of profound change has taken place. Nevertheless, returning to that state of peace and joy seems impossible.

In spite of this 'set-back' my life is good now. I've been left without ambition and this means I live a simple and relaxed life, rather as you describe yourself living. The world seems generally to be a kindly place and I recognise that "This is it and This is enough". In a way it's quite wonderful. But I can't resist asking, do you have any pointers for me?

It doesn't sound from what you write that you need any pointers from me. It sounds instead as if everything there is to be seen has been seen. But perhaps there is still a lingering thought that "If This is it, it should be better than this all the time, with no possibility of negative thoughts or feelings arising."

Some version of this thought can arise for many individuals and can subtly keep searching going. But it's simply bullshit and can end as soon as that is realised. Alternatively it can wither away gradually as the mind becomes less and less interested in it.

✳

RELATIONSHIPS AND LIBERATION

When it is seen that there is no one, my assumption is that conflict in relationships will lessen. After all, the person's buttons will no longer be there to be pushed and the ego will no longer need to be defended. Is this in fact the case?

There are no necessary implications in the seeing of liberation, so anything can happen. However, there is a tendency for neurotic tendencies to decrease, and neurosis can provoke a lot of conflict in relationships. So from that point of view, relationships are likely to improve.

On the other hand, many relationships are glued together by a shared story about The Meaning of Life, such as a religious, spiritual, political or ecological story. In that case, there may be a crisis in the relationship if one individual sees through that story and is no longer able to take it seriously. This might even bring the relationship to an end.

So you see, there are no rules. There are never any rules with liberation. It is the ultimate anarchy and cannot be labelled and put in a box, not even one labelled 'Better Relationships'.

✳

IN DEFENCE OF GURUS

In spite of a certain reluctance, I am drawn to non-duality. I recognise in myself the despair that you write about but it never becomes depression.

But what I actually want to do in writing to you is to defend gurus. It seems to me that gurus offer more than mere intellectual knowledge. I feel that there is an energy or a spirit that can be transmitted through the guru. In the 'guru tradition' this is usually known as Shakti and its transmission is sometimes achieved through a process known as Shaktipat.

So the guru is really engaged in an activity which is essentially non-verbal. And the Shakti energy has its own intelligence, which is also in everything.

I would not see any need to defend gurus. They are after all Oneness doing its 'guru thing', or 'Oneness guru-ing'. In the drama of the relative world, some of them can be helpful. Even when they are not, they can often be very entertaining.

I would also say that intelligence is implicit in everything. This is recognised in the ancient Yogic description of *satchitananda*, one element of which is intelligence, or consciousness.

By the way, many years ago I received Shaktipat from Swami Muktananda via the touch of the peacock feathers, and years before that from a Tibetan Buddhist monk. I enjoyed these rides in the funfair very much.

✷

LIBERATION AFTER BEING ON A SPIRITUAL PATH

I am sure that liberation can happen to anyone. Nevertheless, I feel there is evidence that, if liberation is seen after being on a long spiritual path, it is less of a shock and therefore easier to adjust to.

On the other hand, those who awaken with no previous experience of spirituality can go through many years of difficulties before their seeing is integrated and they adjust to being without a self.

There are no rules. I have met individuals with no history of spiritual seeking who have adjusted smoothly to a sudden awakening.

Some individuals are more neurotic than others. Neurosis tends to make life very uncomfortable. So I suspect that whether liberation is easily adjusted to or not depends more on how neurotic the individual is rather than whether it occurs after a period of spiritual searching or not.

Remember that what is, is. And what isn't, isn't. So being on a long spiritual path happens or it does not happen. There is no one who chooses to set out on a path, to continue on a path or to leave a path.

✸

U.G. KRISHNAMURTI AND YOU

I have been seeking for some years, but now at last some kind of relaxation has taken place. The trouble is that I am now in a sort of limbo state. All my desire to seek has disappeared but in some evanescent way the person is still here. So now sometimes I feel quite relaxed about liberation but sometimes I feel that if I only tried harder, liberation might happen. Perhaps just one more meditation retreat might do it...

I don't have any joie de vivre, but I can't really go back to seeking again.

You've written that searching can give us meaning and purpose, so when that's gone it can leave us in despair. Does it sound to you as if that applies to my current state of 'neither here nor there'? And have you come across U.G. Krishnamurti? What he says is very similar to you only with more swearing.

It sounds as if you are in that state between awakening and liberation which is quite common. The non-existence of the self has been seen, destroying all the stories of searching and meaning, but liberation is not yet realised. This is usually because the emptiness of all phenomena has been seen, but not yet their fullness.

Lacking 'joie de vivre' is a good description of what many feel at this point. And you are right. There really is no going back to seeking after awakening has happened.

I like U.G. Krishnamurti very much. Of course apart from the swearing, there's another difference between him and me at the time of writing this. He's dead.

IN THE TIGER'S MOUTH?

Some time ago I had an awakening. I've heard you talk about the void or emptiness, and that was most definitely what was seen.

Then later on there was another event. This time unconditional love was seen. This was also incontrovertible. Nevertheless, I told myself that this wasn't 'It', because I had a lot of preconceptions about 'enlightenment' which I'd picked up from the TM movement. In TM they'd always implied that enlightenment would come 'with a cherry on top'. And some whipped cream. And a chocolate flake.

Now I've read your book 'Drink Tea, Eat Cake' and the thought keeps coming up "Aha! It really may all be over for me!" Do you think that for me there may be nothing else to see? Is this already it?

One thing we can be sure of. This is most definitely already it. There isn't anything else that this could possibly be.

The earlier experience that you write about is awakening. In this, the emptiness of all phenomena is seen. After that the only thing left to see is unconditional love. You describe this in the second event.

So from what you write, it sounds like your head is at least in the tiger's mouth, but probably the tiger has already bitten your head off. If you haven't already noticed this, that's probably because of your preconceptions about what enlightenment should be like.

❀

AWAKENING AND LIMBO

I am experiencing what I've heard Tony Parsons call 'me-ing and being'. It's extremely painful. In fact I feel like a terminal patient.

It's quite obvious to me that all the paths of seeking that I followed are futile, that there's no medicine which will save me. But my restless seeking energy is still here. I'm still reading the menu even though I've lost my appetite. Does this make sense to you? Have you any comment for me?

Many individuals go through an awakening in which emptiness is seen. This reveals the pointlessness of searching, so it tends to fall away.

However, in awakening the fullness of liberation is not seen. So the individual often feels as if they are in a kind of limbo.

Although for obvious reasons I do not give advice, if you can allow yourself to relax and find some simple undemanding thing that you enjoy doing, that may make life more comfortable.

❋

JOHN ROWAN

I hear that you've had a spat with John Rowan, the well-known humanistic psychologist. What was it about?

John Rowan takes great issue with me over several things that I've said. For me the key point of disagreement between us is that Rowan, like Andrew Cohen and Ken Wilbur, presents enlightenment as evolving. He holds that the enlightenment of 'today' is different and by implication superior to the enlightenment of, for example, the Buddha two and a half thousand years ago.

As enlightenment is the seeing, by no one, of the eternal and unchanging nature of the Absolute out of which all change arises, this cannot be the case. But it might help us to feel a bit smug and superior to believe it.

If you'd like to read my full response to Rowan, and how could you not on a wet Sunday afternoon, you can find it in the Transpersonal Psychology Review, Volume 14, No. 1, Summer 2010 issue.

❋

SPIRITUAL TEXTS

I used to be entranced by beautiful spiritual texts, especially those from the Buddhist and Sufi traditions. Then I came across non-duality! Now the texts that I used to love seem to me to be very obviously dualistic and I no longer delight in reading them. But at the same time I miss them, their beautiful language and the comfort that they used to bring me.

Do you know of anything that I could read to replace them?

For a while I also missed the beauty of the spiritual writings that I used to enjoy and which still sit on my groaning bookshelves. Unfortunately this is just one of the ways in which, as Tony Parsons says, "non-duality ruins your life".

I still occasionally come across bits of writing which hit the mark. For me, these are usually in Zen and Taoist writings. But there's nothing substantial which I know of that I could recommend. Perhaps a walk round the park and a cup of tea could be a substitute?

Yes, it's becoming clear to me that there's nothing for me to get out of reading, not even out of your books! So after all those years of seeking, I'm going to put my books away, go for a walk round the park and then have a nice cup of tea.

❊

WHAT AM I REALLY?

What am I really? Am I the One that simply sees, just as a mirror effortlessly reflects whatever is in front of it? When my mind wanders, is that Oneness being distracted from what is? Whenever I pull myself back and notice what is again, there is a great feeling of relief. It's like being cosseted by a warm blanket.

You are Oneness thinking, you are Oneness feeling, you are Oneness sensing, you are Oneness perceiving. Whatever arises can arise only in and for and as Oneness.

So when you are simply seeing, it is Oneness which is simply seeing. When your mind wanders, it is Oneness which is being distracted. There is no need to pull yourself back, as if you'll miss some moment of Oneness if you do not. But pulling yourself back is also okay. It's just Oneness pulling itself back.

❃

EMPTINESS AND FORM

In 'The Heart Sutra' it is said that "Form is emptiness, emptiness is form". I do not understand how emptiness can be form.

In even a flash of awakening, it may be seen that everything that appears as form is arising out of emptiness. That is how "emptiness is form". Another way of putting this is that emptiness gives rise to all that appears as form.

Two hours of discourse cannot explain this, but a split second of seeing can reveal it.

❃

DEPRESSION AND AWAKENING

I seem to be going through a period of awakening of the kind you've spoken about. It's very difficult for me and for much of the time I feel quite depressed. In your experience, could this depression have to do with awakening? Is there anything helpful that I could do? Do you think any particular kind of intervention might be helpful?

After awakening, people can certainly sometimes experience depression. As to interventions, although I don't give advice, if you know of something that you feel might make this period of time more comfortable, or less uncomfortable, it might be a good idea to look into it.

There were certainly times for me when I found therapeutic practices and transpersonal practices very helpful, as well as simpler things like hanging out with like-minded friends or going for walks in nature.

✾

THE PAIN OF SEEKING

In your book 'I Hope You Die Soon' you write about your decades as a seeker.

I too have spent decades following gurus—in fact many of the gurus who are famous in the West. I was always looking for some special kind of bliss. I collected a great bag of experiences and practices, but my doubts never went away.

Now, looking back, I feel the pain of seeing all that searching as a waste of time. I feel tortured by my past. I see all this desperate searching as a kind of madness. I have heard the truth countless times yet never seen it.

I recognise the impossibility of my doing anything to make 'it' happen, to bring about the seeing of 'This'. I feel despair and complete frustration. Have you any words that might comfort me?

Thank you for your very moving e-mail. You put very well the dilemma of so many people who have seen that searching is futile yet still feel the pain of separation and the agonising pull of the past.

Liberation is very simple. It is indeed just the seeing of 'This', whatever is arising in presence, and the recognition that, as there is no central self, what happens is simply what happens.

I hope that you see This soon.

✾

228

TURMOIL AND THE SHADOW

I am in a state of turmoil. A great deal of very dark shadow material which had been suppressed is now coming to the surface. I've been to therapists about this but I've not found them to be very helpful. I think this is because they do not understand the non-dual take on life which I have.

I have had an awakening event which made abundantly clear the true nature of the self as emptiness. But when I hear you talk about unconditional love, I have no idea what the hell you are getting at! I experience love as a limited human emotion, so I simply cannot see how it can fit into this 'liberation' thing.

To me there is simply Nothing and in this Nothing all the apparent 'stuff' appears.

About unconditional love, all I can say is this. Individuals sometimes experience two events. In the first, the emptiness of all phenomena is seen and this often provokes a crisis of an existential nature. Sometimes this has been referred to as 'the dark night of the soul' or as 'being in the desert'. The shadow material which you are facing is probably being brought to the fore because of this awakening event.

In the second event, which may occur at any time, the fullness of everything is also seen. This is what brings a final end to searching and a final end to the existential crisis. After that, life simply goes on. Before, chop wood. After, chop wood.

The fullness that is seen is beyond words, but 'love' gets nearer to it for me than any other word. The love that is seen is impersonal and goes far beyond limited human emotion.

If this makes no sense to you, all I can add is that when it is seen, it will be unavoidable and irrevocable. As Suzanne Segal puts it, it is a collision with the infinite.

Of course there are no rules and so it doesn't have to be like this. It's just that this is a common enough occurrence to make it worth commenting on.

DO THINGS GET WORSE AFTER AWAKENING?

In your book, you implied that after your first awakening things got worse and you were left in a more painful situation than before.

You also seem to imply that liberation is as simple as enjoying a cup of coffee. Can this be true?

Yes, it really is as simple as enjoying a cup of coffee. As long as there is no one there to enjoy it.

And yes, in a way things did get worse for me after 'awakening'. This was because awakening killed off the hope that 'I' could do anything about my dilemma. This is commonly experienced by many individuals.

✻

WHAT HAPPENS AFTER DEATH?

I'm anxious about death to the point of obsession.

Some people seem to be able to see the spirits of dead people and receive information from the spirit realms of existence. Surely this is good evidence that some essential aspect of ourselves lives on after the body has died. Many people state this, including Douglas Harding for example.

Surely you had spiritual experiences and visited other realms when you were doing your spiritual trip?

There are sufficient phenomena happening, some of them real, some of them imagined, to support any story about reality which we wish to adopt. So if we want to believe in ghosts, we will be able to find 'evidence' to support our belief.

Nevertheless, the dead continue to be remarkably silent about death.

Remember that each story we explore, perhaps about ghosts, or about spiritual experiences, or about multi-dimensional universes, or about attaining gnostic knowledge through the study of the Kabbalah, is simply a different ride in the spiritual funfair. We can get caught up in this funfair for the whole of our life, developing ever more complex esoteric 'understanding'.

Of course it's good to have an open mind, but not so open that our brains fall out. Remember that our perception is a terrible guide to reality. It is constantly fooling us in numerous ways, as most psychologists know. The way memory is created and structured, and our numerous cognitive biases, are just two of the reasons why we should be aware that reality and our perception of reality may be very different to each other.

Yes, I had many spiritual experiences. The clue is in the word 'experiences'. These were simply experiences, of no more importance than any other experience, such as walking round the park. But of course the mind wants to turn them into something highly significant, which makes us special and different for having them.

Liberation is not an experience. It is seeing that out of which all experience arises. Therefore the nature of any specific experience, whether 'spiritual' or not, is unimportant to the seeing of liberation.

❋

BETWEEN BLISS AND DESPAIR

I enjoy the way you share the wisdom of nothingness in your meetings and books. I know it's a difficult thing to do. My own situation is that I find myself caught between bliss and despair.

Between bliss and despair, I hope you're able to enjoy walking round the park, drinking tea, or whatever else would be a simple pleasure for you.

❋

THE RELIEF OF HOPELESSNESS

What you say resonates a great deal with me. But more and more neurosis seems to be manifesting in my life as I pay more and more attention to the message of non-duality. No area of my life is functioning well—it all needs working on.

Yet at the same time I'm becoming lazier and lazier. I just want to sit on my sofa and watch daytime TV. This is completely new for me.

Then suddenly the complete hopelessness of working any of this out with the mind overtakes me and I'm swept up in a deep relaxation for a while. At these times, all the effort of seeking just disappears.

What you are experiencing is similar to what is experienced by many individuals. On the one hand our neuroses can start to manifest even more intensely as we get closer, as it were, to seeing This—although of course we can never really get closer to it nor further away from it.

On the other hand, there may be an increasing tendency to abandon ourselves to laziness, or 'glorious laziness' as I like to think of it. For you that might mean watching day-time TV on a sofa. For me it's likely to be walking round the park.

As we see through the stories of meaning that might previously have kept us in chains, and as the hopelessness of seeking dawns on us, that can leave space at last just to be.

I hope there are more times for you when all the effort of seeking disappears. Realising the utter hopelessness of trying to work This out can be a great relief.

I love that phrase 'glorious laziness'. As I become more and more aware of the total hopelessness of my situation, my neurotic tendencies do finally seem to be dying away.

I'd like to ask you a question about 'resting as awareness'. I've been doing this as a practice for some time, after it was emphasised to me by a teacher that it is invaluable for bringing into awareness the peace and silence that everything arises from, as opposed to the normal content of awareness.

Does this practice have a value? I mean above and beyond simply making the prison more comfortable? I can't help feeling that there must be something which is more helpful than watching soaps on TV, something which goes beyond my normal neurotic behaviour. Or is this thinking just based on my old conditioning?

If you find that 'resting as awareness' as a practice is helpful in terms of your daily comfort, then of course there's nothing wrong with that. But if you find it a strain, you might as well drop it. It is a kind of ersatz version of the natural resting in awareness which occurs when Oneness has been fully seen. This is untouched by whatever arises as experience, so there is no need to do anything about it in order to produce it.

There is no need to go beyond neurotic behaviour or avoid watching soaps on TV, but if either of those happen, that's fine too.

Now that I see how hopeless this is, I'm relaxing more. The utter ordinariness and simplicity of This is becoming apparent.

❊

MEDITATION AND LOSS OF INTEREST IN LIFE

Since starting to practise meditation some time ago, I've lost any interest in the ordinary things in life, such as employment, possessions or even having a family.

Now I'm wondering if it is possible to benefit from meditation and also enjoy life's ordinary pleasures. Can we live in both these realities? Could you give me some advice about this?

I do not give advice. But there certainly does not have to be a conflict between enjoying the benefits of meditation and enjoying the ordinary pleasures of life. These are not two realities but each part of the one and only reality.

Many people find that enjoying something very simple is the easiest way to connect with joy.

233

The seeing of liberation is the seeing of that out of which all experience arises. This embraces everything—meditation, ordinary pleasures and all other experiences.

❀

PHYSICAL BIRTH

Can I ask you how you see your own physical birth from your current perspective?

My best guess is that, if you answer at all, it will be with something like "In actuality, nobody is ever born." But this kind of slippery answer is pretty unsatisfactory, so I'm optimistically hoping for something else.

There is almost no interest left in the personal past anymore, and none whatsoever in the subject of your question. There used to be an interest in psychotherapeutic stories around birth, but these have all died away. Unsatisfactory or not, that is the case. Sorry.

❀

ELECTRONIC VOICE PHENOMENA

You confidently declare that the dead do not communicate with the living. The evidence from research into Electronic Voice Phenomena* proves you wrong.

Well, I'd say that settles it then. Unless of course you happen to know anything about psychology, perception, cognitive biases, self-delusion and wishful thinking.

* Electronic Voice Phenomena (EVP) are random static sounds and other background noises recorded on a variety of electronic devices. They are thought by some parapsychologists to be communications from the dead.

❀

234

TURMOIL

I am still hoping that the story of me may collapse. Reading what you write, it seems so easy, but then I am left feeling amazed at how much I still cling to regrets about the past, nostalgia, fear of the future and unfavourable comparisons of myself with others.

Did you once experience a lot of turmoil? Does seeing This free us from turmoil?

I feel from other conversations that you and I have had that you have a very good understanding of this. But I know that, frustratingly, understanding does not put an end to our searching and our yearning.

The things you mention, the past, the future, regrets, nostalgia, fear, comparisons with others, are likely all to continue to exert a hold over us until it is seen that there is no one who is subject to any of them.

Nevertheless, while there is still the sense of a person, there is often something we can do to make ourselves more comfortable in spite of the presence of these things.

Yes, I had much turmoil in what I once thought was my life. Now turmoil may arise or it may not, but it is seen that there is no one who is subject to it.

❋

LIFE IS A WONDERFUL MYSTERY

I relate very much to what you write. Since childhood it's been seen that form is emptiness and emptiness is form. There is no time. There's only an abyss of silence and stillness in which timeless being expresses itself, ever new and ever fresh.

This is not seen by 'me', the character, but by a kind of presence looking over my shoulder. I don't mean that either literally or metaphorically. Neither word quite fits. Isn't language difficult?

There's always been a character here which has its own flavour. That's never been a problem. It has its own momentum and it usually glides through life with some equanimity.

Life is a wonderful mystery.

That's it!

✸

I'VE GOT IT—WELL NOT ME

After all the questions I've asked you on the phone and all the time I've spent reading your books and listening to your talks I've finally got it. Well, not exactly me, of course. Now I understand why you sometimes say you quite like watching paint dry.

And now I can see that it's so simple but also why neither you nor anyone else has ever really been able to put it into words. As you say, it's like trying to nail custard to the wall. Nevertheless, thank you so much for trying and risking getting custard in your hair.

Now I'm going back to watching paint dry.

It's great to read this. By the way, not only do I quite like watching paint dry, I also like watching paint that's already dry.

✸

IS THIS THE END?

I feel exhausted with seeking. I've developed a lot of therapeutic strategies to make life easier, but though they work to some extent they feel as if they are only dealing with issues on the cognitive level.

I feel I'm in what you call the desert. I go back and forth between relaxation and striving. I feel like I'm in a trap where sometimes I'm fully immersed in life and sometimes I'm a bystander. About a year ago I had a glimpse of what you write about, and since then there has been a big reduction in my neurotic thinking. But my sense of 'doership' is definitely still here to some extent. I still feel like the author of 'the story of my life'. And my sense of longing to finally lose myself is still here.

I feel I've gone as far as I can go with this in terms of my understanding, which has outstripped my experience of this. I understand, as Alan Watts pointed out, that because the ego is fake, no action that the ego can take can resolve the ego's problems. What a paradox! What a bummer! And here I apparently still am, not able to see This as enough.

For example, I fully understand that choice is an illusion. Indeed how could it be anything else? Free will does not even make sense philosophically. Yet I still feel subject to choice. I feel a 'should' or an 'ought' come up for me but then it fades away pretty quickly. Of course this makes life more relaxing than it used to be but it's still a cognitive response, not the 'real deal' of selfless seeing. It's like living with an admittedly beautiful picture of the countryside, which is not the same as actually being in the countryside. There are moments of absolutely clear seeing, periods of complete stillness, times of absolute presence, but then they fade. When they've faded it feels like I, the person, am there again.

Perhaps I'm expecting too much. Perhaps I'm expecting too much permanent clarity when This is really seen. I know that many teachers say "It really is just this. It really is what you already are." But somehow I'm still expecting something more. Is there anything you can say to all of this?

You write very clearly about this and much of what you write is experienced by many other individuals.

A couple of points come to me. Firstly, it is not always the case that when this is seen, it is seen clearly and distinctly. This is because it is subtle, and the mind is a clever little monkey that can make mischief out of any slight doubt. There are cases where everything that there is to be seen has been seen, but the thought still comes up that "This isn't it" or "This can't be it." Usually these thoughts accrete around the sense that "If this is it, it should be better than this!" But liberation contains every possibility, including the ones that the ego considers uncomfortable.

Of course I can't know whether this is the case with you but it may be.

Another possibility is that you are in that state between awakening and liberation which Tony Parsons calls 'me-ing' and 'be-ing', where the seeing of this comes and goes. Sometimes this may be brought to a sudden end by another event, but sometimes there is just a gradual sliding into more 'be-ing' and less 'me-ing' which is hardly noticed.

✺

CHRISTIANITY

What do you think of Christianity?

Christianity is a myth. A myth is a story that many people believe for a long time even though there is a huge amount of evidence that it isn't true.

✺

IN THE DESERT

I feel you will get fed up with me writing to you. I'm still holding on to the drama of my life, still in the desert. I'm still holding on to my old life while wanting desperately to be rid of it.

I used to find comfort and meaning in spiritual paths and 'the guru story'. I spent times in ashrams. But now I feel I've lost all that. I feel like the devotee who felt so calm and peaceful while sitting at the feet of his guru, but when he came down from the mountain and back into the hustle and bustle of everyday life, realised that he had gained nothing that he could hold on to. In the peace of the mountain it felt like the truth, but in the chaos of the subway it's realised that it's not. It was an illusion of being free, dependent on the mountain air. Perhaps it was even oxygen starvation!

I guess I just want to complain to you. You've already answered all the questions I had! But being caught in this in-between place is horrible. No wonder there are so many religions, teachers and gurus out there pandering to the needs of people like me.

The thoughts and feelings that you express are very common among those who feel themselves to be caught in the desert between awakening and liberation. Many individuals experience a similar frustration.

The feeling of regret at the loss of the old spiritual paths is particularly common. You describe very well how many of us, as long as we remain in the rarified ashram air, can feel that we have attained some blessed state. But when we leave the ashram and return to 'real life', we often come down to earth with a bump. Ram Dass (Richard Alpert) expressed this very well.

The amount of despair I feel seems to depend on how much I hold on to my outdated beliefs. But the loss of belief, the existential pain that I feel and my need still to have stories in my life, certainly cause me big trouble! The loss of meaning in my life is especially painful.

I feel caught between wanting to give up control and an addiction to controlling whatever and whoever I can.

My life was always sustained by a vision of what living in enlightenment would mean. This would be a state of perfect peace, perfect harmony, awash with love and light. Realising that this vision has nothing to do with This has also been very painful.

Are there any answers or is there only unknowing?

Finally, the idea of choice really challenges me. But if there is no free will, then is it true that I never made any wrong choices?

You make some very good points about your experiences which I know are shared by many others who have been 'caught by nonduality' but for whom it is not yet all over.

Here are a few brief comments on the points that you raise:

Both holding on to and having to let go of beliefs can equally bring despair.

The loss of meaning is especially potent in bringing about the possibility of despair.

The need to control and the fear of loss of control is almost universal.

Clinging to what you call 'a vision' is also common. The recognition that this is a chimera can be devastating.

There are no answers, but when the self is finally seen through there can be a great relaxation into the complete unknowing that is seen. Then all these apparent problems may fall away and all these questions simply dissolve.

You never made any choices, so you never made any wrong choices. From the point of view of non-duality, what would a 'wrong choice' even mean? That's a rhetorical question by the way. It does not have an answer.

I find myself reminiscing a great deal about the past. I am full of regrets, nostalgia and resentment which I don't seem able to shake off. I recognise that I also have a powerful tendency to idealise the past and to wish, as it were, that I was back there. This deepens my sense of dissatisfaction with the present. I can recognise all this but I seem helpless to do anything about it. Can you help?

Once way in which separation sometimes manifests is in an acute understanding of the ways in which we torture ourselves, for example with thoughts of an idealised past. It is common for us to feel that we cannot stop this self-torture.

I don't make recommendations, but I do notice that many individuals find relief from this when they redirect their attention away from the stories of self-torture in the head towards the visceral feelings that underlie these in the body.

I have tried focussing on my body sensations instead of my thoughts and I've found it helpful up to a point. But eventually I always seem to find my attention being drawn back to my thoughts and my ideas about the past.

You describe the way thoughts or ideas take our attention away from our felt sense when we attend to the feelings in the body. This is very common. In fact I would say it is pretty much universal. It doesn't prevent attending to the felt sense from being effective. We simply return to the felt sense when we are able to and keep on doing that.

I have been listening to Tony Parsons for a long time and also phoning him, asking him many questions at his meetings and in private. Finally he looked at me and said, in quite a kindly way I thought, "There is no answer." Do you agree? Is there an answer?

Tony's "There is no answer" is absolutely right. But we can't expect the mind to be satisfied with this. So although there is no answer, the mind can't help seeking one, until finally the questions dissolve. This happens when it is seen that there is no one asking them.

This really is a mystery, isn't it? I feel like I have been on a journey into the abyss. I think I remember you using a phrase like this in one of your talks that I attended. Sometimes this abyss seems to lead to an incredible peace, sometimes it leads to suffering. But there doesn't seem to be any possibility of escape. Even thought there is still searching, I know that there is nothing to reach.

I think of Shakespeare's description of life as "a tale told by an idiot". I think we are all idiots but now I see the possibility of the idiot living a new kind of life.

The phrases in your message really resonate with me. This is indeed a real mystery. It can be a journey into the abyss, as many mystics have written. And beyond the abyss is sometimes peace.

There is also no escape possible. How could you escape from what is? And there is nothing to reach. Even worse, there is no one to reach it.

"The idiot living a new kind of life" is, I think, how many would describe this too.

A MULTITUDE OF QUESTIONS

Is it possible to live a liberated life if you have a family? Do you have to pretend still to be concerned about others? Are members of your family jealous, thinking that you know a secret that they don't?

How do you know it's all an illusion? And as it's all an illusion, why do you bother to go on living your life?

How can the reality of what you write ever be verified?

As there is no person and no choice and this is a dream, is it okay for me to steal or to commit other crimes?

Should I talk to my parents about this? I can see that it might upset them.

What leads you to the concept of unconditional love?

Unconditional love is not a concept. Unconditional love is revealed in its fullness by direct seeing. This is also the only possible 'verification'.

Life, in general and with one's family, simply goes on. That is why in Zen it is said "Before liberation, chop wood. After liberation, chop wood." It is simply seen that there is no one who any longer owns that life.

An illusion literally means "something which deceives by producing a false or misleading impression of reality". In this proper sense, this could be said to be an illusion but I have never said or written "It's all an illusion". I have used the word 'appearance' and the metaphor that this is 'a waking dream'. I've also said "This is both real and unreal", with apologies for the paradox. This is as real as anything gets. But it can also be likened, in some substantive ways, to a night-time dream.

I am not going to advise you as to whether, as this is a dream, you should steal or not. Do you want to? If so, bear in mind that you might be chased and caught by the dream police and thrown into a dream prison.

It is probably wise to be cautious whom you talk to about non-duality, whether it is your parents, your friends or others. Particularly if you describe an awakening event, those closest to you might mistake it for psychosis and be unnecessarily alarmed. They might even call a psychiatrist.

❋

PHYSICAL PAIN

Although I seem to be experiencing more 'open space' recently, I find that this tends to disappear when I am in physical pain. In fact it seems to me that physical pain almost necessarily takes us away from simplicity and into the ownership of something, even if it's only the ownership of the body.

I'm feeling that I have a further problem arising out of this. I feel that this experience shouldn't be happening to me, that it's a sign that I'm still 'imperfect', and that until it stops my life is fucked. It's as if I'm wanting to find obstacles to simple being at any cost.

By the way, did you feel totally inadequate and that you were going crazy before seeing This?

You comment on your own points very well. Pain is pain, and if there is physical pain the sensible thing to do is whatever might relieve it on the physical level. The experience you have that pain can appear to increase the sense of ownership, or as I would put it, contraction, is very common.

The idea that "This shouldn't be happening to me" is another way we can torture ourselves. It adds a rather grandiose story to the simplicity of what is happening. Then other stories might be added such as "I am imperfect" and "Until this goes away I can't be fine". On and on they go, stories on top of stories, each one keeping us on the hamster wheel of samsara. The fact that you are recognising these stories so clearly is probably a sign that they are loosening their grip on you.

I didn't feel I was going crazy and I didn't feel totally inadequate. I felt despair and hopelessness.

❊

BABBLE

I've read and watched many people talking about non-dual philosophy. It often seems to me like just so much babble and distortion of what is really very simple.

It seems to me that it all just comes down to the realisation that life is living me rather than the other way round. In this realisation, all is well.

Yes, non-duality is actually very simple, but the mind wants to make it complicated so it comes in with all its 'babble' and 'distortion'.

You are right, this is about seeing that life is living you rather than the other way round.

❊

WHAT OTHERS WRITE

Would you agree that U. G. Krishnamurti, Alan Watts and some others are saying the same as you in different words?

It seems to me that no matter what we do, the 'me' goes on trying to survive in numerous ways. Trying to do something about this, or not trying to do anything about it, both seem hopeless to me.

Many others have said and are saying the same thing. I like the basics of what U. G. Krishnamurti says very much, though I think some of his writings are rather 'left field'. I read Alan Watts many years ago and liked him but recently I revisited 'The Book on the Taboo Against Knowing Who You Are'. The first page is great but then it starts getting unnecessarily complicated.

The 'me' can't help trying to survive. It's what it does. But remember, it's an illusion which is trying to survive and when it's gone, it's gone. As you say, it's hopeless. Realising this can be a great blessing.

❊

IS NON-DUALITY A RELIGION?

I feel that what you and others are saying about non-duality is just like another religion. Many people are desperate, so they are following this as if it were a religion. Going to one of your meetings could be compared to a Catholic going to confession.

You offer a comparison between what I am saying and religions. The differences to me are very clear.

Firstly, those who preach religions have an agenda. They wish to persuade you into sharing their beliefs. There is no interest in me in anyone adopting any beliefs about non-duality. To put it bluntly, I don't give a fuck. Popes and priests usually do give a fuck.

Secondly, religions are awash with superstitions. A superstition is an improbable belief held on insufficient evidence. There are no superstitions in my communication about non-duality.

Lastly, religions attempt to construct beliefs. My communication about non-duality attempts to deconstruct beliefs.

❊

IS ANYONE MAKING DECISIONS?

I can't see how it's possible to see that there's no one making decisions and that this e-mail is writing itself. That just seems ridiculous to me. But if it isn't ridiculous, surely there must be a process that can get me to this conclusion. So what can you advise me to do, either to reach this conclusion, or in the meantime while I'm waiting to reach it?

It's not possible to see that there is no one making decisions until the self has been seen through. Then it becomes obvious.

If seeing through the self were a conclusion, it would be possible to get to it through a process. But seeing through the self is simply what happens when there is no one there to see it. Nothing that the mind concludes about it has any bearing here.

I don't give advice. I hope it's obvious why not. But if I did give advice, it would be to relax. No effort of the mind will get non-duality to reveal itself.

❋

AWAKENING CAN BE PAINFUL

I am experiencing a lot of desperation and frustration. You have written that you used to phone Tony Parsons to vent your frustration, and that Tony once said "I hope you die soon" to you. I feel I may be in a similar space to you when you did this. I feel like my life is an empty play. It's very difficult for me to feel any real contact with other people and my communication with them becomes increasingly difficult.

Although the feeling of being an observer of life offers me some protection and comfort, this is now becoming more painful as I increasingly feel the loneliness of being in this situation. I feel more and more desolate and more and more I want 'me' to end. And I know there's no going back to the old ways now.

And in spite of what I have written above, I do sometimes feel that the small details of life are exquisitely beautiful, like the moments I notice my cat purring on my lap.

I would very much appreciate your comments.

You write very clearly about what many individuals experience when they are as it were "caught between seeing and not seeing". I remember myself how frustrating this felt after an initial glimpse of Oneness that then seemed lost. And you're right, I used to phone Tony and he'd suggest that I just do something simple that I enjoyed. It sounds as if you may already be taking this very good 'non-advice'. I can say nothing better than that now. Go on noticing, as you are doing, the simple things and their exquisite beauty.

The difficulties with other people during this period are also very common.

Someone who has just written to me because he is also suffering a lot at the moment told me that Claire, Tony's wife, said to him the other day: "Remember. It can end in a moment."

Thank you very much for your reply. Your 'non-advice' has encouraged me to notice the simple enjoyable things in life even more. And I like what Claire said.

❀

NEGATIVE THOUGHTS

I think I've heard you say at a meeting that negative thoughts can still continue after liberation. Is that correct?

To name certain thoughts 'negative' is to make a value judgement about them which implies a story. I prefer to use the phrase 'uncomfortable thoughts'. This simply describes their emotional impact.

Anything can occur when liberation is seen because there are no rules. To declare that "Uncomfortable thoughts are impossible after liberation" would be imprisonment, not liberation.

So yes, uncomfortable thoughts can still occur. The likelihood, though, is that these will become less frequent and less compelling.

First thoughts may be written in concrete. Then they may be in written in sand, then in water and finally in air.

❀

DETERMINING YOUR TRUE NATURE

A well known non-duality teacher recently said to me that if I determined what my true nature was, that would constitute realisation.

Do you agree? Also, what is your day-to-day experience like now? For example, is it filled with tranquility?

It is not possible for you to determine your true nature, because it is the sense of 'you' that is the problem. When you are not there anymore, the true nature of everything reveals itself.

Go back to the well-known non-duality teacher and ask them how you would set about determining what your true nature is. Also ask them whether this is what they did. If they say it was, ask them how they did it.

I would also be cautious of anyone who described themself as a non-duality teacher, as non-duality cannot be taught.

There is nothing special about the day-to-day experience once non-duality has been seen. Sometimes there is tranquility here, sometimes there isn't. Everything is impermanent so no experience lasts for long. In fact, impermanence is one of the most obvious facts of existence.

❀

DOUBTING AWAKENING

When I was a young boy, everything you talk about seemed obvious to me. I even thought to myself that one day I will tell people that death doesn't exist.

When I was older I started seeking. Whether as a result of this or not, I went through a dramatic awakening experience and after that there was suddenly only This and it was seen that Nothing and Everything are the same and there is only Presence. Life is a kind of dream. Unconditional love is the case.

Later on it seemed that I was back in duality and seeking started again. Although sometimes there was still just Presence, the mind with its stories seemed to get more and more of a grip on me again. So now it feels like I have lost something of great value and this is very painful. It makes me feel inferior. But when I listen to you or Tony it feels like I am remembering what it is again.

I remember you saying to me once that I should consider writing about this. I lack confidence in doing this, but nevertheless perhaps now finally I will.

I relate to what you write and I know of others who would too.

It sounds from your description as though everything that there is to be seen has been seen. But the mind has a habit of reasserting itself and seeding doubts. So even though it's clearly seen that "This is it", thoughts arise that say "No, it isn't! There must be something more!" In this way, seeking manages to gain a foothold again and we're back on the hamster wheel of becoming.

You may find that in the act of writing about this, more clarity comes and doubts may fall away. If you're doubtful about your writing, it's probably best to write spontaneously and in an uncensored way and then only go back to edit what you've written later.

❋

IS THIS AWAKENING?

I know that I understand a great deal about non-duality intellectually, but I also know that this intellectual understanding is pretty much worthless.

I once saw clearly that there is simply causeless joy and that this is what gives rise to everything. It was obvious that there was no such thing as a separate person—or indeed even any separate object. After a time, the sense of my being a separate person came back.

Ever since then I've been frantically trying to get back to that experience (which I know is not an experience. Even trying to write to you about this is frustrating!). I've been reading everything about this I can read, watching everyone I can watch, going to see anyone who seems to understand something about this.

I've got to the end of my tether with this. I want an end to the frustration. I want 'me' to be finished. Do you think that when this will happen is predestined? Is there any point in my spending time with someone who is awakened?

I suspect that I know pretty much how you're going to answer this. But the temptation to write to you is too strong.

Yes, you probably know that I am going to reply "Who is there who predestination could happen for?" and "If spending time with someone who is awakened happens, it happens." And I know how profoundly unhelpful that can sound to the one who still feels that they are searching.

From what you describe, I wonder whether for you everything that there is to be seen has already been seen, but that there is still a thought hanging on that "This isn't It." This occurs for quite a number of individuals because of a belief that "If this is It, it should be better than this." But 'this' is always exactly what it is and after liberation life simply goes on. Before, chop wood. After, chop wood, as they say in Zen.

Your reply feels as if it may be right in my case. There's a kind of recognition that This is it, despite the thought that it isn't. I know this sounds paradoxical.

Nevertheless I still miss the event when 'I' simply wasn't there, when there was just absolute love and silence and stillness. Now people, objects and 'I' feel separate again. It seems natural to want to get back to that experience of non-separation.

I make the distinction between contraction and localisation. Both disappear in a liberation event. After a while, localisation always returns, but contraction does not. I feel from what you write that this may be the case with you, but I can't be sure. It's worth considering though.

After there had been the total disappearance of separation here, and then a return to a sense of location, I phoned Tony Parsons. One of the things he said to me was "It will probably never be like that again." That was profoundly helpful and allowed me to let go of any expectation the mind had of returning to that 'state' (which is not a state). It also proved accurate, both for myself and for many other individuals that I have talked to.

CONTEMPLATING NAVELS

I believe what you say about non-duality is true, but I can't see how it's possible to live in a non-dual way other than intellectually.

And why are you so driven to hold meetings about it all the time? Surely if non-duality is really a lived actuality for you, then you shouldn't need anything more than your 'walk round a lake and a cup of coffee'!

All that non-duality does for me is reinforce my unhappiness as I endlessly contemplate my navel.

Belief and living this intellectually have no value. This is either seen or it is not seen. If it is seen, then life simply goes on.

I am not "driven to hold meetings about it all the time". But occasionally talking about this happens and it can be fun. The trouble with 'Why' questions is that they always assume a reason, often where there is none. Your question is "Why hold meetings?" The obvious answer is "Why not?"

I don't make recommendations, but if I did it would be to relax and do some small simple thing that you enjoy, rather than endlessly contemplating your navel.

CONTRACTION AND LOCALISATION

Dear Richard, I have been experiencing fewer and fewer thoughts lately. My identification with any sense of a separate person is fading.

Yet on a very subtle and non-dual level, and even though identification with the old self has gone, there still seems to be someone here. Out of nothing still arises the sense that 'I' exist even though there is stillness and peace. I feel that I exist not as a person that can be labelled, but simply as pure existence.

This subtle sense of 'I' doesn't cause any suffering, but I believe that my ego still has to completely die. It's as if the ego needs to kill the ego. But another part of me believes that this remaining part of 'me' cannot and does not need to disappear. Can you help me with this? Best wishes, Thorsten

Dear Thorsten, The ego, which is only a series of thoughts, cannot kill the ego, nor does it need to.

It sounds from your description that what you are experiencing is simply the sense of location, which always returns after a 'liberation event' during which all sense of bodily location may be lost. The sense of location is simply the sense that awareness is localised where the body-mind organism is, rather than 'everywhere'.

If the sense of contraction has been lost, then it is all over, even when this sense of location returns. Best wishes, Richard

Dear Richard, It's as if my old habits of mind are slowly losing their momentum. In your experience, can this happen? Best wishes, Thorsten

Dear Thorsten, Yes, this often happens. After liberation is seen, any neurotic energy or old habits of thinking that remain tend to wind down either gradually or quickly. But there are no rules, so anything can happen, and it doesn't matter whether they wind down or not. It just makes life more comfortable if they do. Best wishes, Richard

❁

AWAKENING OR SICKNESS?

I thought I was sick but now I think it's awakening. It's taken me a long time to realise this. Some of the time it's fun.

Perhaps I'll write a book about it now. The sun is shining and I'm putting on weight. What are you up to?

Great! The sun is shining here as well, though I'm not putting on weight. Good luck if you write a book about this.

✻

WHAT PRECIPITATES NON-DUAL SEEING?

Non-duality is familiar to me from Zen Buddhism and I've even come across it in Christianity. There have been a few 'flashes' here but I feel a mounting frustration because a real seeing of non-duality seems as far away as ever. I know a great deal of theory about it, but any door I try to go through seems to turn into a brick wall.

What enabled you to bridge the gap between theory and practice and precipitate the seeing of This? Can you help me to bridge that gap?

I know it's frustrating, but I can't tell you what precipitated the seeing of This here. Awakening and liberation are spontaneous events in which it's seen that the past that apparently led up to them is a kind of waking dream. So everything that we think we're doing to achieve liberation loses its meaning in even a split second of seeing.

I love your metaphor of any door through which we try to get to non-duality actually turning into a brick wall.

I hope it's obvious why I offer no advice, although if it is possible to relax and enjoy the small things in life, that tends to make life more comfortable.

Are you still practising as a psychotherapist? I'm thinking of training but I'm worried in case seeing non-duality makes it difficult to practise.

I've heard you say that liberation ruined your life, because everything that you thought you had learned lost its meaning. Did this impact on you as a psychotherapist? There is another part of me that thinks that seeing through separation might be very helpful when working psychotherapeutically with people. Do you have any comment on this?

For many years I was involved with therapy and counselling but mostly as a lecturer and trainer rather than as a practitioner. A lot of my work was in psycho-education.

I have come across some people working in psychology and psychotherapy who have had a crisis about the value of their work when they became interested in non-duality. But for me there is definitely no conflict. In fact I agree with you that it is probable that seeing non-duality would improve an individual's work as a psychotherapist.

It would be more accurate to say that seeing liberation ruins what we thought was our life. It also reveals, of course, that there was in any case no one who ever had a life.

If you decide to do your training, I wish you well in it and hope you enjoy many years of practice.

❈

PRIMAL AND CAUSAL

What do you think of Ken Wilber's idea that there is the primal and the causal? Can Oneness evolve? And can the nature of our seeing of enlightenment evolve?

What do you think of the work of Stan Grof and of regression therapy?

I don't know a great deal about Wilber's idea of the primal and the causal, but from my limited viewpoint I do not see it as anything other than a clever modern re-telling of the good old story of the Absolute and the Relative, or of Brahman and Atman. And as we all know, Brahman and Atman are One. And so are Nirvana and Samsara. And so are the Absolute and the Relative.

I think 'primal' and 'causal' is just a way of putting a psychological spin on the Vedanta and Buddhist insights in order to retell them in a way that will make them sound up-to-date for a twentieth and twenty-first century audience. And nothing wrong with that.

In my wild transpersonal therapy days I was very keen on Stan Grof, William Emerson and pre-birth regression, past-life regression and rebirthing. You name it, I did it. And very entertaining it was.

As for Oneness evolving, or 'evolutionary enlightenment' as it is sometimes called, the unchanging Absolute cannot evolve, and it's a bit of a stretch to claim that our seeing of Oneness can or has evolved. How could we possibly know whether we were more sophisticated in our understanding or seeing than five thousand years ago? It's just that we tell different stories about the same thing and then get a bit arrogant about them.

❀

COULD THIS BE LIBERATION?

Dear Richard, When I think of who I really am, I know and feel that I am not the body or the mind. Nevertheless, fear and other concerns still sometimes come up, so I feel I can't have realised freedom yet.

I realise that a person can't make themselves wake up, so what can be done to bring about the freedom that you describe? Best wishes, Rosemary Cochran

Dear Rosemary, When liberation is seen, any kind of feeling and thought can still arise, including fear or sorrow or other concerns. There are sayings in the mystical traditions pointing this out, for example "No one knows sorrow like a Zen master." As long as we think that uncomfortable feelings or thoughts have to be banished, we are caught in the trap of non-acceptance.

I wish I could give you a prescription but I can't. When our head is caught in the tiger's mouth, either the tiger bites our head off or it does not. Maybe yours has already been bitten off. Best wishes, Richard

Dear Richard, Thank you so much for your answer. I had the idea that when liberation is seen, these feelings and thoughts would no

longer be possible, but I have already been thinking that maybe this was just a false idea that I had picked up reading about 'spiritual' stuff.

Whenever I looked for who I am, I found nothing. But I still thought that this couldn't be liberation if there were such 'human' feelings coming up.

Now I've read your answer, that stuff has just dropped away, I'm very happy to say! And while I was walking on the beach this morning with my dog it dawned on me that it has absolutely no importance whether liberation has been seen or not anyway! Best wishes, Rosemary Cochran

❁

OUR ORIGINAL STATE

During your recent talk I believe that you said that there was an original state of openness which was then removed by adult treatment, but that this Oneness was somehow remembered. Have I got that right?

It's very difficult to put this into words, but I probably said that there is only Oneness but within this at a certain very young age a sense of separation or self-consciousness arises.

Rather than Oneness being somehow remembered, I would say that there is a sense of loss, or incompleteness, without there being the possibility of knowing what that sense of loss is really about. From this begin all the different kinds of searching for satisfaction, whether through material, spiritual, psychological or emotional means.

Although this searching can be colourful, dramatic, entertaining and even for a while fulfilling, ultimately we are still left with the sense of loss until the sense of being a separate individual drops away and there is the direct seeing that All Is One.

Surely it's impossible to say anything about the non-dual from the position of the non-dual. In order to say anything about it, people like you have to move back into the dual. Otherwise there's nothing to talk about and no one to talk about it.

So when you talk about this, what you really do is move into the non-dual and then come back and say something. This only approximates to what you would have said from the non-dual if you could have said anything while you were there—which you can't!

I'm not sure exactly how a person "moves into the non-dual". Do they need a bicycle? And what should they pack?

Your confident assertions about non-duality obviously imply that newborns are incomplete and not real persons. In what way is this the case?

No, newborns are complete. Or rather they are completeness.

It is 'real persons' who are incomplete, or rather who face the problem of feeling incomplete. This is because they feel separated from Oneness.

You are suggesting that the great spiritual teachers say that before birth we were whole and part of the Oneness, that we were truly present then without distortions of any kind. This is not the case.

This is a great misunderstanding of what I am saying.

There is no chance that we were ever whole or ever will be. We are not whole, there is only wholeness. This cannot be seen while we are there—that is, while there is still a sense of being a separated person.

Likewise, we are not "part of the Oneness" because Oneness does not have parts. What we are is Oneness appearing as an individual. And we were never truly present, there is only presence. Paradoxically and frustratingly this can only be known in our absence.

Then we seem to agree that the Oneness did not exist at birth.

When was there ever a time when there was not Oneness? There is only Oneness, in which apparent differentiation arises.

There is evidence that children can be spiritual, but this is not at its peak at or before birth and then tails off, as you suggest.

I do not suggest this. But in any case, Oneness has nothing to do with being spiritual or not being spiritual. In non-duality, all distinction between 'spiritual' and 'non-spiritual' disappears. It therefore makes as much sense to say that everything is spiritual or to say that nothing is spiritual.

The world in which the Buddha lived two and a half thousand years ago is not the same as the world today. Our understanding has pro-gressed, so the fullness experienced now has more to it than then.

All the levels which various traditions have postulated are not pre-existing and eternal. They change and develop. Enlightenment changes and develops.

In Oneness a dream of time arises and the dream apparently changes. So what?

Oneness has absolutely no interest in levels nor in enlight-enment. Levels and enlightenment are invented by humans to flatter our egos.

❋

A COURSE IN MIRACLES

What do you think of A Course In Miracles?

I can do no better than to quote Michael Graham about ACIM: "For the life of me, I could never find anyone who had got the least demonstrable benefit from the Course [In Miracles]."

❋

THE COSMIC JOKE

Liberation seems to me to be a great cosmic joke. Part of the joke is that it turns out that liberation has nothing to do with bliss. Come to think of it, it doesn't really have anything to do with anything, does it? It's just life doing its thing, whatever that happens to be.

Yes, it's a great cosmic joke. And seeing This definitely has nothing to do with bliss, although of course bliss may sometimes arise. Your description is very good. There's an energy shift and then life just goes on doing its thing, whatever that is.

❀

DESPAIR ON AWAKENING

I've been feeling like writing to you for a while. Now I don't know if I'm communicating with you directly or through one of your staff.

I know you've talked about the possibility that after an awakening event there might be both despair and a loss of motivation.

I don't know whether for me there have been some awakening experiences. I don't really know how to distinguish these from phenomena that are just psychological in their nature. I am quite a sceptical person, but I have had what I would call 'non-ordinary' experiences.

For example, there was an experience of loving emptiness. That left me in great peace, with everything that was happening afterwards seeming empty.

On another occasion I took a hallucinogenic drug and was left knowing that "nothing mattered". The absolute knowing of this went on for some time and re-configured who I was. Many of my beliefs and inhibitions fell away leaving me a much less ego-centred person. Could you comment on any of this?

Luckily your message bypassed my dozens of staff including my under-butler and came directly to me.

These sound like 'awakening events', although I'd be a little wary of the post-hallucinogenic drug one, purely for that reason.

Seeing liberation can be quite undramatic and, once it's established, very ordinary. It may be that it's already all over for you.

The loss of ordinary motivation is quite common after awakening. So is despair, but this usually dies away with a lot of other junk once liberation is seen.

❋

DIFFERENCES IN INTERPRETATION OF NON-DUALITY

Recently I've become very interested in non-duality so I've been watching a lot of interviews on the internet. In one of these you were in discussion with Timothy Freke on conscious.tv. Would you agree that there are differences of interpretation between you? If there are, what lies at the core of them?

Many of those who say they are speaking about non-duality are actually engaged in teaching paths and practices or in teaching a philosophy of 'how to live in an Advaita way'. They are selling hope.

Others are simply offering a description of what it is like when the sense of self has been seen through. With these, I have not really noticed any substantive differences, except that each has their own flavour, depending on their character.

❋

AWAKENING

For some reason that I don't fully understand, I find your approach to Advaita very congenial to me. I've just finished 'The Book of No One' and I've finally realised that there is nothing for me to do. So no more paths and techniques for me—I've started to genuinely feel that there is no 'I' to practise any of them.

Some time ago I had what may or may not have been an awakening. There was the recognition of something vast and boundless, something which somehow had always been known. Time no longer existed and, in a way I can't explain, neither did place. It was as if all places were simply one place. There was no longer any 'here' and 'there'.

This lasted for a very brief moment during which 'I' was completely absent. Then 'I' came back. In some ways this leaves me feeling like a lunatic and in some ways as if I am sane for the first time in 'my' life.

I don't know whether that was an awakening. If it was, then somehow I feel gratitude to your book.

By the way, I love the quotation you give from Max Furlaud—"At death there is only liberation. It is just more chic to see liberation when you are alive." As a seeker, I find that very comforting.

I love your description and recognise it clearly. That was an awakening.

❀

U.G. KRISHNAMURTI

Have you read U.G. Krishnamurti? If so, what do you think of him?

Do you find communication with others difficult after seeing This? Talking about trivial things is okay, but once things go deep, I often feel like I am walking on eggshells, trying not to hurt people's feelings—especially if they have strong spiritual beliefs. It's like the "Don't mention the war" sketch from 'Fawlty Towers'.

I've read U.G. Krishnamurti. He is very uncompromising and I like him. But his account of awakening is quite weird with a few strange and extraneous ideas woven into it.

I relate to what you say about communication—especially with those still following a spiritual story whose feelings you don't want to hurt.

❀

DEATH AND ATTACHMENTS

If all I am is 'a soup of energy' why do I feel attachments? When I die, how meaningful will those attachments be?

What is death? Are you afraid of it?

I don't recognise the description that we are 'a soup of energy'. I'd need to think about that metaphor before I commented on it further, but my off-the-cuff response is that it doesn't mean much to me.

Attachments are attachments. They are part of the stuff that arises in this. They often accrete around neurosis. When liberation is seen, a lot of neurotic energy tends to dissipate, so attachments are quite likely to become less sticky.

Death is the end of the dream of separation. When liberation is seen concerns about death often fall away. This is partly because it is seen that what we really are was never born and so can never die. The recognition of unconditional love also plays a part in the disappearance of concerns about death.

However, this has nothing to do with feelings about the body-mind organism going through the process of dying. It is natural for the organism to want to be comfortable and to seek to avoid discomfort.

❄

IDENTIFYING THE DESIRES BEHIND SUFFERING

A non-duality teacher has advised a friend of mine to overcome her suffering by identifying the desires behind it. I can't see any point in this advice. Can you comment?

I can't see any point in this teacher's advice either.

Coincidentally I've just received a phone call from someone in the US who is in a pleasurable relaxed state at the moment. He wants to know how it can be maintained. But seeing non-duality is not about being in any particular state. It is seeing that which all states arise out of. It contains pleasurable states and not-so-pleasurable states, joy and sorrow, pleasure and pain.

❊

PASSING ONE'S TIME AND SUFFERING

You have said that it doesn't matter how one passes the time—that all activities are equal. That might sound fine and dandy from a mystic's viewpoint, but I'm sure it's not appreciated by those who are suffering.

I have not said that "It doesn't matter how one passes the time". I have said something far more radical—that there is no one who has a life with time in it to pass. The sense that there is a separate person who can make meaningful choices about how they pass their time is an appearance somewhat like a night-time dream. Just as a night-time dream can suddenly end, so can the dream of separation. Then it is seen that there is only This, in which time and activities apparently arise.

You raise the issue of suffering. Very little sense has ever been written about this. Religions and spiritual doctrines try to explain suffering, usually by saying either that the ways of God are mysterious to mankind, or that suffering is the result of karma, the sour fruit of negative actions committed in this or in a past life. Both of these explanations are equally stories, best summed up in the phrase 'baseless speculation'. While we are engaged with them, we are probably missing the miracle of whatever is arising in This, within apparent time.

❊

IS LIBERATION ACAUSAL?

Dear Richard, I resonate very much with your description that liberation is a return to experiencing the world in the same way that we did as a child. I also like the way you seem to value laziness.

I've recently been having some discussions with a friend who has the opinion that you have to do a practice or follow a path to become liberated. He doesn't like what Tony Parsons and you and a few others say. He calls you neo-advaitans.

My view is that liberation is acausal—it lies beyond the relative world. I'm aware that many individuals seem to have awakened by accident or chance. These include Ramana Maharshi, U.G. Krishnamurti, J. Krishnamurti, Nisargadatta, Eckhart Tolle and Byron Katie. Even the Buddha became realised only after he'd given up all practices. Other individuals speaking about this today say that enlightenment happened only after they'd given up practice, often in despair.

My friend says that maybe all these individuals were simply ready to make the final leap, but most people aren't, so they shouldn't just sit back and do nothing. But I don't think you are saying people should actually stop doing anything. My friend likes to quote the well-known words "Enlightenment is an accident, but practice makes you accident-prone."

My view is that Tony Parsons is right:– seeking happens until it doesn't, and that's got nothing to do with who we think we are. But I have to add that for myself, I am very drawn to going to meetings about this, so perhaps that's my practice after all. I'm also drawn to Zen and have practised it, intensively in monasteries at times. But I've noticed that although the monks seem very calm, when they leave the monastery they seem to have a lot of problems and find life outside very hard. Best wishes, Jay

Hi Jay, Your message encapsulates very well a lot of the discussion that goes on around whether practice is necessary or not. There is also a third view that generates a lot of heat on the internet. This is that there is simply no such thing as liberation. I have an acquaintance who is very strongly of this opinion.

Dennis Waite calls these three views traditional advaita (represented by your friend), neo-advaita (represented by Tony and myself among others) and pseudo-advaita (represented by my acquaintance). These views could be summed up in the following three short sentences:-

"There is liberation and a path to liberation."

"There is liberation but no path to liberation."

"There is neither liberation nor a path to liberation."

By the way, Dennis is a convinced traditional advaitist and has written a book denouncing the likes of Tony and myself.

Ultimately all of this is a story which becomes irrelevant if the self drops away and Oneness is seen. Then it is known that nothing 'I' ever did could have had any relevance because there is no 'I' and no time in which the non-existent 'I' could have done anything.

But often the self comes back after an initial awakening and then lays claim to what is now seen as an experience, perhaps the experience of enlightenment. After that it's quite likely that the self will start teaching misleading ideas about how this experience can be attained by others.

Of course none of this matters. It's all simply Oneness doing its sweet, colourful, confusing thing. Best wishes, Richard

Dear Richard, Thanks so much for your reply. I think you are right. I've noticed that the traditional advaitans can get quite angry about the neo-advaitans. I sometimes have to placate my friend to calm him down.

I've been listening to Tony and you lately and a kind of relaxation into being seems to be happening. I don't understand it and it doesn't seem to have anything to do with me.

My friend likes Ken Wilber a lot, but I find him very tough going. Best wishes, Jay

Dear Jay, If you spend a little time on the internet, you'll see that a lot of web-rage is generated around these three kinds of advaita, or three kinds of not-two-ness!

I'm glad you are experiencing some relaxation. The park can be a beautiful place at this time of year and a cup of tea a great joy.

Ken Wilber is extremely complex. Liberation is extremely simple. Best wishes, Richard

❀

DEATH

Tell me everything you can about death.

Death is liberation from the dream of separation.

However, as long as we live with a sense of separation and feel we are living an autonomous life, death may seem like an affront, an insult to our precious individuality, the snatching away of the most valuable of our belongings, 'myself'.

Of course actually the individual dies every night in dreamless sleep, yet in spite of this, the mind cannot imagine its own annihilation.

The easiest way for the mind to deal with death is to make up stories about its continuation after dying. So death becomes seen as a doorway through which the individual passes in the guise of a soul or a spirit. These stories are rich, colourful and enchanting. They are also often mutually contradictory. And for all their variety they tend to revolve around only two key elements.

One of these elements is the idea that we are given one chance to pass the test of life. If we succeed, we will proceed to a joyful eternal life beyond this one. If we fail, we will get no second chance and will be consigned to eternal torture or (a more recent idea) annihilation. Passing the test of life may require faith, belief, good works, rituals or all of these. The three Abrahamic religions in their multifarious forms favour this story though they disagree wildly about the details.

The other element is the idea of spiritual evolution proceeding through numerous rebirths as the soul gradually learns the lessons that will refine and perfect it, eventually carrying it to a state of ultimate enlightenment. A modern fashion is for individuals who are entranced with this story to declare themselves to be 'old souls', meaning that they are nearing the end of their evolutionary path.

A common cultural phenomenon is that it is possible to make a very good living out of the mind's fear of death. Through the invention of Purgatory, the Church was able to boost its earnings enormously. In the Middle Ages priests sold indulgences and in the twenty-first century you can go to a 'future-life therapist' who will help you work through the karmic difficulties that are due to you in your next lifetime. In that way you can deal with them in advance and thus get ahead of the game.

Even Buddhism, which declares clearly that there is no self, generates countless stories of lifetimes past and lifetimes future, in which you may take rebirth in any form from a hungry ghost to a buddha in a heavenly realm. The sangha or community of monks needs to keep these stories alive as otherwise it loses much of its raison d'être.

However, when it is seen that there is no person, that separation is a dream, death ceases to be an issue. No one was ever born, so no one will ever die. What we are is the pure mystery of Being itself. Being is timeless and therefore untouched by birth and death.

We are the light of consciousness and the light of consciousness cannot die.

Death is the end of time and space. Death is the end of the story. Death is the great return to what we already are and always have been. The dying wave returns to the ocean, but the wave was never anything but the ocean.

Even this answer is already a story. And anything else that can be written about death is simply more story.

❀

GURUS

Can gurus help?

No, but they can provide a lot of entertainment.

❀

RELIGION

Would you agree that non-duality is becoming a religion?

Yes, that is simply the way of the world. Non-duality is seen in its simplicity, and then the mind comes in and turns it into a religion.

I think that religion is poisonous. Non-duality appeals to me partly because it doesn't seem to need churches, traditions, scriptures or priests.

Yes, liberation needs nothing.

❀

DREAMS

You suggest that dreams are artificial or fake, that they simply disappear when we wake up. I strongly disagree. The body needs very little sleep for physical rest, so the majority of sleep is devoted to dreaming. They are extremely important.

I have not said that dreams are 'artificial' or 'fake'. They are as real as any other phenomenon that arises. But of course they do indeed 'simply disappear when we wake up'.

Whether we view dreams as important or not depends on the story that we tell about them. In Freud's story, dreams are 'the royal road' to a knowledge of unconscious activities, and are therefore extremely meaningful. Your own story, that dreams are so important that most of sleep is devoted to it, may be scientifically very plausible. There are many other stories about dreams that we can become entranced by. The shaman might say that dreams allow us to visit other dimensions and even engage in 'soul retrieval'. The priest might say that God may speak to us and give us guidance in dreams. The New Age healer might say that the Divine Goddess may come to us in our dreams. The guru might say that dreams enable us to work through our past karma in an effortless way—that it is better to be skewered by a sword in a dream than to have to take rebirth and be skewered by a sword in our next life because of some karmic comeuppance. The psychologist might say that dreams are necessary to eliminate the stresses of the day.

But a dream is simply a phenomenon. Then we might add a meaning to it. The meaning that we add is also a phenomenon, a thought arising in This.

A dream also provides a very good metaphor for awakening and liberation. When liberation is seen, it is realised that this waking state is also a kind of dream, and that like a night-time dream it is both real and unreal. It may be utterly convincing but of course so is a night-time dream—until we wake up in the morning.

❋

DOING AWAY WITH THE SELF

Westerners find it almost impossible to do away with the self or ego. But in the East there is a long tradition that says we must lose the self.

It is not "almost impossible" to do away with the self or ego. It is utterly impossible. This is because we are trying to do away with something that does not exist.

Whether or not we are Westerners has no relevance to this. Since no one has an ego, no one can do away with it. This includes the Indian ascetic living on a small bowl of rice a day. His waist-line might diminish, but not his ego. He cannot diminish what he hasn't got.

You are right that in the East there is a long tradition that says that we must lose the self. This is founded on a belief that is shared by the West, that we are inadequate and must do something to become someone other than who we are right now. The swami, the priest, the mullah, the rabbi are always on hand to instruct us on what we must do about ourself, and of course to take a fair payment for this valuable information.

But there is no one who is inadequate. There is no one who has a self that they can do anything about. There is no one who needs to become someone other than who they are right now.

There is already only the light of consciousness in which everything arises.

❀

THE BENEFITS OF LIBERATION

What are the main benefits of liberation? What is the best way of searching for it? Can you give some examples of people who have found it?

Liberation has no benefits.

Spiritual seekers who are entranced by stories about personal enlightenment might expect great benefits and feel that these can be earned by arduous work, or perhaps by self-denial. These benefits might be imagined as an end to suffering, perpetual bliss, a greatly enhanced aura, magical powers and the envy of our friends. Some spiritual paths offer the promise of enlightenment as the ultimate party-bag.

Religions sometimes promise us eternal delight after death, and spiritual paths sometimes promise us eternal delight in this life, or the next one, or the one after that.

In other words, religions and spiritual paths may appeal to us as a business deal, as something we can negotiate with as we seek to profit from life. But liberation is the one thing we cannot negotiate with. We can't get anything out of it because when liberation is seen, we aren't there.

In some ways liberation can be considered a catastrophe, as it is the end of what we thought had been our life. Whatever had sustained us in our life, whether it was following the guru or going shopping, accumulating wealth and power or being a humble servant of the Lord, is seen through in liberation. It is seen as a story. It may be still enjoyed but it can no longer be taken seriously.

As to ways of searching for liberation, there are many of these but unfortunately they are futile. The one who is seeking liberation is an unreal person. An unreal person cannot discover the reality that there is only Oneness appearing as everything. This can only be seen when the sense of being a person falls away. And nothing precipitates that. Or rather, Nothing precipitates that.

Of course the mind hates hearing this. The mind believes there must be something it can do to discover Oneness, just as it can discover a recipe for a better salad dressing. No matter how often the mind hears that there is nothing it can do, it will misconstrue this into a task, a path or a religion.

Thus there arise the many colourful roads to enlightenment with their gaily-painted stalls offering chakra-clearing workshops, shaktipat, darshan, and opportunities to do karma yoga, meditate on the third eye or hug the divine mother. Much of this provides fun and entertainment, and none of it has any more (or any less) to do with liberation than walking on the beach and throwing a stick for your dog to chase.

I can't give you any examples of people who've found liberation, because no person has ever found it. Liberation is only seen when the person is no longer there obscuring the view. Then it is seen that what we have always been searching for was never lost. It has always been the case. This is the biggest joke of all. What we have been searching for has always been closer to us than we are to ourself.

THE POPULARITY OF NON-DUALITY

How many people are interested in non-duality? How many followers does it have worldwide? Does it matter whether it is popular or not or whether it has a tradition which is maintained?

In general, few people are interested in non-duality. However, amongst spiritual seekers it has become very popular in recent years. As a result, many gurus and spiritual teachers have felt the need to recast their message into an apparently non-dual form. Often this involves the creation of complex stories that feed the seeker's sense of inadequacy and keeps them searching. In other words, they are given yet more complex stuff to do, and may spend many years self-enquiring or experiencing being in The Now. The promise is that eventually there will be enlightenment at the end of the spiritual rainbow. The simple description of Oneness is still very much resisted.

Of course none of this matters in the least.

I don't know how many followers non-duality has. Followers tend to turn it into a religion, with modern versions of pogroms, witch-burnings, the denouncing of heretics and the Inquisition all taking place on the internet. Non-duality generates its fair share of 'web-rage' and there are quite a few non-duality trolls out there in cyberspace.

No, it doesn't matter whether non-duality is popular or not. As to tradition, if everything that had ever been thought, said or written about non-duality were to disappear in a moment, the seeing of liberation would simply arise spontaneously again. There is no teaching or scripture that needs to be preserved for non-duality to be seen over and over again. There is no need for a non-duality church, or for non-duality holy tablets or relics— no need for bejewelled silver reliquaries housing the blackened rotting fingers of non-duality saints.

EGO AND FREE WILL

What are the implications of non-duality for Western notions of the ego and free will? My guess is that many people will not react well if we talk to them about non-duality.

Non-duality undermines these notions. There is no one who has ego or free will.

It is probably a good idea to avoid talking to people in general about non-duality.

❋

RELIGIONS

Does non-duality reveal all religions and philosophies as interchangeable, as valuable or as valueless as each other?

Yes. It's possible that in the seeing of non-duality, we may stop killing each other in arguments over which mythical being we believe created the universe.

Buddhism, existentialism and a cup of tea are equal—except to the mind.

❋

NON-ACTION

Can non-duality bring us to a place of non-action?

No. There is no one who can be brought to such a place. The idea that non-action can be achieved by a person, and that this is a higher state than action, is another spiritual story. This story has gripped many minds in the East and is now infecting many minds in the West.

Try not acting. Let me know when you've achieved it.

NO SELF

You say that there is no self. How do you know?

No answer that I give will be satisfactory to the mind. Nevertheless, I am going to assert that, when This is seen, it is incontrovertible. If you want to reply that I am making a baseless assertion, that is up to you.

When the person is present, Presence is hidden. When the person is absent, Presence is revealed.

As long as there is a person searching for This, it cannot be found, because the person searching for it believes that this isn't it. As liberation can only be seen in the absence of the person, it can never be owned by anyone. Another way of putting this is that liberation is always impersonal. It does not belong to me or to you.

All stories about the finding of personal enlightenment are pointing in the wrong direction, although many of them are very entertaining. We might love the story that, if we give all our money to our guru, live with him in his ashram and meditate on his holy beard, we will become enlightened. This is much more dramatic than the simple noticing of a swallow as it defies the non-existence of time by swooping across the sky.

❀

TIME AND NO SELF

Was there always a time when there was no self?

There is only timeless being. There is only eternity. Eternity is not, as a person might try to imagine it, a very long time and then a little bit more. Eternity is outside time so it is neither very long nor very short.

In timeless eternity a dream of individuality arises in which the self and time come into being together. It is the emergence of self-consciousness that sets the clock ticking. The great game is now underway and from this arises all the joys and sorrows, the gifts and burdens, of being a person.

Self-consciousness brings a sense of separation, a sense of individual identity and even destiny. Now there is the sense that there is time to be filled and, whether it is consciously recognised or not, the existential problem of how to fill it emerges. We may structure the time between birth and death in a thousand noble and ignoble ways—by shopping, by killing heathens for the Lord, by running soup kitchens, by following our beloved guru, by accumulating wealth and power. All solutions to the problem of how a person fills time and gives their life meaning are in a sense equal. And when it is seen that there is no individual and there is no time, all are seen to be equally and gloriously meaningless. In liberation that meaninglessness can be celebrated as all the stories about the importance of our life, our successes and our failures, fall away and what is left is the simple wonder of This.

Time ends when self-consciousness ends. Time ends every night when we go to sleep, and time ends at the death of the person.

❋

DEATH

Is death a concept? Is it an experience? Is it something we have to go through? Is it always going to happen to everyone everywhere?

Of course there can be concepts about death. In fact death has probably generated more concepts and stories than any other subject. As an individual living with a sense of separation we may be fascinated by death, puzzled by death, appalled by death. Death confronts us with the limits of our individual identity. Those who wish to cling to the preciousness of individuality have made up stories throughout history about the continuation of personal identity in some form after death, whether as a soul or spirit, or as a bundle of karmic influences.

Our willingness to give credence to these stories has also proved very profitable to both popes and princes.

What we are, Oneness itself, was never born and therefore can never die. Death is not an experience because in death there is no one to have an experience. Therefore, although in the story of a person the dying process may take place, death itself does not take place. In the story, this is indeed 'always going to happen to everyone and everything everywhere'. But in Oneness it is seen that, as there is only This, nothing is happening, including death.

Does death not get everyone in the end?

In the story, death gets everyone in the end. But when it is seen that actually there is no one for death to get, death loses its fascination. It may even become quite uninteresting.

Does death actually exist?

What we call death is simply the end of the dream of individuality.

❋

LIKING LIBERATION

You have said that even if we find liberation we probably won't like it. Could you comment?

No, I have not said this. I have just pointed out that this is a possibility that is worth considering. For anyone who is desperately seeking, realising the absolute futility of seeking might take some of the desperation away. Although that won't bring liberation closer (because it is already here), it might produce some relaxation and a less stressful life.

❋

UNDERMINING THE FOUNDATION OF EXISTENCE

Your idea that there is no self surely undermines the whole foundation of our existence.

Yes, you are right. The suggestion that there is no self undermines everything in our lives and so there is great resistance to this idea. It undermines all our beliefs, all our achievements, all our moral principles. It undermines all notions of personal freedom, of choice and of responsibility. It undermines all the stories we tell ourselves to give our lives significance, including all stories of progress whether spiritual, psychological, historical, social, political, scientific, technological or economic. It's even undermines our neuroses and the meanings we give to them.

So to most people the suggestion that I do not exist, that I am simply a set of phenomena arising in this, with no unitary self at the core, is complete madness.

But I am not talking about the *idea* that there is no self. I am talking about *seeing* that there is no self, a confrontation with the absolute, a confrontation with the actuality that there is only emptiness at the core of the person. Before we fall into existential despair about this, let me quickly add that the emptiness at the core of the person is a very full emptiness, for it is the emptiness from which everything, every phenomenon, arises.

❋

THOUGHTS ABOUT DEATH

What are your thoughts about death?

I have no thoughts about death, although thoughts about death may arise here. But if they do, they arise impersonally. Actually, it's the same for you and for everyone else, but added on to those impersonal thoughts may be another impersonal thought, "These thoughts are mine. They arise from me."

But if I take your question autobiographically, all I can say is that since the dream of individuality has been seen through here, concerns about death no longer arise in a troubling way. Death is simply the end of the dream of individuality. Anything we add to that statement is a story made up either to comfort or to intimidate the apparent individual. It is obvious from their abundance and diversity that there is a deep fascination with these stories, but nevertheless stories they remain.

Death is a mystery, but so is this simple cup of tea that I am drinking while I write these words. The individual cannot understand how a blade of grass can arise from nothing, so what chance is there for the individual to understand death?

❈

LIVING BY THE TENETS OF LIBERATION

Do you live by the tenets of liberation?

"Living by the tenets of liberation" would just be an idea. It would be living in another story, just like "living by the tenets of Catholicism" or "living by the tenets of Buddhism". It would have no value.

❈

BEING ONE WITH A TRAMP

You write about everyone being one, but I don't think that I want to be one with, for example, the tramp who roots around in the rubbish bin outside my house.

You are not one with the tramp who roots around in the rubbish bin outside your house, nor is he one with you. That would only make sense in a story of individuality where there were different people who could become one with each other. However, the desirability of becoming one with others is a part of many stories of religious and spiritual unfoldment.

Both you and the tramp are already simply Oneness expressing itself as difference.

❀

HAS ANYONE BEEN ALIVE?

Has anyone ever been alive? Or is this simply the wrong question?

There is no such thing as a wrong question. But your question is about time, which does not exist. There is only This and in This aliveness happens.

❀

CAN YOU DO ANYTHING IN LIBERATION?

Does liberation mean that you can do anything because nothing makes any difference?

There is no you, so you cannot do anything.

❀

TERROR OF DEATH

Why are we terrified of death? Does liberation make a difference to this? Does acknowledging the non-existence of the self take away the fear of death?

To the separated searching individual, it seems that what we are was once born and so will one day die. But when non-separation is seen and it is known that what we are is awareness itself, pure being, Oneness, it is known that this was never born and so can never die. Just as a night-time dream ends when we awake in the morning, so this day-time dream ends at death. But the dreamer, Being itself, exists outside time and so is without beginning or end.

Because personal annihilation can seem terrifying, the mind creates many stories about what happens after death. So we develop delusions and elaborate constructs about it. One glance at the many bookshelves of volumes on religious and spiritual philosophies shows how much energy we put into creating stories about a personal life after death, and what we need to do to ensure that our personal continuation will be a happy one.

That so many of these stories deeply contradict one another simply fuels our search. Yet in spite of all their complex rules of behaviour, no one has ever bettered the simplicity of the golden rule. This states "Don't do to others what you would not have them do to you." It is simple enough for a child of seven to understand and provides any moral guidance that may be needed until separation is seen through, whereupon moral guidance becomes irrelevant.

"Acknowledging the non-existence of the self" may be a useful watchdog over fears about death for a person, but it cannot be more than that. When the person is seen through, there is no need for a watchdog any longer.

If there is still a self to be concerned about death, I like the words of Sogyal Rinpoche. He said, heaving with laughter in his inimitable way, "The trouble with you Westerners is that you don't think about death until you're dying, and by then it's rather too late!" Of course, once the self is seen through, this may sound a little too purposive.

❇

MISUNDERSTANDINGS

Do you agree that, where non-duality is concerned, we have to be very careful what words we use, because it is so easy to give rise to misunderstandings?

It doesn't matter if misunderstandings occur. Understanding is no better than misunderstanding. It is certainly no more helpful. And sometimes misunderstandings give rise to more fun.

❋

MEETING THE BUDDHA

What do you think of the Buddha? To my mind he was a being of great wisdom. I would dearly have liked to have met him.

The Buddha is a thought arising in This.

❋

NON-DUALITY AND RELIGIONS

There is a problem for me when non-duality is related to religions such as Buddhism or Hinduism. These bring in moral and religious teachings, and cultural and historical issues, which to me have nothing really to do with non-duality.

Yes, but it does not matter. Until "the lightning strikes" and "the eye blinks" this is in any case incomprehensible, however it is expressed.

❋

INDIVIDUALITY AND SURVIVAL

Does individuality not have an important evolutionary function? Are not things like pain, fear and a sense of individuality crucial for our survival?

Part of the surprise when non-duality is seen, is that survival, like everything else, is quite capable of going on without anyone causing it. Pain, fear, a sense of individuality and all other phenomena simply arise. Individuality could be called the ultimate non-necessity, the dream of dreams.

❀

SEPARATENESS AND THE SELF

I don't agree with your concepts of separateness and non-separateness. But I do think that it is the self that gets in the way of liberation.

I do not have concepts of separateness and non-separateness. It is simply seen that there is no separation.

Nothing can get in the way of liberation. There is only liberation. But when the self drops away, it is seen to be the case. What is more, it's seen that it always was the case.

❀

A PHILOSOPHICAL EXCHANGE

I see some similarities between what you write about and the philosophies of Ingmar Bergman and Samuel Beckett. They express the view that life is hopeless. Beckett in particular sees that life is awful and empty.

Bergman and Beckett are concerned with the dilemma that occurs when meaning is seen through but the sense of being a person remains.

I am concerned with the gift that occurs when the sense of being a person drops away and therefore meaning is seen through.

The difference is that existentialism sometimes leads to despair and the view that life is awful and empty, while liberation sometimes leads to laughter and the realisation that life is wonderful and full.

My favourite Beckett quote is "There's man all over for you, blaming on his boots the faults of his feet."

It seems to me that both the existentialists and the post-modernists have a lot in common with what you are saying. By the mid-twentieth century many writers were emphasising hopelessness, pointlessness and despair.

That was a natural point for many individuals to reach after being battered by the shocks of Darwin, Marx, the Russian Revolution, Freud, two world wars, the Holocaust, the death of God and the dropping of two atomic bombs. But the post-modern abandonment of the old meaningful stories, the Grand Narratives of Western civilisation, is itself yet another story. It has nothing to do with what I am saying. The seeing of non-separation can arise at any time, in any place, in any circumstances. It has no reference to anything which may or may not be happening.

In general, the existentialists and the post-modernists saw through the stories, but they didn't see through separation. This can lead to depression.

Do you think that the belief in purpose and progress through striving and effort will ever be eradicated in the West? It doesn't seem to grip the East, with their Taoist and Buddhist concepts, in the same way.

As long as there is a sense of separation, there will be dissatisfaction and notions of striving to achieve progress and purpose.

Striving is not the exclusive preserve of the West. There is plenty of striving in the East. Striving is striving, whether it is for a better car or for better karma and an improved rebirth.

What about Heidegger's problem of being and doing? Does that relate to what you say?

When the separate self is seen through, there is no problem of being and doing. There is only being, in which doing apparently arises. Heidegger couldn't see this because he was an existentialist, not a communicator of non-duality.

Maybe we should just be.

Who is there who could just be? You already are whatever is.

I think that Tat tvam asi *sums this up. "Thou art that". I relate it to what you say; "This is already what you are looking for."*

The mind cannot comprehend *Tat tvam asi*, however much it tries. But when non-separation is seen, *Tat tvam asi* is simply seen to be the case. It is seen to be a statement of the obvious.

What do you think of Joseph Campbell's phrase "Bliss is now"?

Yes, bliss is now. There is no other time that it could be. But this is not about bliss. Everything is always and only ever 'now'. Bliss, headaches, ice-cream, wasp stings are all only now. Non-duality embraces everything and in that bliss may or may not arise.

But shouldn't you be encouraging ideas such as "bliss is now"? And the importance to that of creativity and art?

I'm not interested in encouraging anything. Creativity and art are as important or as unimportant as everything else. There are no conditions or causations for the seeing of non-duality. It can arise in any conditions at any time anywhere.

I suppose the wonder is in everything.

Yes, the simple ripples on the lake as I write this on the verandah of the park café are a wonder.

But what is the purpose of being human?

There is no purpose, although the mind will often invent one. Nevertheless, Oneness seems to delight in manifestation.

Or to put it another way, the purpose of this copper beech by the lake is this copper beech by the lake.

Surely consciousness must have a purpose?

Consciousness needs no purpose. It simply is. *satchitananda.* Energy, consciousness and love simply are.

284

Many scientists regard consciousness as a by-product of the brain. It would be more accurate (although still inaccurate) to regard the brain as a by-product of consciousness.

I suppose the self is an enormous barrier to seeing Oneness.

Yes, it is a barrier which it is impossible for the false self to overcome.

I am confronted by the problem of doing nothing.

As there is nothing to be done, it isn't a problem.

Would you agree that what you are talking about could be seen as madness? Non-duality seems to lead to a great dissociation.

Oh yes, this can definitely be seen as madness in the ordinary world.

But there is nothing dissociative about seeing through separation. There is nothing to be dissociated from, nor anyone to be dissociated.

Nevertheless, the disappearance of the self can be perceived by some as psychosis. Kindly friends and concerned relatives may suggest the seeing of a psychiatrist. It is wise to be cautious about how this is shared, if at all, and with whom it is shared, if with anyone.

The problem seems to be about the relationship between the person and the world, between the one who does things and the things they do.

In liberation everything goes on functioning without a doer. In fact, it is seen that this always was the case.

Ultimately, I don't see that either liberation or this communication of yours about it is particularly helpful.

It is possible that the ending of the self may be experienced as the dropping of a great burden.

I am not trying to be helpful.

Can depression arise once liberation has been seen, once there is no person to be depressed? Does depression lessen or disappear entirely?

Anything can arise. Nothing is excluded. As a matter of fact depression no longer arises here but that doesn't mean that it couldn't.

Depression does not need a person. Nothing needs a person. Everything is already happening without a person.

Depression is less likely to arise when liberation is seen partly because depression is a manifestation of the neurotic self. When the neurotic self has lessened or faded away, feelings manifest in a more raw and natural way. They then tend to process themselves rather than coagulating into depression.

Another reason depression is less likely to arise is because, in the seeing of liberation, the simplest thing, like the way a leaf moves in the wind, becomes fascinating. The appreciation of simplicity makes life less depressing.

What is your goal in giving your talks? I notice that whatever language you use, people tend to become confused.

I have no goal in giving my talks.

Alas, we have to use language. I try to be clear without torturing language so much that it becomes unbearable.

What is a human being? What is its meaning?

A human being is Oneness expressing itself as a human being. It has no meaning.

How can I be in the present?

You cannot be in the present, but presence may be seen.

I was at your recent talk. I don't agree with what you said about dreams. I think that dreams are very important. And I don't get your comparison of dreams with awakening.

Dreams may be interpreted by the mind as very important. That's just the mind doing its own sweet thing. The mind makes up stories to entertain itself and to convince itself that it actually exists and has importance.

Yes, I know that this last sentence is paradoxical.

My comparison was about lucid dreaming. Lucid dreaming, in which the dream goes on but it is recognised that it is a dream, is a good metaphor for awakening. In both lucid dreaming and awakening, whatever appears is known to be both real and unreal.

What do you think of the central image of Christianity, a dead man nailed to a cross? I prefer a laughing Buddha.

Yes, it's a strange icon for a world religion, isn't it? And remember, it's *your* fault that he's nailed to that cross! It's because of *your* sin!

I like Ganesh, the elephant-headed god. An elephant. And a God. What's not to like? And I like dancing Shiva. And Kali.

In Buddhism, Taoism and Hinduism, absence or emptiness is emphasised. Would you agree that it is the same in non-duality?

Yes, although paradoxically when the self is seen to be empty, This is seen to be full. Emptiness and fullness, silence and sound, stillness and movement, are the same.

What is consciousness?

Consciousness is the light in which you and I and everything else arises.

I ask myself why I and some other people go to meetings about non-duality. The only answer that I can come up with is that it resonates. What do you think?

Yes, for some of us it resonates so we go to meetings or read books about it. For others of us, buying a new hat resonates so we do that instead. Neither is better or worse. It's all Oneness doing its thing. It's all stuff happening.

I've recently become fascinated by non-duality. It seems to me that it's clearing away a lot of metaphysical junk that I've accumulated over the years.

Yes, this cuts through the clutter of all the stories that seek to teach us what life should be about. All those dusty shelves packed with meaning and purpose are swept clear, leaving glorious empty space.

Is non-duality useful? Is it helpful?

No, it is not useful. No, it's not helpful. Isn't that great? Nothing left to do but relax!

Can Oneness be found more easily in certain places, such as Rishikesh rather than Manchester?

Everywhere is Oneness doing everywhere excellently. Paris is Oneness doing Paris wonderfully. London is Oneness doing London marvellously. And you are Oneness doing Jeremy fantastically.

Is there anything I can do to bring Liberation closer?

No. But we like to be told that there is something we can do and there are plenty of prescriptions available. These include watching the gap between your thoughts, staying in the now, touching your guru's feet, drinking your guru's bath water, counting your breaths, clearing your chakras, doing good works, wanting liberation more than life itself and giving up wanting liberation entirely.

We do not like to be told that there is nothing that we can do and, what is worse, there is no one who can do anything.

As Tony Parsons says, this communication is reassuringly unpopular.

I was brought up in an evangelical sect. Perhaps as a result of this, I now have a very strong antipathy towards religion. Would you agree that religion is more of a curse than a blessing?

We are addicted to stories of meaning. Religion offers us these. In spite of their colourful variety, most of them seduce us with promises of imaginary heavens if we obey their priesthood and threaten us with torments in imaginary hells if we disobey or ignore them.

But in liberation all of this is revealed as a story. Every story is undone in liberation.

What kind of reaction do you generally get to your suggestion that there is nothing we can do?

Some people find this notion ridiculous. Others become angry. These are both natural reactions for someone who has only ever known living in separation.

But I am not suggesting that there is nothing we can do. I am saying that there is no one who can do anything, which is quite different. "There is nothing we can do" suggests the presence of an impotent person. "There is no one" describes the absence of the person. This has entirely different implications. The reaction to this may also sometimes be anger. But others feel relief on hearing this and recognise a deep truth which is beyond the understanding of the mind.

Have you ever had a discussion about non-duality with a fundamentalist Christian?

No. Waste of time. I'd rather have a cup of tea and a walk round the park.

What is your estimate of the number of people who have seen Oneness?

There are no people, of course, who have seen Oneness. But taking your question in the spirit in which I think you're asking it, and using language carelessly, quite a lot. Perhaps there always were, but it wasn't much spoken about. We can never know. In the past this could get you burnt as a heretic, and even now it might attract the unwelcome attention of a psychiatrist or an evangelical preacher.

Do those who have seen Oneness have anything in common as a result?

Not really. Being awake and being asleep are the same thing. And there can be no rules because liberation encompasses every possibility.

Nevertheless, some things may change. For example, a certain level of neurosis may fall away. Some relaxation may take place. A sense of satisfaction in small pleasures may arise. Stories will probably not be taken seriously anymore.

The essential glorious meaninglessness of everything will probably be appreciated once the nature of everything as unconditional love is seen.

Do some people react violently when they come across nonduality?

Some people become very angry at even the suggestion that there is no person. I have witnessed a Ramana Maharshi devotee physically threaten someone who was giving a talk on non-duality. He was ejected from the building by force. In Germany, a psychotic-looking young man stared at me ferociously throughout my talk, waited afterwards till everyone else had gone, then said to me "What you are saying is total bullshit! There are a thousand people inside your head!"

Generally I am not very interested in these reactions. If someone wants to get disputatious with me about non-duality I tend simply to leave. There is nothing in me that cares whether people understand this or 'get it'. I do not have that agenda.

Can you explain the connections between what you write about and traditional Advaita?

I could explain a little about that, but I won't because I would find it boring. There are some excellent books and websites about traditional Advaita, but after you've read them you'll just have a head full of concepts about non-duality. These have nothing to do with the seeing of Oneness, so I'd rather keep my head clear for concepts about where my next patisserie might come from.

Does the seeing of Oneness have anything to do with what might be reported in sudden religious conversions or mystical epiphanies?

Awakening is the sudden temporary seeing that there is no one. After awakening the person comes back and may interpret awakening in any number of personal ways. If they had been following a spiritual path or one of the world religions, they might interpret it in those terms. They might see it as caused by their devotion to their guru or to their god.

But in liberation, all the stories that the person may previously have invested their belief in tend to be seen through. It is difficult then to take these stories seriously anymore.

There are descriptions of liberation within the world religions. These descriptions can be separated from the "background noise" of the religion that surrounds them. Most commonly these descriptions are found in Taoism, Buddhism including Zen, and Advaita Vedanta. But they are also found in the mystical streams of Christianity, Islam, Judaism and other faiths.

Mystics of all faiths and of no faith are able to see that the mystical apprehension has no connection with any particular faith. So mystics generally remain uninterested in either converting or slaughtering members of other faiths.

This is one reason why non-mystics are sometimes interested in slaughtering the mystics of their own faith. They see the mystics as a threat and as letting down the side by not wishing to kill infidels.

What is the connection between seeing Oneness and the major world religions?

There is none. The seeing of Oneness can occur within any religion or outside all religions.

However, if it occurs within a religion, that may give rise to 'background noise' or 'static' which might confuse any description given.

Could you comment on the difficulties of communicating about non-separation?

Wittgenstein wrote "Whereof one cannot speak, thereof one must remain silent." Nevertheless an urge to "eff the ineffable" arises. It's a mystery.

Could you sum up liberation in as few words as possible?

There is no self. This is it and this is sufficient. There is unconditional love.

Fifteen words is the best I can do.

Does the mind get in the way of seeing non-separation?

No, that would be a confusing description. Firstly, there is no mind, there are only thoughts arising, creating the impression that there is a mind. Secondly, those thoughts are themselves simply Oneness thinking. Therefore they cannot obscure Oneness if the person drops away.

The idea that the mind, or thinking itself, gets in the way of liberation is a very common one in some schools of enlightenment and on some spiritual paths. Some gurus and teachers encourage their devotees and students to attempt to stop their thoughts. At least one contemporary teacher has stated that thinking is a disease.

This can lead to terrible mental constipation. Some would call it 'poisonous pedagogy'.

What happens to the mind in awakening and liberation? Does the mind realise Oneness?

There is no mind, so nothing happens to it in awakening and liberation. Being non-existent, the mind does not realise Oneness.

A great deal of the mental energy that was contracted in the person may explode outwards in the seeing of liberation. Please understand that this is only a metaphor. What is consequently seen is that there is no mind, there is only the process of thinking (and perceiving etcetera).

The mind is an illusion which is created because thinking can be so powerfully energised. In actuality, thoughts arise out of nothing just like everything else.

Once liberation has been seen, can it be forgotten?

Because your question is in the past tense, it is difficult to answer. Liberation is either seen or it is not seen, so the past tense does not apply.

Nevertheless, if I answer your question in the spirit in which it is asked, I have to say that anything is possible in liberation. However, and pretending for a moment that there is time, once the fullness of emptiness and the nature of unconditional love has been seen, it is unlikely to be forgotten.

Has liberation been seen throughout history?

Pretending that there is such a thing as time, there have been unmistakable reports of liberation occurring many times.

Did the Buddha see Oneness?

The Buddha saw nothing, or 'no thing'. He saw the 'no thing' from which everything arises, the emptiness which is also fullness. The Buddha saw that this manifestation, and the emptiness from which it arises, are the same. This is what is meant in Buddhism by "Samsara and nirvana are one."

Do children see Oneness more easily than adults?

"Unless you become as little children, you shall not enter the kingdom of heaven."

For the child, as self-consciousness is gained, Oneness is usually lost. The child develops a sense of separation at quite a young age, and thus starts the great adventure of owning a life and having to negotiate with others who own lives.

In your meetings I've heard you talk about tuning into feelings in the body, especially to fear. Can you say more about that?

When liberation is seen, there is a natural tendency for all feelings, including fear, to be experienced in a raw form as sensation in the body rather than in a processed form as a story in the head. When feelings are experienced in this raw unblinkered way, they process themselves more quickly and cause fewer problems. Instead of weeks of anxiety and neurotic story-telling about the terrible events that might happen or have happened, there might be a much shorter more intense period of feeling fear.

One of the important insights of psychotherapy is that focussing on the body-sensations of feelings, rather than on the rat-run of the stories that go with them, is likely to help the client process those feelings more easily. This is sometimes called 'experiential non-avoidance'. It can be very much more fertile than endlessly and tediously re-telling the story, either to the psychotherapist or in the client's own head.

Many psychotherapists have developed ways of encouraging clients to be more 'experientially non-avoidant'. In liberation this simply tends to happen as a natural process.

You have said that unconditional love allows everything to be. When you consider some of the events that it allows to be, isn't this statement highly problematic? Some people might even see it as outrageous, or even blasphemous.

Yes, it is highly problematic to the mind. Intelligent minds are likely to reject it. However, when it is seen it becomes incontrovertible and undeniable. Then questions of outrage or blasphemy become irrelevant.

In some ways, this non-duality stuff is hell! I feel like apologising to you on behalf of Oneness. But of course you should really be apologising to yourself.

The problem for the mind with the phrase 'unconditional love' is not the love, it's the unconditionality. The mind works by dividing reality into 'this' and 'that' in numerous ways, including 'this which is approved of' and 'that which is disapproved of'. As the mind always excludes something from its approval, it can only ever experience conditional love. Unconditional love can only be seen when the person, and therefore the mind, is not there. If the mind comes back to argue about this, it will win. Oneness has no arguments against the mind.

I'd like to know what led you to becoming interested in non-duality and whether you see your spiritual searching as relevant to this.

There is no cause for awakening. Everything that apparently happens is irrelevant because nothing actually happens. The realisation of this can sometimes elicit relief although it can equally often elicit despair.

You have written that unconditional love can only be seen when there is no one and no mind to see it. Do you really think this?

What I think is unimportant. It is simply another thought arising. It will fall away again pretty quickly and has no more significance than the purring of my cat as she sits on my lap while I write these words.

A thought is always provisional.

When the person is seen through, then unconditional love is just seen to be the case. The mind with all its fascinating stories is seen to be unimportant. This is perhaps why mystics are sometimes famously disengaged from political and social issues, to the great annoyance of those who are engaged.

You have said that in awakening the mind is seen through. That's set me wondering whether people who are mad, who are said to have lost their minds, are more likely to awaken than we sane ones.

There is no causation at work in the seeing of liberation so even madness is no help. 'Losing our mind' in that sense does not relate to awakening. The mind is not lost in liberation but it is seen through, which is quite different. In any case 'losing our mind' is just a metaphor.

Nevertheless, some of the phenomena associated with awakening can also be associated with psychosis. This can give rise to what is sometimes termed 'spiritual crisis'. Anyone concerned about this might find assistance from www.spiritualcrisisnetwork. org.uk.

Am I right in thinking that you have said that animals see Oneness? If so, how do you know?

No, I have not said that animals see Oneness. Animals are Oneness, expressing itself as animals. A dog does not see Oneness, a dog is Oneness chasing sticks and burying bones.

What is the relationship between Oneness and plants, animals, even the universe?

All those things—plants, animals and the universe—are Oneness manifesting as everything.

Do you think the mind can ever accept Oneness?

The mind can never accept Oneness. The mind lives in time. In time there is always separation and there is always something happening.

That which sees Oneness is beyond time, the mind and the individual. It is That which gives rise to all of these.

You seem to be saying that there is no difference between doing and not doing, between effort and laziness. I cannot accept this.

The mind can only know separation. It can never know non-duality but it cannot bear the thought of this. So it seeks and it seeks and it seeks, often with great effort. When it is exhausted it sometimes takes a little rest. Often it then becomes guilty about this.

The mind never gives up seeking. But when the mind finally drops away, it is seen that there never was anything to seek.

What do you think of culture and civilization? A lot of what you write seems to negate the importance of these.

Culture and civilization are a wonderful colourful dream arising in This. They are as important or as unimportant as you think them to be. The importance you assign them is a passing thought, sometimes lasting no longer than a sip of tea.

Celibacy is often extolled as a great virtue, even a necessity, on many spiritual paths. What do you think of this?

If someone is drawn to celibacy, then celibacy is quite likely to arise. There is no need to make a great song and dance about it.

There is a French Buddhist monk who ascribes his happiness partly to thirty years of celibacy. I ascribe my happiness partly to fifty years of non-celibacy. As the Americans say "Go figure."

❀

AWAKENING OR LIBERATION?

In a movie the next scene simply replaces the last one. That is how time seems to me now. I've also become very forgetful. Thoughts just appear and disappear. It feels like a game when I was a child.

Sometimes the feeling of being a person arises again, and then it feels like a game again. Is this awakening? Or liberation? What is liberation anyway?

Your description reminds me of other descriptions that I have heard. The change in how time is seen, the forgetfulness, the knowing that thoughts simply appear out of nothing, the remembering that it's a 'game', are all commonly reported in awakening and liberation.

You ask what liberation is. Liberation is the end of searching because it is seen that there is nothing to search for as This is already it. This is already what we are searching for. In liberation, the fullness of emptiness has been seen. That fullness is known to be love. Because of this, gratitude tends to arise. Then life goes on, it is simply seen that there is no one living that life.

❋

NEGATIVE FEELINGS

I am experiencing very powerful negative feelings. At times I feel very fearful, at other times very angry. My anger seems to be mostly produced by certain specific people in my life. At times I become concerned about what I might do as a result of these feelings.

Would you associate these strong emotions with a process of awakening? Can you recommend any particular way of dealing with them? Would you recommend seeing a therapist about them? I should add that I have very limited financial resources.

I'm sorry you're having such a hard time.

No, I wouldn't necessarily associate what you describe with a process of awakening. It sounds more likely that these profound feelings are crying out for attention. Because they are distressing, it's important that you find a way of managing them either for yourself or with the support of someone else.

If you're able to, you might find it helpful to spend some time paying attention to these feelings as sensations—in other words noticing where they arise in the body and just staying with them for a while on that physical level. This may be more therapeutic than getting caught up in any story that you attach to these feelings in your head, especially stories which involve you projecting your anger onto other people.

You may also be able to find the support of a therapist. If you are not able to pay for this privately, it's possible to obtain therapy free through the National Health Service IAPT scheme.

I hope you find a way of managing these feelings and I wish you well.

Thank you for your reply. I'd like to ask you one more question. Some people recommend expressing and releasing anger in an energetic way, by for example beating cushions or chopping wood. Other people say this only increases the anger. Do you have an opinion about this?

It's a very individual thing. Some people derive psychological benefit from vigorous physical anger release, some do not. So it's best to experiment for yourself. In any case, some fairly vigorous exercise has excellent health benefits, psychologically as well as physically. Chopping wood might suit you but even brisk walking has benefits.

This is not an alternative to spending some time sitting quietly and noticing the feelings in the body. You can try both—many people find both beneficial.

❋

GOD

Dear Richard, Just out of interest, how do you know that there is no God? Best wishes, Jonny

Dear Jonny, There is no satisfactory answer for the mind to your question. Essentially "There is a God" in all its many forms is a story. In liberation all stories are both seen through and seen clearly for what they are—simply stories. But if someone wants to have God or a god in their universe then of course they're quite welcome to have her. Best wishes Richard

Dear Richard, When it is seen that there is no one there, does rethinking decisions still arise? Best wishes, Jonny

Dear Jonny, That's a good way of describing what can happen. Rethinking decisions may arise, although as a matter of fact that doesn't happen very often here. For example, in a restaurant:- "I think I'll have the steak. No, I'll have the fish." Life goes on, wood is still chopped. This really makes very little difference. Best wishes, Richard

❀

PROGRESS

Are things getting better? Can we look forward to human progress?

Within this dream-story, sometimes things appear to improve, sometimes they appear to deteriorate. We cure smallpox and invent the Kalashnikov.

The notion of human progress is a grand narrative in whose name much mischief has been done.

And notice how "looking forward" takes us away from presence. As long as we are looking forward, we cannot notice the wonder of This.

But we seem addicted to utopian ideals.

The mind is forever dissatisfied with what is. So it is always vulnerable to being seduced by stories of progress, utopias and heavens to come.

The mind is always projecting some desire or some dread onto the future.

So what is 'presence'?

Presence is This, always fresh and new. The cup of coffee that I sip as I write these words is the first cup of coffee that has ever been tasted. This is always and eternally the first morning of the world.

❀

CHILDREN AND GRATITUDE

Are children nearer to This than adults? Does seeing This bring gratitude?

Children have a natural appreciation for the mystery of existence. Watch how a child can remain fascinated by an ant crawling over a leaf, the flame of a candle or life in a rock pool. Seeing liberation could be described as a return to experiencing life directly as a child does.

Seeing This tends to bring gratitude and an appreciation of life and its mystery. Often, near-death experiences do the same. The violinist Paul Robertson described how, after a major heart attack and several strokes, he felt great appreciation for the simplest things in life and gratitude for every moment.

So can the simple awareness of death bring gratitude?

It may or it may not.

On the treacherous mountain road out of Leh Ladakh to Kashmir, for the encouragement of motorists, there are frequent signs announcing "Death Waits With Icy Hand On Srinagar Highway".

❁

ACCEPTING ONENESS

Can the mind accept Oneness?

No, the mind can never accept Oneness except as an idea, which has no value.

I have another question. What do you mean by "There is no mind" and "There is no person"?

There is no mind, there is only a stream of passing thoughts and other perceptions. There is no person, there is only life happening.

STORIES

You say that in the seeing of liberation all the stories are seen through. But I quite like my stories. I would see their disappearance as a loss.

Liberation is a death, a loss, the ruination of a person's life. If we want to hold on to our stories, we should run away from non-duality as fast as we can.

Many people come close to non-duality, recognise this and run away from it never to return. Non-duality is the great destroyer of stories.

A friend of mine took an acquaintance to a talk on non-duality. Afterwards, the acquaintance said rather plaintively "But I *like* my stories!" He didn't go back.

Are the mind with its stories and unconditional love incompatible, mutually exclusive?

The mind with its stories is unconditional love, appearing as the mind with its stories. And in liberation the mind is seen to be non-existent.

MADNESS

Do you think that the mad and the psychotic are more likely to see Oneness because they are less restricted by the usual conventions of the mind?

Generally speaking, the mad and the psychotic, although they may see reality differently, are still lost in duality. The notion that the mad have access to a deeper reality than the sane is a romantic one which appeals to many people who have been influenced by

Ken Kesey, R. D. Lang and Thomas Szasz. But a story is still only a story, even when it is generated by psychosis.

Is the mind a hindrance to seeing liberation? Would it be better not to have a mind?

No one has a mind so the mind is not a hindrance. Thoughts are often considered to be a hindrance and there are many people who make a good living out of teaching ways in which thoughts might be reduced or eliminated. These methods can sometimes be highly stressful, in which case they are best avoided in favour of a cup of tea and a pastry.

However, simple mindfulness techniques and 'experiential non-avoidance' may be helpful in dealing with uncomfortable thoughts and feelings.

❋

TIME

Does the mind live in time?

There is no such thing as a mind. The mind is a process of thoughts. A thought has a beginning, a middle and an end, so it can only take place in the appearance of time. Of course it is also true that any process, such as a bird winging its way across the sky, can only take place in the appearance of time.

A night-time dream appears to take place in time. But when we awake in the morning, that time is immediately seen to be unreal. When non-duality is seen, this day-time dream is revealed to be an appearance taking place in an unreal time.

There is no past, there is no future, there is no 'now'. There is not even a moment, because a moment has duration. How long is a moment?

There is only presence. There is only eternally This.

❋

SEEKING

Can the person give up seeking? What happens to the mind when Oneness is seen?

The tendency of the person is to constantly seek. While the seeking of liberation is going on, liberation cannot be seen.

When Oneness is seen, the mind continues to do its own sweet thing. This is the same as saying that Oneness continues to appear as thoughts. But in liberation the mind tends to do its own sweet thing more quietly and with less neurosis. However, this is only a tendency, not a rule.

❄

NEGATIVE REACTIONS TO NON-DUALITY

I imagine that hearing about Oneness can be very irritating. What's the most negative reaction you've had?

If you think that you are a person, it can be understandably irritating to be told that you are not a person. However, most people are simply bored by this. Unless someone's expressing a great interest, it's probably better to talk about the weather or the football or to have a cup of tea.

By the way, I have noticed a common thread running through all the Eastern philosophical and spiritual practices that I have come across. When practised in groups, they all involve a half-hour tea break. Perhaps it's worth considering that this may not be a coincidence.

❄

OBSESSIVE ABOUT LANGUAGE

I notice that you often 'correct' individuals at your meetings when they use the words 'person' or 'people', as in when someone asks you

"How many people have become liberated?" Don't you think you're being a bit over-zealous about this, not to say obsessive?

I'm sorry if I seem to be nit-picking, but the mother of all misconceptions is that a person can become liberated or enlightened, or even worse, Liberated or Enlightened.

This misconception leads to a great deal of misery, self-abnegation and guilt as the seeker tries to make themself worthy of finding the pot of gold at the end of the spiritual rainbow. It also leads to a lot of grandiosity, narcissism and exploitative behaviour in some of those who think that they have become enlightened or, even worse, Enlightened.

❁

ART

Do you think that any particular forms of art express Oneness more than others?

All art is Oneness expressing itself as art.

❁

CHANGING YOUR LIFE

Has seeing Oneness changed your life?

I don't have a life. Neither do you. There is just life happening. Nevertheless, when Oneness is seen, there is a tendency for there to be less anxiety and for certain neuroses to drop away.

It's more difficult to maintain neuroses and anxiety when unconditional love is seen. But it's not impossible.

❁

BUDDHIST CONCEPTS

What do you think of Buddhist concepts such as samsara, nirvana and karma?

There is only Oneness. Samsara and nirvana are one. This is already nirvana but, as long as there is a person looking for nirvana somewhere else, that cannot be seen.

Karma is a story told by the mind. It seduces and delights the mind because it seems to promise justice and to right all wrongs. Justice is chocolate gateau for the mind. It is mouth-watering to contemplate that our oppressors will get their just desserts.

❈

MUSIC

Can music be a way into Oneness?

Music is the sound of Oneness. The roar of traffic is also the sound of Oneness. It is silence making a noise.

When Oneness is seen, there may be more liking for silence. Or not.

❈

TRICKS

You have written "Oneness plays a trick on itself to convince itself that it is separate". How do you know this? I don't accept it or its implications.

"Oneness plays a trick on itself" is a metaphor. It is an attempt to express the dilemma that people find themselves in. We are searching for wholeness, with no possibility of knowing what that really is. Wholeness cannot be known until the person has disappeared. So what we really seek is our own disappearance.

I do not know this. No one can know this. It is simply seen when the person is no longer there. It can be directly apprehended by no one, but it can never be known by someone.

❀

ANOTHER PHILOSOPHICAL EXCHANGE

You write about being in a non-dual mode. Then you refer to specific experiences, such as the sound of the breeze rustling in the trees. But to have a specific experience, you must be in a dual mode, because in a non-dual mode no experiences are happening.

There is no difference between 'a dual mode' and 'a non-dual mode'. There is only non-separation, in which Oneness arises as everything that is, including the sound of the breeze in the trees.

The traditional metaphor that may help with this is that of the waves and the ocean. The waves appear different to the ocean but we know that they are actually the same. Before you start picking holes in this, remember that it is only a metaphor.

Oneness and the stuff that arises in Oneness are not different from each other. As the Buddhists sometimes put it "Samsara and nirvana are one".

How can a baby arise out of nothing? It requires two parents. These two parents come together either out of free-will or because they are destined to or because they are scripted to.

A baby arises out of nothing. Everything arises out of nothing. There is no free-will, destiny or script. There is only what is apparently happening.

Another traditional metaphor may help here. In a night-time dream, all kinds of things might appear to be happening. But it is known on awakening that nothing at all has been happening. Again, this is only a metaphor. If you want to pick holes in it, you'll be able to.

I've been trying to understand what you write about non-duality, but I don't feel I'm being successful. Can you clarify the main points so that my mind can be satisfied? That's really what I want to get out of this.

You say that what you want is understanding of non-duality by your mind. But I don't have much interest in the mind's understanding of non-duality, so we may not have much of a dialogue here.

The mind tends to do with non-duality what it always tends to do. That is to complicate, mystify, misunderstand and fight for one set of ideas while denigrating others. The mind spins complexity out of simplicity and erects great edifices of unnecessary interpretations which obscure rather than clarify. This leads to ferocious exchanges with other minds and their different interpretations and stories. The mind cannot help doing this. It is its nature.

My interest is rather in trying to give a description of what it is like when Oneness is seen, although even this can sound too grandiose. This interest arises even though it is an impossibility, because Oneness is always beyond words and beyond thought.

Some writers talk about 'realisation'. Does realisation change the individual in any way? Are these changes preferred? Is Oneness itself changed in any way by realisation?

The ultimate paradox is that realisation does not exist, but that cannot be known until there is realisation. Nevertheless, I'll answer your question in the spirit in which it is asked.

Realisation has no necessary implications for the character that remains behind. But in the story of that character, changes may take place. For example, a certain level of neurosis may fall away, so the character may spend more time staring at a leaf and less time fretting over a shopping list. Yes, it does sound a little like the effects of ganja, doesn't it?

My experience of talking to individuals where the person has been seen through, is that what remains is generally preferred to what went before. But as nothing can be done about this, we might be tempted to add "So what?"

I follow the various controversies about non-duality on the internet. One line of argument particularly appeals to me. I can sum it up in the following question:- Is not a statement about "the dropping away of the person" or "the seeing of Oneness" just another story?

Any statement could be described as a story. Nevertheless, to say that the seeing of Oneness is just another story is like a blind man denying that there is such a thing as colour. If you don't recognise that metaphor, it is from Tony Parsons.

You suggest that Oneness is eternal, unchanging. Yet you also write about the falling away of the person in which separation is seen through, such as happened to Tony Parsons when walking through a park or Nathan Gill when cycling down a lane. These are clearly changes. Isn't there a contradiction here?

Oneness is unchanging and in Oneness the appearance of change arises. This is the same as saying that Oneness arises as everything that is, as all the stuff that happens.

Let me try a traditional analogy again. In a night-time dream many things may happen and many changes may take place. On awakening it is known that nothing happened and no changes took place. Or we could say that there appeared to be changes in the mind of the dreamer but actually nothing happened. Or we could say that the changes that appeared to take place were actually a story.

I don't know if any of that helps, but now I've run out of metaphors.

"All is One" seems to me to be a concept or an assumption. Can you explain that concept or assumption further?

For you, "All is One" may be a concept or an assumption. For me "All is One" is a description which cannot be grasped by the mind. So there is no point in trying to explain it further.

By the way, trying to understand non-duality and trying to describe it are both impossible. So we are both on a road to nowhere.

But I can see no evidence that "All is One".

The mind expects to find evidence. There is no evidence that can satisfy the mind. When it is simply seen that All is One, no evidence is required. It becomes irrefutable.

I think that maybe this view was first developed by somebody with depression who wanted to make themself feel better.

Who knows? How could that ever be known? What does it matter?
    It isn't a view.

Would you say that all separation is illusory?

It is illusory in the sense that it is not what it appears to be. I prefer to say that all separation is an appearance which is both real and unreal.

You say that there is no such thing as liberation but this cannot be seen until there is liberation. Is this not unclear, contradictory and confusing?

No, it is a paradox which is impossible for the mind to understand. But where liberation is concerned, the mind is irrelevant.
    We could also say that being asleep and being awake are the same thing, but this cannot be seen while we are asleep.

Don't you feel that your description of non-duality encourages people to search?

Searching will happen or not happen. It has nothing to do with me or you or anyone else.

You seem to imply that seekers lack something that they need to find. If that's the case, I don't agree with you. Is it the case?

No, the seeker lacks nothing. Yet they feel that they do and this is what fuels seeking.

It could be said that the seeker possesses something that they need to lose—themself.

I think that there are many illusory beliefs—for example that we'll go to heaven when we die. I think that 'realisation' is another illusory belief.

You're welcome to your point of view.

What's the point of searching for liberation? What's the point of liberation?

There is no point. That's the point.

What in your view is enlightenment? Is it the same thing as realisation, liberation or seeing Oneness? Can enlightenment be personal?

All these words and phrases attempt inadequately to 'eff the ineffable' and describe the dropping away of the sense of self and the seeing that there is no person. At the core of what seems to be a person there is only emptiness.

Because the word 'enlightenment' is associated with many misleading stories, I tend to avoid it. In the literature of spiritual paths it is often suggested that it is possible for an individual to attain a state of personal enlightenment, and that this will bring great rewards such as a permanent state of bliss, or magical powers like the siddhis that are spoken about in some yogic traditions.

As no state of personal enlightenment exists, this is all highly misleading. In fact it is seen in liberation that there is no person who could enjoy the fruits of personal enlightenment.

Then how come you and others talk of enlightenment events?

In the story, 'enlightenment events' happen. First there is Nathan Gill cycling down a country lane, then there is just cycling down a country lane but no one cycling. First there is Tony Parsons walking through a park, then there is just walking through a park but no one walking.

The very essence of these events is that the person is absent. Therefore they preclude any possibility of personal enlightenment.

Why do you give talks about realisation or liberation? What is it about realisation that you find interesting?

The fundamental problem that many of us face is a core sense of dissatisfaction with whatever is the case. This can persist no matter what may be happening in our lives.

We may seek to end this dissatisfaction in many ways, for example by taking drugs or buying fast cars or changing our partner or our decor. We might strive for a more just and equal world, or seek to improve ourselves through self-development, following a spiritual path or worshipping some god or other.

At a deep level, this sense of dissatisfaction manifests as a search for meaning, an insistent and persistent feeling that there must be more than 'just this', that 'just this' must be about something. Oh, if only we could find out what that meaning is, at last we would feel fulfilled!

An individual's search for meaning can be seen as both a blessing and a curse. It can provide relief from existential angst but it can only ever be provisionally satisfying.

Liberation brings an end to this search for meaning. In liberation it is seen not only that there is nothing to be found, but more fundamentally that there is no one to find it. The 'secret' is seen to be not that there is something unknown that can be discovered, but that there is no one who was ever searching.

Then This is seen for the first time for what it is, sufficient in itself, already complete.

To go back to your question, I think that the end of a lifetime of searching in the disappearance of the person is interesting.

A liberation event can only happen in a story, right? Apart from that liberation does not exist. So liberation does not really exist, right?

Events happen in a story, of course, because the mind can only place events in time and time belongs to a story. It would be more precise to say that events appear to happen in a story.

Liberation is the direct seeing that there is no person or self who could be liberated. It is seen by no one. The mind (which also does not exist) might describe this as an event or not, which happens or does not, within a story or not. None of that description matters or makes any difference. It's just the mind doing its own sweet thing and trying to pin down and define that which the mind can in any case never understand.

❀

TWO KRISHNAMURTIS

Do you think that liberation was seen by either J. or U.G. Krishnamurti? I've heard you say that you think J never felt separate, but what about U.G.? When they spoke, were they both pointing to non-duality?

Many contemporary speakers about non-duality seem to be teaching people lessons in how to become liberated. I see this as bull-shit. What do you think?

I can't give you a definitive answer about either J. or U.G. Krishnamurti. I never met either of them. But my best guess to your question is "Yes" in both cases. From what I've read of U.G., I think he is 'pointing'. I have never read much of J., as I found the little that I did read very tedious.

Many individuals are giving a teaching about this. It is tempting to do this, but I have no patience with it. A German woman I met said she had seen many individuals talk about this. Her view was that at first they all gave a very clear communication, but as time went by most of them started to turn what they were saying into a teaching. I don't really know why this is but there may be a clue in that a teaching is what most people want.

I feel that J. Krishnamurti is suggesting self-enquiry. What do you think?

It's so long since I looked at J. Krishnamurti's writings that I can't comment. I just remember finding him very tedious.

Can someone who has really seen non-duality suggest that others self-enquire, or even drift between suggesting this and rejecting it?

Anything is possible. I have been told that one speaker, when challenged about this, said "I make compromises." Many speakers seem to drift eventually to teaching self-enquiry or some other practice. As I've already said, I have no patience with this.

You can teach people how to have an experience. But awakening and liberation are not experiences.

❋

DESPAIR

For many years I was searching. Then suddenly a few months ago, searching stopped. This seems to have happened partly because I read your little book 'I Hope You Die Soon'.

Now it seems that I am able to absolutely see that separation is an illusion, but this leaves me feeling deeply dissatisfied and in despair. Even on a good day like today, I find it hard to bear that nothing has any meaning. I don't really have any hope that you can help me to 'disappear' but something in me makes me write to you.

I'm sorry that you're having such a hard time. I remember when I felt the kind of despair that you write about. I would sometimes phone Tony Parsons about it. By this time I was a psychologically sophisticated person who had already explored many psychotherapeutic pathways.

Tony would simply suggest that if possible I find some simple thing that I enjoyed doing and do it—such as a taking a walk, going for a drive or eating a good meal. At the time a part of me felt that this response was naïve, but now I find myself saying the same thing to people who contact me in despair.

There are quite a few of them because despair is a common reaction to an initial opening to This.

❀

NEUROSIS, PSYCHOSIS AND LIBERATION

I think I remember coming across a reference of yours where you state that, after liberation is seen, neurosis and psychosis might both still continue.

I respect your intuitive powers, but psychosis? *Surely you can't be serious!*

I have no specific memory of that reference. However, in liberation anything is possible. There are no rules. So yes, this is at least theoretically possible.

The causes of psychosis are at best poorly understood. Nevertheless, I'd risk a punt that psychosis has at least something to do with the brain. So going out on a limb here, I'm prepared to say that psychosis becomes impossible in cases where the brain has been removed.

Interestingly, signs of psychosis and of spiritual breakthrough can often be confused or inter-twined or ambiguous. This is sometimes expressed as the question "Is it breakdown or break-through?" There is an organisation which deals specifically with this area called Spiritual Crisis Network.

By the way, in general I am not able to respond to e-mails anymore but I found yours too intriguing to ignore.

❀

RELATIONSHIPS

Dear Richard, I have recently started a new relationship with a woman. I am wondering what changes if any you noticed in 'relationships' when non-duality was seen.

For me, it seems like there is no effort to change anyone anymore. It's as if there is relating but no relationship. It feels very free. Best wishes, Jonny

Dear Jonny, That sounds great. I wouldn't make any generalisations about what happens in relationships when non-duality is seen. Nevertheless, as there is likely to be a reduction in neurosis, things might go more smoothly and there might be less trauma when they don't.

I describe things in the same way that you do. There's no such thing as a relationship, there's only relating. There is a verb but no noun, a process but no entity.

I wish you well in your new relationship. Best wishes, Richard

Dear Richard, You say that neurosis tends to drop away when non-duality is seen. But I notice that here neurosis still pretty much arises—thoughts and feelings such as jealousy, inferiority, anger.

Of course I don't expect bliss. But shouldn't neurosis simply drop away along with the person? Even though you say there are no rules, I still wonder about this. Best wishes, Jonny

Dear Jonny, I've said that there's a tendency for neurosis to drop away or diminish over time but it's only a tendency. And where neurosis doesn't drop away there's a tendency to be less concerned about it.

The thoughts and feelings that you mention may fade in time, or they may not. But if we think any particular state of mind or emotion must be achieved in 'the future', then we have accepted the mind's invitation to climb back onto the hamster wheel of becoming. In that case, my invitation to you would be to simply climb back off it, having told the mind to go fuck itself. Best wishes, Richard

Dear Richard, Thanks for your message, I really appreciated your words and your clear speech really made me laugh.

Do you think psychotherapy reinforces the idea of being a person? On the one hand it seems to help, but on the other it seems to be exactly doing that. Best wishes, Jonny

Dear Jonny, There are many kinds of psychotherapy. Some of them, particularly the more psychoanalytically orientated ones, encourage the development of a story and therefore may tend to reinforce the idea of a person.

I am more drawn to the psychotherapies that address issues and problems more directly rather than focussing on a story about the past.

But either way, if it seems to help, why not have it? Best wishes, Richard

Dear Richard, At the moment I'm experiencing a heavy dose of "going in and out of the person" again. One moment I'm getting caught up in stories but the next moment they're all falling away. Did you go through this kind of experience? Do you have any thoughts on it? Best wishes, Jonny

Dear Jonny, Many individuals report this. It could be called going in and out of the story. It's quite likely that this will become weaker. If it does not, then probably there will be less and less of a sense of anyone 'inside' who cares anymore whether this is going on or not.

In other words, if no one is listening, a heavy dose of going in and out of the person becomes seen as simply what's happening. Best wishes, Richard

Dear Richard, Thanks for always answering. I enjoy the resonance.

Doesn't any psychological technique that is intended to help deal with problems tend to reinforce the person?

For me, relaxing into the moment seems to offer the only relief. Best wishes, Jonny

Dear Jonny, If relaxing into the moment happens, that's great. There might even be a danish pastry involved.

For the one who feels separate, anything can reinforce the sense of being a person. Nevertheless some psychotherapeutic techniques and other practices can make us feel more comfortable. And some can have the opposite effect.

Of course it may eventually be seen that techniques and practices happen or they do not, just like everything else.

The mind frequently has a disposition to make things wrong, or to pick a fight with things. But there is nothing wrong with doing techniques and practices, just as there is nothing right with them. They are simply what they are. Best wishes, Richard

✺

DOES ANYTHING MATTER?

Does anything really matter? And are you 'writing' another book?

It might be simpler to ask the question "Does anything matter to me?" Many things may or may not matter to Mike the character. But the question "Does anything really matter?" sounds like it is actually about meaning and purpose as in "Does anything ultimately have any meaning or purpose?" In that case, the answer is no. Nothing needs to have a meaning or a purpose because everything is already complete in itself.

Yes, I'm writing another book. I hope it will be available soon.

✺

DESPAIR AND ANXIETY

There has been a sense of despair here for some time. There is also anxiety underlying the despair. I've experienced this for as long as I can remember and it seems to make it impossible for me to relax.

Nevertheless, there is sometimes a sense that this is enough and a tendency not to want to do much. At these times I appreciate life more, especially the stunning russet and red colours of this autumnal time of the year.

What to do? Nothing?

What to do about despair and anxiety? As you say, maybe nothing. Nevertheless, you may be drawn to doing something. Despair and anxiety are experiences. As such, some orientations to them may be more helpful than others. Many people find that spending some time paying attention to these feelings where they emerge in the body is helpful. This could be thought of as a kind of 'emotional mindfulness'.

What you report in your second paragraph are typical characteristics of sinking more into This. Enjoy.

❋

"I AM A PERSON"

Dear Richard, If anything can arise in liberation, is it not possible for the thought "I am a person" to arise from time to time? Best wishes, Jonny

Dear Jonny, Of course. In fact the thought "I am a person" arises in some form or other rather often for most individuals. But in liberation such thoughts tend to be seen through and to gain less and less purchase. Best wishes, Richard

Dear Richard, You were right when you said that there can be a slow transition into liberation—for no one of course. Everything is becoming dreamlike, but it is a very convincing dream. And it is full of love. Yes, I know that sounds very esoteric. Best wishes, Jonny.

Dear Jonny, That's a very good description—dreamlike, convincing, full of love. And of course containing whatever else is arising as well. Best wishes, Richard

WOULD AN ENLIGHTENED ONE WEAR LIPSTICK?

In the Spring of 2014, nondualitymagazine.org invited contributors to submit articles in answer to a long series of questions that they had posed. Most of these questions were about how an 'enlightened person' would or would not behave.

For the purposes of my reply, I summarised their numerous questions as follows:-

What happens to the mind at death?

Is there rebirth?

Could an enlightened person fear death or spiders?

Would an enlightened person wear lipstick or have liposuction?

Could an enlightened person feel anger or anxiety or make disclaimers about their 'offer'?

nondualitymagazine.org received and published several replies. Here is mine.

The assumption underlying these questions is that there may be such a thing as an enlightened person, or even worse an Enlightened Person, who might manifest certain characteristics by which they could be recognised. These characteristics might include knowing what happens to the mind at death and whether there is such a thing as rebirth, not fearing death or spiders, not wearing lipstick or having liposuction, not losing their temper or getting anxious and definitely not making legal disclaimers!

We only have to grant some of these characteristics and we have started to create the idea of a God Man or a God Woman. I would suggest that by and large God Men and God Women are very bad news. They are likely to lead us a merry dance during which we may lose our relationships, our credit cards and possibly our minds. Like other lovers, they often break our hearts.

But a God Man or a God Woman is only an idea and there is no such thing as an enlightened person or an Enlightened Person. This is why we can dismiss anyone who proclaims themself to be in any of these categories.

'Enlightenment' is a weasel word which I usually avoid, but as nondualitymagazine.org has posed its questions using this term, I'll stick to it. Your magazine, your rules.

Enlightenment consists precisely of the direct seeing that there is no person, so there cannot be any enlightened people. There is no self, so the quest for selflessness is futile. We are seeking to lose something which we do not have, because there is no one to have it.

Although there are no rules, the direct seeing of Oneness tends to leave a deep recognition of unknowing. Questions such as "What happens at death?", "Is there rebirth and karma?" and "Is it vain to wear lipstick? If not, what shade suits me best?" dissolve in this great unknowing. The mind, pretending for a moment that there is such a thing, simply loses interest in topics about which nothing but baseless speculation can take place. Instead of asking unanswerable questions, relaxation may happen.

There is no method, but if there were, relaxation would be it. That is why my recommendation is to drink tea and eat cake.

Let me end with a quotation from Longchenpa. "A fool…trusting in his dogma…is trapped; losing his way [in] intellect, he fails to see the real meaning." And from his translator, Keith Dowman, there is this: "Relaxation is the key to Buddhahood here-and-now."

❊

INDEX OF CHAPTER TITLES

330

Richard Sylvester is a humanistic psychologist, therapist, and lecturer. For thirty years he engaged with a variety of spiritual practices while training in psychotherapeutic techniques and teaching counseling. Sylvester has written three previous books on non-duality: *I Hope You Die Soon*, *The Book of No One*, and *Drink Tea, Eat Cake*. He holds meetings about non-duality in London, England, and elsewhere. To learn more, please visit www.richardsylvester.com.

MORE BOOKS from NON-DUALITY PRESS

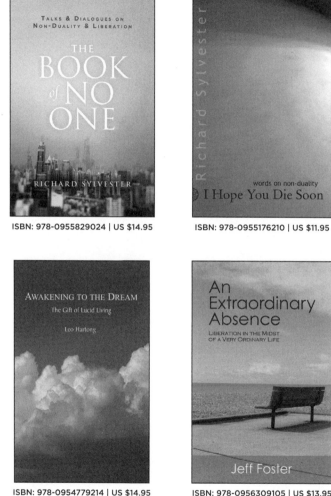

TALKS & DIALOGUES ON
NON-DUALITY & LIBERATION

THE
BOOK
of NO
ONE

RICHARD SYLVESTER

Richard Sylvester

words on non-duality
I Hope You Die Soon

ISBN: 978-0955829024 | US $14.95

ISBN: 978-0955176210 | US $11.95

AWAKENING TO THE DREAM
The Gift of Lucid Living

Leo Hartong

An
Extraordinary
Absence

LIBERATION IN THE MIDST
OF A VERY ORDINARY LIFE

Jeff Foster

ISBN: 978-0954779214 | US $14.95

ISBN: 978-0956309105 | US $13.95

NON-DUALITY PRESS
An Imprint of New Harbinger Publications
www.newharbinger.com